DEFENSE, SECURITY AND STRATEGIES

CYBER RESILIENCY, SECURITY, AND CLOUD COMPUTING SUITABILITY IN MILITARY INFORMATION TECHNOLOGY

DEFENSE, SECURITY AND STRATEGIES

Additional books in this series can be found on Nova's website under the Series tab.

Additional E-books in this series can be found on Nova's website under the E-book tab.

DEFENSE, SECURITY AND STRATEGIES

CYBER RESILIENCY, SECURITY, AND CLOUD COMPUTING SUITABILITY IN MILITARY INFORMATION TECHNOLOGY

JESSE A. FLANAGAN
EDITOR

nova publishers
New York

For permission to use material from this book please contact us:
Telephone 631-231-7269; Fax 631-231-8175
Web Site: http://www.novapublishers.com

Additional color graphics may be available in the e-book version of this book.

Library of Congress Cataloging-in-Publication Data

ISBN: 978-1-62948-868-4

Published by Nova Science Publishers, Inc. † New York

CONTENTS

PREFACE

This book provides recommendations for a workable framework; details about how the Department could prepare to operate in a cyber-contested environment; and the task force describes the specific aspects of the cloud computing configuration that are relevant to avoid the simple choice of public or private clouds.

Chapter 1 – The United States cannot be confident that our critical Information Technology (IT) systems will work under attack from a sophisticated and well-resourced opponent utilizing cyber capabilities in combination with all of their military and intelligence capabilities (a "full spectrum" adversary). While this is also true for others (e.g. Allies, rivals, and public/private networks), this Task Force strongly believes the DoD needs to take the lead and build an effective response to measurably increase confidence in the IT systems we depend on (public and private) and at the same time decrease a would-be attacker's confidence in the effectiveness of their capabilities to compromise DoD systems. We have recommended an approach to do so, and we need to start now!

While DoD takes great care to secure the use and operation of the "hardware" of its weapon systems, these security practices have not kept up with the cyber adversary tactics and capabilities. Further, the same level of resource and attention is not spent on the complex network of information technology (IT) systems that are used to support and operate those weapons or critical cyber capabilities embedded within them. This Task Force was asked to review and make recommendations to improve the resilience of DoD systems to cyber attacks and to develop a set of metrics that the Department could use to track progress and shape investment priorities.

Over the past 18 months, the Task Force received more than 50 briefings from practitioners and senior officials throughout the DoD, Intelligence Community (IC), commercial practitioners, academia, national laboratories, and policymakers. As a result of its deliberations, the Task Force concludes that:

- The cyber threat is serious, with potential consequences similar in some ways to the nuclear threat of the Cold War
- The cyber threat is also insidious, enabling adversaries to access vast new channels of intelligence about critical U.S. enablers (operational and technical; military and industrial) that can threaten our national and economic security
- Current DoD actions, though numerous, are fragmented. Thus, DoD is not prepared to defend against this threat

- DoD red teams, using cyber attack tools which can be downloaded from the Internet, are very successful at defeating our systems
- U.S. networks are built on inherently insecure architectures with increasing use of foreign-built components
- U.S. intelligence against peer threats targeting DoD systems is inadequate
- With present capabilities and technology it is not possible to defend with confidence against the most sophisticated cyber attacks
- It will take years for the Department to build an effective response to the cyber threat to include elements of deterrence, mission assurance and offensive cyber capabilities.

Chapter 2 – Cloud computing is viewed by many as the next major step in the evolution of computing infrastructure. Very large commercial cloud computing data centers have emerged around the world with petaflops of processing capacity, hundreds of petabytes of data storage, and wideband network access. Services, including electronic mail, data storage, database management, application hosting, very large dataset processing, and high performance computing, are globally available today from many cloud computing data centers. Cloud computing advocates promise on-demand delivery of these massive, warehouse-scale computing resources simply and easily through a network browser.

Much of the technology and computer architecture that enable modern cloud computing has roots in the mainframe, client-server, and early internet computing eras. What has emerged in recent years, however, differs from all of these in many attributes. Cloud computing data centers have different capabilities, risks, and security concerns than conventional networks, as well as different cost and efficiency models.

These differences are substantial, and have resulted in a wide variety of realistic and unrealistic claims for cloud computing, as well as a good deal of hype and confusion. With the proper implementation and operations, cloud computing data centers have demonstrated as good or better cyber security, capabilities, and cost than is currently available in Department of Defense (DoD) data centers. These improvements, however, are by no means guaranteed for every case and very much depend on the specific details of the implementation and operations. Cloud computing offers the DoD new, agile computational capabilities to support increasingly multifaceted missions. Some DoD missions likely to benefit from cloud computing services will involve varying or unpredictable computing requirements, or the integration of many, high-capacity data feeds from sensor networks and other sources. Other missions may include the analysis of very large data sets or those that require the ability to move computational resources. An additional benefit is the productivity gained from a ubiquitous connection to common cloud-based services, such as email, shared calendars, unclassified training, or document preparation.

This study investigates the suitability of the cloud computing approach for addressing the DoD enterprise and operational computing needs. Over the past few years, DoD has transitioned some of its computing needs to cloud computing data centers. The main factors driving this transition include enhanced mission capabilities, potential reduction in data center costs, and potential improvement in cyber security. This study has investigated these factors in detail and has analyzed the characteristics that should be considered when DoD contemplates moving applications onto cloud computing data centers. The study also investigated ways for the DoD to manage the cyber security risks and benefits associated with cloud computing.

In: Cyber Resiliency, Security …
Editor: Jesse A. Flanagan
ISBN: 978-1-62948-868-4

Chapter 1

RESILIENT MILITARY SYSTEMS AND THE ADVANCED CYBER THREAT*

Defense Science Board

October 11, 2012

MEMORANDUM FOR UNDER SECRETARY OF DEFENSE
FOR ACQUISITION, TECHNOLOGY & LOGISTICS

SUBJECT: Final Report of the Defense Science Board (DSB)
Task Force on Resilient Military Systems

I am pleased to forward the final report of the DSB Task Force on Resilient Military Systems. This study comprises one part of a DSB Cyber Initiative. A study on Cyber-Security and Reliability in a Digital Cloud is the other component of the initiative and will be forwarded shortly.

The Task Force on Resilient Military Systems provides a set of recommendations to improve the resilience of DoD systems to cyber attacks. The overarching strategy aims to enhance the Department's defenses against known vulnerabilities; decrease the effectiveness of, and increase the cost to, adversaries attempting to introduce new vulnerabilities; and deter the most sophisticated actors by ensuring the US maintains the ability to deliver desired mission capabilities in the face of a catastrophic cyber attack.

In addition, the Task Force identified a framework to implement a metrics collection system and then develop appropriate performance metrics that can be used to shape the Department's investment decisions. The framework can be adjusted to accommodate alternative implementation plans and should prove a powerful tool for the Department's leadership.

---

* This is an edited, reformatted and augmented version of Defense Science Board; Department of Defense, dated January 2013.

I fully endorse all of the Task Force's recommendations contained in this report, and urge their careful consideration and soonest adoption.

Dr. Paul Kaminski
Chairman

October 10, 2012

MEMORANDUM TO THE CHAIRMAN, DEFENSE SCIENCE BOARD
SUBJECT: Final Report of the Defense Science Board (DSB)
Task Force on Resilient Military Systems

The final report of the DSB Task Force on Resilient Military Systems is attached. This report is based on the perspective of 24 Task Force members who received more than 50 briefings from practitioners and senior officials throughout the Department of Defense (DoD), Intelligence Community (IC), commercial sector, academia, national laboratories, and policymakers.

This Task Force was asked to review and make recommendations to improve the resilience of DoD systems to cyber attacks, and to develop a set of metrics that the Department could use to track progress and shape investment priorities.

After conducting an 18-month study, this Task Force concluded that the cyber threat is serious and that the United States cannot be confident that our critical Information Technology (IT) systems will work under attack from a sophisticated and well-resourced opponent utilizing cyber capabilities in combination with all of their military and intelligence capabilities (a "full spectrum" adversary). While this is also true for others (e.g. Allies, rivals, and public/private networks), this Task Force strongly believes the DoD needs to take the lead and build an effective response to measurably increase confidence in the IT systems we depend on (public and private) and at the same time decrease a would-be attacker's confidence in the effectiveness of their capabilities to compromise DoD systems. This conclusion was developed upon several factors, including the success adversaries have had penetrating our networks; the relative ease that our Red Teams have in disrupting, or completely beating, our forces in exercises using exploits available on the Internet; and the weak cyber hygiene position of DoD networks and systems. The Task Force believes that the recommendations of this report create the basis for a strategy to address this broad and pervasive threat.

Nearly every conceivable component within DoD is networked. These networked systems and components are inextricably linked to the Department's ability to project military force and the associated mission assurance. Yet, DoD's networks are built on inherently insecure architectures that are composed of, and increasingly using, foreign parts. While DoD takes great care to secure the use and operation of the "hardware" of its weapon systems, the same level of resource and attention is not spent on the complex network of information technology (IT) systems that are used to support and operate those weapons or critical IT capabilities embedded within them.

DoD's dependence on this vulnerable technology is a magnet to U.S. opponents. In fact, DoD and its contractor base have already sustained staggering losses of system design information incorporating decades of combat knowledge and experience that provide adversaries insight to technical designs and system use. Despite numerous DoD actions, efforts are fragmented, and the Department is not currently prepared to effectively mitigate this threat.

Cyber is a complicated domain. There is no silver bullet that will eliminate the threats inherent to leveraging cyber as a force multiplier, and it is impossible to completely defend against the most sophisticated cyber attacks. However, solving this problem is analogous to complex national security and military strategy challenges of the past, such as the counter U-boat strategy in WWII and nuclear deterrence in the Cold War. The risks involved with these challenges were never driven to zero, but through broad systems engineering of a spectrum of techniques, the challenges were successfully contained and managed. Similarly, by employing the systems approach detailed in the report, the Task Force believes the Department can effectively manage and contain the risks presented by the cyber threat.

The report details an overall risk reduction strategy, which includes a combination of deterrence, refocused intelligence capabilities, and an improved cyber defense. Pursuing this strategy will enable the Department to credibly defend against known vulnerabilities; decrease the effectiveness of, and increase the cost to, adversaries attempting to introduce new vulnerabilities; and deter the most sophisticated actors by ensuring the US has a critical set of segmented conventional systems that will deliver desired mission capabilities in the face of a catastrophic attack. Taking these steps will provide DoD with a ladder of capabilities, ensuring the President has multiple response options to a catastrophic cyber attack. It also removes the requirement to protect all of our military systems from the most advanced cyber threats, which the Task Force believes is neither feasible nor affordable.

In addition, while the Task Force did not find metrics available today to directly determine or predict the cyber security or resilience of a given system, the Task Force was able to create an implementation plan to develop measurement systems to help the Department execute the proposed risk reduction strategy and then measure performance within that structure.

Ultimately, this Task Force report makes a case for implementing a broad systems approach (that is grounded in its technical and economic feasibility) to effectively address the cyber threat. It will take time to build the capabilities necessary to prepare and protect our country from present and future cyber threats, therefore DoD must act now.

We fully endorse all of the recommendations made in this report and urge their adoption.

Mr. James R. Gosler
Co-Chair

Mr. Lewis Von Thaer
Co-Chair

EXECUTIVE SUMMARY

The United States cannot be confident that our critical Information Technology (IT) systems will work under attack from a sophisticated and well-resourced opponent utilizing cyber capabilities in combination with all of their military and intelligence capabilities (a "full spectrum" adversary). While this is also true for others (e.g. Allies, rivals, and public/private networks), this Task Force strongly believes the DoD needs to take the lead and build an effective response to measurably increase confidence in the IT systems we depend on (public and private) and at the same time decrease a would-be attacker's confidence in the effectiveness of their capabilities to compromise DoD systems. We have recommended an approach to do so, and we need to start now!

While DoD takes great care to secure the use and operation of the “hardware” of its weapon systems, these security practices have not kept up with the cyber adversary tactics and capabilities. Further, the same level of resource and attention is not spent on the complex network of information technology (IT) systems that are used to support and operate those weapons or critical cyber capabilities embedded within them. This Task Force was asked to review and make recommendations to improve the resilience of DoD systems to cyber attacks and to develop a set of metrics that the Department could use to track progress and shape investment priorities.

Over the past 18 months, the Task Force received more than 50 briefings from practitioners and senior officials throughout the DoD, Intelligence Community (IC), commercial practitioners, academia, national laboratories, and policymakers. As a result of its deliberations, the Task Force concludes that:

- The cyber threat is serious, with potential consequences similar in some ways to the nuclear threat of the Cold War
- The cyber threat is also insidious, enabling adversaries to access vast new channels of intelligence about critical U.S. enablers (operational and technical; military and industrial) that can threaten our national and economic security
- Current DoD actions, though numerous, are fragmented. Thus, DoD is not prepared to defend against this threat
- DoD red teams, using cyber attack tools which can be downloaded from the Internet, are very successful at defeating our systems
- U.S. networks are built on inherently insecure architectures with increasing use of foreign-built components
- U.S. intelligence against peer threats targeting DoD systems is inadequate
- With present capabilities and technology it is not possible to defend with confidence against the most sophisticated cyber attacks
- It will take years for the Department to build an effective response to the cyber threat to include elements of deterrence, mission assurance and offensive cyber capabilities.

Report Terminology

To discuss the cyber threat and potential responses in more detail, it is important to establish some common language. For purpose of this report, Cyber is broadly used to address the components and systems that provide all digital information, including weapons/battle management systems, IT systems, hardware, processors, and software operating systems and applications, both standalone and embedded. Resilience is defined as the ability to provide acceptable operations despite disruption: natural or man-made, inadvertent or deliberate. Existential Cyber Attack is defined as an attack that is capable of causing sufficient wide scale damage for the government potentially to lose control of the country, including loss or damage to significant portions of military and critical infrastructure: power generation, communications, fuel and transportation, emergency services, financial services, etc.

The Task Force developed a threat hierarchy to describe capabilities of potential attackers, organized by level of skills and breadth of available resources (See Figure ES.1).

- Tiers I and II attackers primarily *exploit known* vulnerabilities
- Tiers III and IV attackers are better funded and have a level of expertise and sophistication sufficient to *discover new* vulnerabilities in systems and to exploit them
- Tiers V and VI attackers can invest large amounts of money (billions) and time (years) to *actually create* vulnerabilities in systems, including systems that are otherwise strongly protected.

Higher-tier competitors will use all capabilities available to them to attack a system but will usually try lower-tier exploits first before exposing their most advanced capabilities. Tier V and VI level capabilities are today limited to just a few countries such as the United States, China[1,2] and Russia.[3]

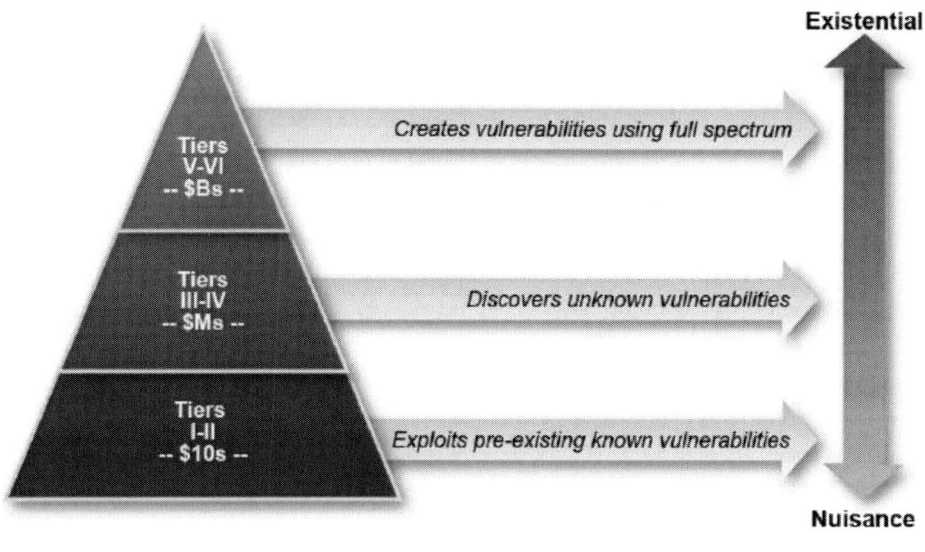

Figure ES.1. Cyber Threat Taxonomy.

Background

The adversary is in our networks. Then Deputy Secretary of Defense William Lynn's 2010 Foreign Affairs article documented a significant compromise of DoD classified networks in 2008 through the simple insertion of an infected flash drive. Moreover, adversaries exploit more than military operational systems, but intellectual property relevant to our commercial industries as well.

The DoD, and its contractor base are high priority targets that have sustained staggering losses of system design information incorporating years of combat knowledge and experience. Employing reverse engineering techniques, adversaries can exploit weapon system technical plans for their benefit. Perhaps even more significant, they gained insight to operational concepts and system use (e.g., which processes are automated and which are person controlled) developed from decades of U.S. operational and developmental experience—the type of information that cannot simply be recreated in a laboratory or factory environment. Such information provides tremendous benefit to an adversary, shortening time for development of countermeasures by years.

In addition, there is evidence of attacks that exploit known vulnerabilities in the domestic power grid and critical infrastructure systems.[4,5] DoD, and the United States, is extremely reliant on the availability of its critical infrastructure.

Exploitation is not a new threat. For years adversaries have infiltrated U.S. systems, sometimes detected, sometimes deflected, but almost never deterred. A recently declassified Soviet Union operation against the United States serves as an effective example. Starting in the late 1970s, the Gunman operation exploited an operationally introduced vulnerability resulting in the transmission to Soviet intelligence of every keystroke in 16 IBM Selectric typewriters located in the U.S. Embassy in Moscow and the U.S. Mission in Leningrad. More recently, in 2010, the 2nd International Conference on Information Engineering and Computer Science (ICIECS), published an article titled “Towards Hardware Trojan: Problem Analysis and Trojan Simulation” authored by members of the Department of Computer Science and Technology Zhengzhou Institute of Information Science and Technology, in Zhengzhou, China which outlined the technical approach elements for developing covertly modified hardware. The concept of hardware modification is so prevalent now that criminal elements routinely insert modified or replacement card readers to steal customer information from automated teller machines (ATMs), and other commercial activities.

Recent DoD and U.S. interest in counterfeit parts has resulted in the identification of widespread introduction of counterfeit parts into DoD systems through commercial supply chains. Since many systems use the same processors and those processors are typically built overseas in untrustworthy environments, the challenge to supply chain management in a cyber- contested environment is significant.

Identification of operationally introduced vulnerabilities in complex systems is extremely difficult technically, and as a result, cost prohibitive. The United States only learned of Project GUNMAN via a tipoff from a liaison intelligence service. The ability of intelligence to provide unique and specific information provides some mitigation against a Tier V-VI adversary’s ability to introduce vulnerabilities.

DoD is in the process of institutionalizing a Supply Chain Risk Management (SCRM) strategy that prioritizes scarce security resources on critical mission systems and components, provides intelligence analysis to acquisition programs and incorporates vulnerability risk mitigation requirements into system designs.

The success of DoD red teams against its operational systems should also give pause to DoD leadership. During exercises and testing, DoD red teams, using only small teams and a short amount of time, are able to significantly disrupt the “blue team’s” ability to carry out military missions. Typically, the disruption is so great, that the exercise must be essentially reset without the cyber intrusion to allow enough operational capability to proceed. These stark demonstrations contribute to the Task Force's assertion that the functioning of DoD's systems is not assured in the presence of even a modestly aggressive cyber attack.

The DSB 2010 Summer Study addressed the issue of degraded operations and the need to include cyber attacks in realistic exercises. The Chairman, Joint Chiefs of Staff, issued an instruction in February 2011[6] mandating that all DoD exercises begin to include realistic cyber attacks into their war games. If this level of damage can be done by a few smart people, in a few days, using tools available to everyone, imagine what a determined, sophisticated adversary with large amounts of people, time, and money could do.

New is the wide spread knowledge of the destructive ability of cyber attacks (e.g. Aurora, Stuxnet, etc.). The cyber world has moved from exploitation and disruption to destruction.

The benefits to an attacker using cyber exploits are potentially spectacular. Should the United States find itself in a full-scale conflict with a peer adversary, attacks would be expected to include denial of service, data corruption, supply chain corruption, traitorous insiders, kinetic and related non-kinetic attacks at all altitudes from underwater to space. U.S. guns, missiles, and bombs may not fire, or may be directed against our own troops. Resupply, including food, water, ammunition, and fuel may not arrive when or where needed. Military Commanders may rapidly lose trust in the information and ability to control U.S. systems and forces. Once lost, that trust is very difficult to regain.

The impact of a destructive cyber attack on the civilian population would be even greater with no electricity, money, communications, TV, radio, or fuel (electrically pumped). In a short time, food and medicine distribution systems would be ineffective; transportation would fail or become so chaotic as to be useless. Law enforcement, medical staff, and emergency personnel capabilities could be expected to be barely functional in the short term and dysfunctional over sustained periods. If the attack's effects were reversible, damage could be limited to an impact equivalent to a power outage lasting a few days. If an attack's effects cause physical damage to control systems, pumps, engines, generators, controllers, etc., the unavailability of parts and manufacturing capacity could mean months to years are required to rebuild and reestablish basic infrastructure operation.

The DoD should expect cyber attacks to be part of all conflicts in the future, and should not expect competitors to play by our version of the rules, but instead apply their rules (e.g. using surrogates for exploitation and offense operations, sharing IP with local industries for economic gain, etc.).

Based upon the societal dependence on these systems, and the interdependence of the various services and capabilities, the Task Force believes that the integrated impact of a cyber attack has the potential of existential consequence. While the manifestation of a nuclear and cyber attack are very different, in the end, the existential impact to the United States is the same.

To address the widespread cyber threats, the Task Force defined cyber risk (Figure ES.2) as a function of the following parameters: threat, vulnerabilities of the systems you need to protect, and consequences of losing the systems. The threat broke into two categories: adversary intent and their capabilities. Vulnerabilities are described as either inherent or operationally introduced, and consequences either fixable or fatal to the impacted systems.

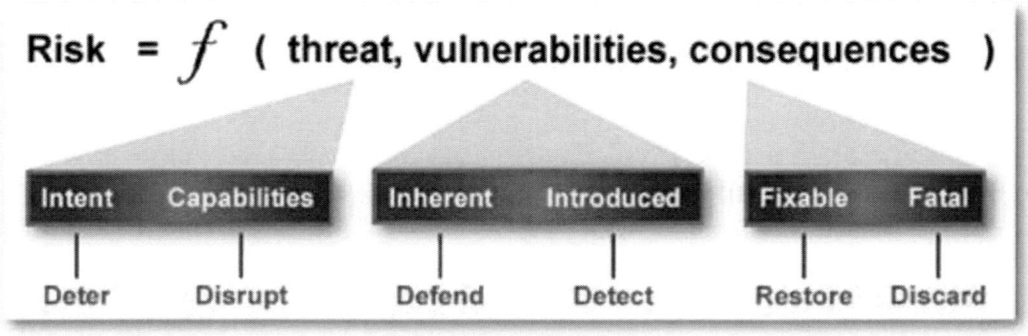

Figure ES.2. Risk Management Parameters.

The Task Force could not discover a credible mechanism to reduce the value of any of the three parameters alone or in conjunction with the other parameters, to zero. Therefore, the threat, vulnerability and consequence parameters cannot be managed in isolation. A systems solution is required. Today, much of DoD's money and effort are spent trying to defend against just the inherent vulnerabilities which exist in all complex systems. Defense-only is a failed strategy.

The Task Force developed a layered approach for managing cyber risk:

- Since it will be impossible to fully defend our systems against Tier V-VI threats, deterrence must be an element of an overall risk reduction strategy.
- Defending against known vulnerabilities is an insufficient strategy against Tier III and IV threats. Additional measures are required, such as consequence management.
- When properly executed, defensive strategies can defend against Tier I and II threats.

The White House and DoD each published a cyber strategy in 2011. Both strategies note the importance of the threat and the increased diligence required to protect the country. Each strategy provides a high-level framework for a response to the cyber threat, but they lack essential details necessary to guide the DoD through execution. The Task Force believes the recommendations provided within this report offer a workable framework and fill in some of the detail about how the Department could prepare to operate in a cyber-contested environment.

The Task Force could not find a set of metrics employed by DoD or industry that would help DoD shape its investment decisions. A qualitative comparison of resources and DoD level of effort in relation to the success rate of red teams is clear evidence of the lack of useful metrics.

The Task Force addresses the lack of metrics in Chapter 4 by providing a conceptual framework to put in place of metrics to improve the Department's cyber resiliency. In addition, the Task Force also proposed an initial set of performance measures that could be used to align the Department to the strategy and then measure progress toward implementation.

Recommendations

An overview of the Task Force's recommendations is included in this executive summary. Recommendation details, including proposed organizational assignments and due dates, are described further in the main body of the report.

1. Protect the Nuclear Strike as a Deterrent (for Existing Nuclear Armed States and Existential Cyber Attack)

- Secretary of Defense (SECDEF) assign United States Strategic Command (USSTRATCOM) the task to ensure the availability of Nuclear Command, Control and Communications (C3) and the Triad delivery platforms in the face of a full-spectrum Tier V-VI attack – including cyber (supply chain, insiders, communications, etc.).

Our nuclear deterrent is regularly evaluated for reliability and readiness. However most of the systems have not been assessed (end-to-end) against a Tier V-VI cyber attack to understand possible weak spots. A 2007 Air Force study addressed portions of this issue for the ICBM leg of the U.S. triad but was still not a complete assessment against a high-tier threat.[7]

The Task Force believes that our capacity for deterrence will remain viable into the foreseeable future, only because cyber practitioners that pose Tier V-VI level threats are limited to a few state actors who have much to hold at risk, combined with confidence in our ability to attribute an existential level attack.

2. Determine the Mix of Cyber, Protected-Conventional, and Nuclear Capabilities Necessary for Assured Operation in the Face of a Full-Spectrum Adversary

- SECDEF and Chairman, Joint Chiefs of Staff (CJCS) designate a mix of forces necessary for assured operation.

To ensure the President has options beyond a nuclear-only response to a catastrophic cyber attack, the DoD must develop a mix of offensive cyber and high-confidence conventional capabilities. Cyber offense may provide the means to respond in-kind. The protected conventional capability should provide credible and observable kinetic effects globally. Forces supporting this capability are isolated and segmented from general purpose forces to maintain the highest level of cyber resiliency at an affordable cost. Nuclear weapons would remain the ultimate response and anchor the deterrence ladder. This strategy builds a real ladder of capabilities and alleviates the need to protect all of our systems to the highest level requirements, which is unaffordable for the nation. Similar to the prior argument regarding the cyber resiliency of the nuclear deterrent, DoD must ensure that some portion of its conventional capability is able to provide assured operations for theater and regional operations within a full-spectrum, cyber-stressed environment.

Because of the expected cost of implementation, the protected-conventional capability must support a limited number of cyber critical survivable missions. This Task Force recommends improving the cyber resiliency of a mix of the following systems for assured operation in the face of a full spectrum adversary: global selective strike systems e.g.

penetrating bombers, submarines with long range cruise missiles, Conventional Prompt Global Strike (CPGS),[8] survivable national and combatant command (CCMD) C2.

- Segment Sufficient Forces to Assure Mission Execution in a Cyber Environment

Segmentation must differentiate only sufficient forces required to assure mission execution; it is not required across an entire capability. For example, if long range strike is a component of the protected-conventional capability, then DoD should segment a sufficient quantity that is designated as a cyber critical survivable mission. Notionally, 20 aircraft designated by tail number, out of a fleet of hundreds, might be segregated and treated as part of the cyber critical survivable mission force. Segmented forces must remain separate and isolated from the general purpose forces, with no dual purpose missions (e.g. the current B-52 conventional/nuclear mission).

DoD must engage multi-agency counterparts for an updated Strategic Deterrence Strategy, including the development of cyber escalation scenarios and thin lines.

3. Refocus Intelligence Collection and Analysis to Understand Adversarial Cyber Capabilities, Plans and Intentions, and to Enable Counterstrategies

- SECDEF in coordination with the Directors of CIA, FBI, and DHS, should require the Director of National Intelligence (DNI) to support enhanced intelligence collection and analysis on high-end cyber threats.

Intelligence must include the identification and understanding of adversarial cyber weapon development organizations, tools, leadership, and intentions, and the development of targeting information to support initiatives to counter cyber weaponization. Mitigating a Tier V-VI threat is impossible without filling these intelligence gaps. Therefore, the Intelligence Community (IC) should increase the priority of its intelligence collection and reporting requirements in this domain.

4. Build and Maintain World-Class Cyber Offensive Capabilities (with Appropriate Authorities)

- United States Cyber Command (USCYBERCOM) develop capability to model, game and train for full-scale cyber warfare.
- Under Secretary of Defense for Personnel and Readiness (USD(P&R)) establish a formal career path for civilian and military personnel engaged in offensive cyber actions.

Today, the United States is a leader in cyber offensive capabilities. However, most training and engagements are very limited and in controlled environments. Preparing for full-scale force-onforce cyber battle is not well understood. Challenges range from the scale of numbers of expected sorties to uncertainty of triggering mechanisms, trust and capability recovery timelines, and potential blowback of attacks all happening within the fog of war. To prepare, DoD must first begin to understand the full complexities of cyber war.

Recommendations include developing the capability to model, war game, red team and eventually train for full scale peer-on-peer cyber warfare. A policy framework should be established for offensive cyber actions, to include who has the authority and under what circumstances and controls to act.

Finally, DoD needs to significantly increase the number of qualified "cyber warriors" and enlarge the offensive cyber infrastructure commensurate with the size of threat. Professionalizing the cyber offense skill set and providing career ladders in this new field will be a key element toward growing the human resources required to compete effectively. This report is especially concerned with developing top-tier talent who can be certified to perform at the elite or extreme cyber conflict levels. The United States needs such world class performers in substantial numbers--some of whom may not be eligible for security clearances.

5. Enhance Defenses to Protect Against Low and Mid-Tier Threats

- DoD Chief Information Officer (CIO) in collaboration with the Military Departments and Agencies establish an enterprise security architecture, including appropriate "Building Codes and Standards", that ensure the availability of enabling enterprise missions.

Some adversaries will not be deterred (e.g., terrorist organizations and lone wolves); DoD must defend its systems against these low- and mid-tier threats. Therefore, the Task Force recommends that the DoD CIO establish a DoD-wide "Enterprise" architecture, including "building codes and standards" that ensure availability of mission operations during peace-time and full-spectrum wartime events. The building code analogy suggests that DoD should not make every network across the DoD identical, but instead should ensure that all networks, even when tailored by the Military Departments and end-users, meet a robust set of minimum standards that ensure a reasonable system network defense can be provided. U.S. networks also need requirements for instrumentation to increase the probability of detection of attacks and create situational awareness to speed remediation. Existing acquisition programs should be influenced, to the maximum extent feasible, with the new requirements. Audits should be conducted to the standard, and conducting in-process reviews to develop migration and mitigation strategies are critical. Legacy systems that cannot be maintained in a timely manner, (and DoD has many of them) must be enclaved and firewalled from the Global Information Grid (GIG).

Commercial technologies that enable the automation of some network maintenance activities and provide real-time mitigation of detected malware are available today. The Task Force believes that use of these technologies would actually drive network operation costs down and free up resources to hunt on the network for intruders.

6. Change DoD's Culture Regarding Cyber and Cyber Security

- SECDEF/CJCS establish a DoD-wide policy, communication, education and enforcement program to change the culture regarding cyber and cyber security

Establish a DoD-wide policy, communication, and education program to change the cyber culture. When focused, DoD can be one of the most disciplined large organizations in the world. It is this discipline that enables DoD to establish and execute processes that ensure the physical fitness of the armed forces, the safe and secure handling of weapons and the effective management of classified material. The same level of importance and discipline has not been applied to cyber hygiene and security. We will not succeed in securing our systems against even low- and mid-tier threats without changing this dynamic.

Communication of the critical importance of DoD cyber hygiene must be led by the SECDEF, CJCS, and their direct reports. Updated policies and training programs, and providing clear, punitive consequences for breach of policy will be necessary to move DoD to a higher level of cyber readiness.

7. Build a Cyber Resilient Force

- Deputy Secretary of Defense (DEPSECDEF) should direct specific actions to introduce cyber resiliency requirements throughout DoD force structure to include:
- Build a set of standards/requirements that incorporate cyber resiliency into the cyber critical survivable mission systems identified in Recommendation 2, (Under Secretary of Defense for Acquisition, Technology and Logistics (USD(AT&L)), DoD CIO)

The DoD CIO, in coordination with USD(AT&L), should establish a resiliency standard to design, build and measure capability against. The Joint Staff will use the standard to inform the requirements process. The cyber resiliency standard should be applied to sufficient segments of the force structure identified as the conventional components of the escalation ladder (see Recommendation 2) to achieve a credible deterrent effect.

- Apply a subset of the cyber resiliency standard developed above to all other DoD programs (USD(AT&L), DOD CIO, Service Acquisition Executives (SAEs))
- Increase feedback from testing, red teaming, the Intelligence Community, and modeling and simulation as a development mechanism to build-out DoD's cyber resilient force (USD(AT&L), Undersecretary of Defense for Intelligence (USD(I)), DOT&E, SAEs, CJCS)
- Develop a DoD-wide cyber technical workforce to support the build out of the cyber critical survivable mission capability and rollout to DoD force structure (USD(AT&L), CIO, SAEs, Director, Operational Test and Evaluation (DOT&E), USD(I), USD(P&R))
- Science and Technology community establish secure system design project with Federally Funded Research and Development Centers (FFRDCs), University Affiliated Research Centers (UARCs), academia, commercial and defense industry (Assistant Secretary of Defense for Research and Engineering (ASD(R&E))
- Intelligence community should initiate a supply chain collection activity (USD(I))

Investment Requirements

While it is difficult to project investment costs within an organization as broad and diverse as the DoD, the Task Force attempted to predict the ranges of cost and approximate time frames for which these recommendations could be accomplished, as shown in Table ES.1

Table ES.1. Estimated Investment Requirements for Study Recommendations

		ROM	Timeframe
1 & 2	Protect the Nuclear Strike as a Deterrent (for existing nuclear armed states and existential cyber attack). Determine the Mix of Cyber, Protected-Conventional, and Nuclear Capabilities Necessary for Assured Operation in the Face of a Full-Spectrum Adversary.	$$$$	36-60 mo.
3	Refocus Intelligence Collection and Analysis to Understand Adversarial Cyber Capabilities, Plans and Intentions, and to Enable Counterstrategies.	$	12-24 mo.
4	Build and Maintain World-Class Cyber Offensive Capabilities (with appropriate authorities).	$$	12-24 mo.
5	Enhance Defenses to Protect Against Low and Mid-Tier Threats.	$	6-18 mo.
6	Change DoD's Culture Regarding Cyber and Cyber Security.	$	12-48 mo.
7	Build a Cyber Resilient Force.	$$	12-24 mo.
ROM Costs $ <$50M/yr, $$ $50M-$100M/yr, $$$ $100M-$500M/yr, $$$$ >$500M/yr			

The good news is, even within the difficult current budget environment, much can be done to address challenges faced in the cyber domain. The Task Force believes the Department must move quickly to better understand the interrelationship between the cyber threat, national defense, and deterrence. The only recommendations requiring a large amount of resources are that of ensuring the strategic deterrent is protected to a high degree of confidence, and building a protected set of conventional capabilities. While the basic components of these systems exist today, understanding their cyber vulnerabilities, and separating their C2 systems, providing backup or war reserve capabilities to ensure available operation, will require time and resources.

Measuring Progress

The Task Force unsuccessfully searched for cyber metrics in commercial, academic, and government spaces that directly determine or predict the cyber security or resilience of a given system--which could ultimately be used by the Department to manage and shape its cyber investments. Instead, the Task Force provided an implementation plan to develop the measurement systems to help the Department execute the strategy defined within this report and then measure performance within that structure. If the Department chooses a different path, the implementation plan can be tailored to address alternate choices. Fundamentally, any metrics based approach must establish a mechanism to determine what will be measured, develop an appropriate collection system and construct appropriate performance measurements.

In any enterprise, metrics are only successful if their application is driven from the top leadership down through the organization, and followed up with consistent, determined attention. The measures recommended herein serve as a starting point for the Department, but ultimately, experience shows that in any enterprise, metrics will develop and evolve over time as experience is gained. This may seem like a trivial action, but from an historical and cultural aspect, this would be very new to the DoD.

The proposed framework enables leadership to first monitor the establishment of the collection systems, processes and activity created to implement the Task Force recommendations. Figure ES.3 below shows the first of two proposed metric panels, identifying the establishment of the metric collection systems to implement the Task Force recommendations. Within each recommendation (deterrent, intelligence, world-class offense...), a series of steps, from least to most complicated, are defined with the objective to track the systematic development of enterprise cyber resiliency capability. A maturity level approach is used to ensure the Department can prepare a solid foundation for achieving cyber resilience and allow flexibility if the Department chooses alternative paths to achieving cyber resiliency.

At a minimum, each component of the metric collection system in Figure ES.3 must define a common language and standards that can be used across the enterprise and identify reporting and tracking mechanisms that allow leadership the ability to track progress toward the intended goal. Without a common language, any effort will probably fail due to the inability to compare performance across the enterprise. For example, if the Department immediately leapt to an automated intrusion detection collection system without knowing the components of each separate network, or understanding how to detect an intrusion, or how to identify which network architectures supported automation, or when intrusions should be reported, etc. then comparing collected data would involve significant amounts of work just to ensure Network A is looked at the same way as Network Z.

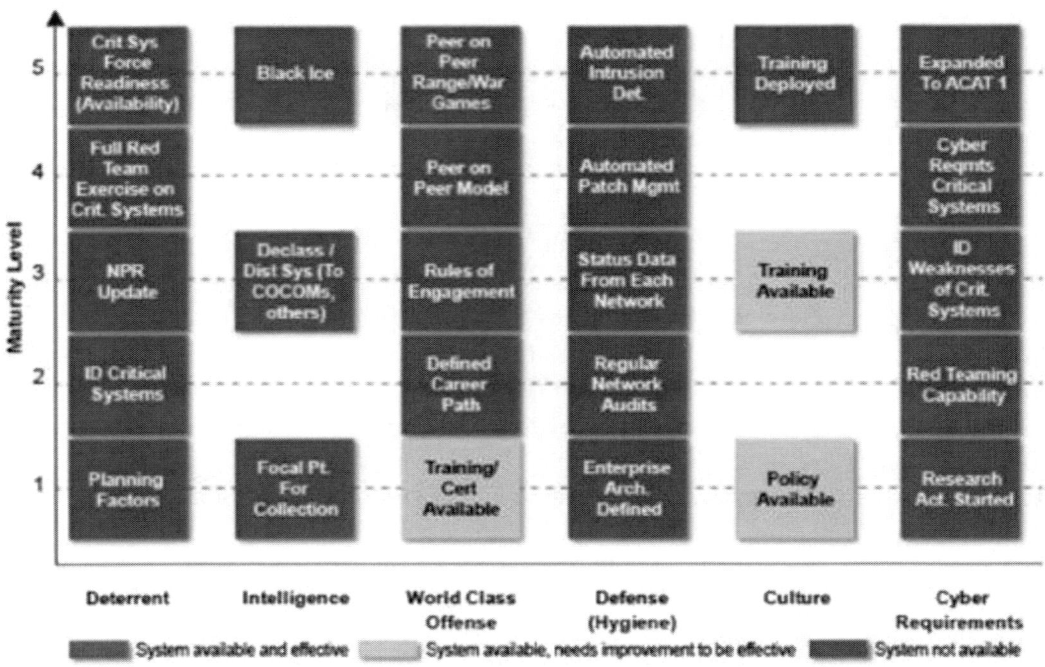

Figure ES.3. Notional Dashboard – Metric Collection System.

Once the metric collection systems are identified and in place, performance metrics can be defined to give the Department an understanding of its cyber readiness (Figure ES.4). When properly defined, performance measures provide better insight into actual status. Accurate information gathered from the bottom up can be used to tie the data to expenditures and enable visibility into the actual costs of managing network elements. For example, a set of defense/cyber hygiene performance metrics start with a simple count of audits. A line manager could look at the graph and tell immediately how much of the network was audited and the results of the audit. Since definitions are common across the enterprise, upper level managers are alerted to danger areas when too many audits result in failure. Audits also expose network components because properly conducted audits require a high fidelity inventory of network components. This creates an ability to measure the cost to manage network elements. Other performance metrics identify the time to patch a system and the time to detect an intruder once a vulnerability is identified.

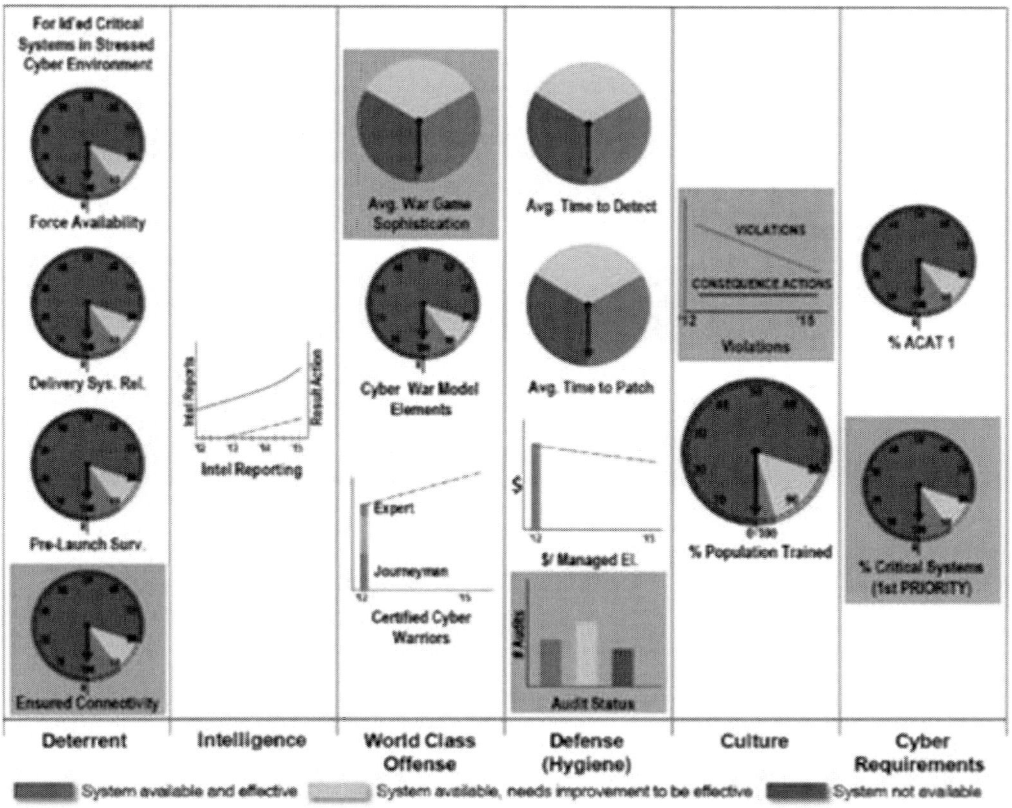

Figure ES.4. Notional Dashboard – Performance Metrics.

Ultimately, performance metrics identify best practices that can then be shared across the organization. Peer pressure between network owners will encourage improved performance by those responsible.

The Department will do best to measure outcomes, such as the average time it takes to detect a successful attack that breaches the network perimeter defenses, and the amount of time it takes to recover a system that is lost as a result of a cyber attack. Little value would be generated by jumping to outcome metrics without the common enterprise standards, audit definitions, and an understanding of what the metrics mean. The Task Force estimates that the DoD would have an experience base within two years of gathering data that would begin to allow comparisons of architectures, networks, and system elements for their cyber resilience and cost to operate. That data would provide DoD insight to inform predictions of performance of various architectures and elements versus available budgets. However, the Department must be disciplined and thoughtful about its use of metrics. Poorly defined and improperly used metrics may prove as harmful as no metrics at all.

Conclusion

The network connectivity that the United States has used to tremendous advantage, economically and militarily, over the past 20 years has made the country more vulnerable than ever to cyber attacks. At the same time, our adversaries are far more capable of conducting such attacks. The DoD should expect cyber to be part of all future conflicts, especially against near-peer and peer adversaries. This Task Force believes that full manifestation of the cyber threat could even produce existential consequences to the United States, particularly with respect to critical infrastructure. To maintain global stability in the emerging area of cyber warfare, the United States must be, and be seen as, a worthy competitor in this domain.

This Task Force developed a set of recommendations that, when taken in whole, creates a strategy for DoD to address this broad and pervasive threat. Cyber is a complicated domain and must be managed from a systems perspective. There is no silver bullet that will reduce DoD cyber risk to zero. While the problem cannot be eliminated, it can and must be determinedly managed through the combination of deterrence and improved cyber defense. Deterrence is achieved with offensive cyber, some protected-conventional capabilities, and anchored with U.S. nuclear weapons. This strategy removes the requirement to protect all of our military systems from the most advanced cyber threats, which the Task Force believes is neither feasible nor affordable. It will take time to build the capabilities necessary to prepare and protect our country from the cyber threat. **We must start now!**

1.0. Introduction

1.1. Identification of This Report

This document (and its companion appendices) constitutes the final report of the Defense Science Board (DSB) Task Force study on Resilient Military Systems. This effort was one component of the DSB Cyber Initiative. The other component is addressed by the DSB Task Force on Cyber Security and Reliability in a Digital Cloud. This report is the culmination of a year-plus study by a Task Force comprised of over 20 topic-knowledgeable members selected from the private sector. (See Appendix 2 for a listing of the Task Force membership and structure.)

As described in Appendix 3, the Task Force received briefings from civilian, military and private sector personnel from across the spectrum of research, development, acquisition, administration, operation, and use of automated systems.

1.2. Study Purpose

The DSB study on Resilient Military Systems and the Advanced Cyber Threat was commissioned by the Deputy Secretary of Defense, the Hon. William J. Lynn, on May 19, 2011 to:

- Study, and if possible, define meaningful measures and metrics to evaluate and monitor the level of DoD operational system resiliency in the face of a cyber attack.
- Identify strategies and techniques that could improve DoD system resiliency in the face of a cyber attack.

The study Terms of Reference (TOR) (Appendix 1) focused on maintaining the global ability to defend the Nation in the face of increasingly sophisticated and potentially devastating, cyber exploitation and attack. Some portions of the TOR are repeated below for clarity and emphasis.

Recognizing that the superiority of U.S. military systems is critically dependent upon increasingly vulnerable information technology, the Department requested assistance from the DSB in seeking a new perspective on the ways it manages and defends military systems against cyber exploitation and attack.

> "Innovative use of modern information and communications technology (ICT) (e.g. networks, software and microelectronics) in military systems plays a key and vital role in making the U.S. military second to none. However, the effectiveness of these military systems is extremely dependent upon the information assurance provided by its ICT underpinnings and of the personnel who operate and maintain the systems. An unintended consequence of the reliance on ICT to sustain superior U.S. capability is that our adversaries can erode or eliminate our advantage by targeting and exploitation at both the system and component level."
>
> "...To continue to take advantage of modern technology to increase our military effectiveness, we must possess sufficient confidence that these systems are not compromised to such a degree that we lose the benefit. In addition, we want to actively decrease the confidence of our adversaries that their clandestine operations targeting our systems would be effective enough to eliminate our advantage."

The challenges of mounting an effective cyber defense are well-appreciated by the Department's civilian and military leaders. However, the continually evolving environment of cyber threat and increasing system vulnerabilities poses a worsening situation that demands a more comprehensive and pro-active risk management approach. Effective management entails the ability to measure the relative strengths and weaknesses of cyber capabilities as well as organizational progress toward improvement implementation.

> "...Based in part on the complexity of modern software and microelectronic systems, very small and difficult to detect defects or subversive modifications introduced at some point in the life cycle of the systems can create debilitating effects...As a result of the great and growing complexity of DoD systems, cyber resiliency is an extremely broad and difficult attribute to guarantee."
>
> "...An important step toward designing, implementing and maintaining more resilient systems is to understand how to effectively measure the resiliency of those systems

relative to various cyber attacks and adversaries...[to ensure that] they will perform as expected in a hostile environment."

Recognizing the importance of effective measures or metrics and the difficulty in creating good metrics, the DSB was asked to seek any such cyber-relevant measures currently in use as well as to suggest areas where useful metrics might be developed.

1.3. Study Background and Special Circumstances

For the past three decades, the United States has led the world in developing and leveraging networks and embedded cyber capabilities to build a significant advantage across a number of linked National Security areas (e.g. military capabilities, intelligence, and the defense industrial base). The resulting DoD doctrine (Joint Vision 2010, 2020) of Full Spectrum Dominance envisioned information superiority to great advantage as a force multiplier. The power of this doctrine and its near total reliance on information superiority led to networking almost every conceivable component within DoD, with frequent networking across the rest of Government, commercial and private entities, and coalition partners in complex, intertwined paths. While proving incredibly beneficial, these ubiquitous IT capabilities have also made the United States increasingly dependent upon safe, secure access and the integrity of the data contained in the networks. A weakness of the implementation of this doctrine is its focus on functionality, connectivity and cost of information superiority over security--similar to the development of the Internet.

The performance of U.S. military forces over the last decade has demonstrated the superiority of networked systems coupled with kinetic capabilities and well-trained forces. While it is doubtful that the United States will face a peer force in the immediate future, "our" adversaries have discovered that the same connectivity and automation that provides great advantage to the US, is also a weakness that presents an opportunity to undermine U.S. capabilities in a very asymmetric way. The same network attack tools that are available on the commercial market are available to our adversaries. In addition, adversaries with financial means will invest to improve those tools and build more capable weapons to attack U.S. military systems and national infrastructure. Recent reports of Iran building cyber capabilities and Al Qaeda video releases with how-to instructions encouraging attacks on U.S. infrastructure are troubling.

In addition to state sponsored attacks against U.S. military capability, a wide range of actors (e.g. criminals, state sponsored economic espionage, etc.) employ cyber tools to pursue illicit economic gain. The almost daily release of new press reports and studies describe the risk and economic harm created by constant cyber attacks against commercial (e.g. financial, social, email, etc.) and government systems. Symantec reports blocking over 5.5 billion attacks with its software in 2011 alone finding that the average breach exposed 1.1 million identities and nearly 5,000 new vulnerabilities were identified in the calendar year.[9] Over 400 million unique variants of malware attempted to take advantage of those vulnerabilities, up 40% from 2010. Attack toolkits are easy to find and available in web forums or on the underground black-market and cost only $40-$4,000 to procure. Use of these widely-available tools allows almost anyone to exploit any known and uncorrected vulnerability.

Over the last several years, concern over America's cyber risk has made regular headlines and has been the subject of many studies. In January 2008, President Bush launched the Comprehensive National Cyber Security Initiative. In May 2009, President Obama accepted the recommendations of the Cyberspace Policy Review to ensure an organized and unified response to future cyber incidents; strengthen public/private partnerships to find technology solutions that ensure U.S. security and prosperity; invest in the cutting-edge research and development necessary for the innovation and discovery to meet the digital challenges of our time; begin a campaign to promote cyber security awareness and digital literacy from our boardrooms to our classrooms; and begin to build the digital workforce of the 21st century. With the establishment of various cyber initiatives and strategies, the standing-up of USCYBERCOM, and the development of greater cyber capabilities within the DoD Military Departments and our Nation's intelligence agencies, the United States is moving in the right direction. However, to date, this increased activity lacks coordination and consistent strategic intent.

This is not the first time the DSB has addressed the subject of cyber security. Indeed, the DSB has repeatedly warned of increasing vulnerabilities of information and communication technologies, the growing cyber threat from state actors as well as smaller groups, and the lack of adequate priorities placed on cyber matters by Department management (Table 1.2 Previous DSB Studies That Have Addressed the Cyber Theme).

Table 1.2. Previous DSB Studies That Have Addressed the Cyber Theme

February 2011	2010 Summer Study on Enhancing Adaptability of our Military Forces
September 2007	Mission Impact of Foreign Influence on DoDSoftware
April 2007	2006 Summer Study on Information Management for Net-Centric Operations, Volume I
April 2007	2006 Summer Study on Information Management for Net-Centric Operations, Volume II
January 2007	Critical Homeland Infrastructure Protection
February 2005	High Performance Microchip Supply
June 2001	Defensive Information Operations, Vol. II, Part 2
March 2001	Defensive Information Operations, Vol. II
February 2001	2000 Summer Study on Protecting the Homeland: Report on Defensive Information Operations
November 1996	Information Warfare Defense
October 1994	1994 Summer Study on Information Architecture for the Battlefield

The topic of cyber exploitation and attack has been openly addressed in public policy as well as in the press, and the tempo is escalating. Due to the sensitive nature of facts and background data related to cyber, versions of this report were prepared at appropriate classification levels.

1.4. Working Terminology, Scope, and Definitions for this Study

For the purposes of this DSB study, the term **Cyber** is broadly used to address all digital automation used by the Department and its industrial base. This includes weapons systems and their platforms; command, control, and communications systems; intelligence, surveillance, and reconnaissance systems; logistics and human resource systems; and mobile as well as fixed-infrastructure systems. "Cyber" applies to, but is not limited to, "IT" and the "backbone network," and it includes any software or applications resident on or operating within any DoD system environment. (See Appendix 4 for a more complete listing of acronyms used in this report.)

Cyber encompasses the entirety of digital electronic systems and devices used by DoD. In today's world of hyper-connectivity and automation, any device with electronic processing, storage, or software is a potential attack point and every system is a potential victim–including our own weapons systems. Cyber is not the exclusive purview of USCYBERCOM, the DoD Chief Information Officer (CIO), the Defense Information Systems Agency (DISA), or the individual system support activities of the Military Departments and Commands. Neither can it be discounted by resource planners or system research, development, and acquisition authorities as somehow beyond their responsibilities. Cyber provides an area of common concern for all these organizations (and more) – an area where all must work together in addressing this rapidly emerging threat.

Resilience is the ability to continue or return to normal operations in the event of some disruption: natural or man-made, inadvertent or deliberate. A goal of DoD is to have **mission resiliency** in the face of all forms of failure (including espionage and attack). Thus, commanders must develop alternative mission plans, emergency procedures, and reinforcements and resupply options. Similarly, for **cyber system resiliency** there must be alternative system plans, emergency back-up procedures, and reconfiguration/restart options. In modern warfare, effective mission resiliency requires that all systems critical to mission accomplishment be resilient.

In this study, the Task Force deliberately viewed DoD as a globally networked enterprise – a complex entity of highly interconnected and interdependent components, each of which may contain embedded cyber capabilities-where failure to accomplish a mission can have far-reaching impact with potentially serious national security consequences. Because of the nature of cyber exploitation and attack, failure to protect the enterprise at any possible point of entry can expose the entire enterprise to potentially devastating results.

1.5. Report Structure

This report is laid out as follows. Following this Introduction, Chapter 2 provides an explanation of the growing cyber threat to our military mission. Chapter 3 offers a comprehensive strategic approach for addressing system resiliency in the face of the ongoing cyber threat, and Chapter 4 addresses approaches to measuring progress in implementing the strategy. Chapters 5 through 10 address key aspects of the strategy, namely: ensuring deterrence through our nuclear and conventional military strike capability, collecting intelligence on peer adversaries' cyber capabilities, developing broader cyber offensive capabilities available to the United States, enhancing the U.S. military's cyber defense to thwart low- and mid-tier threats, changing DoD's cyber culture to take security more seriously, and building a cyber-resilient force. Chapter 11 provides order of magnitude cost estimates for implementing the proposed strategy. Chapter 12 provides a summary of the study conclusions and recommendations. The document concludes with a series of appendices containing ancillary, technically detailed and/or classified information.

In this study, the Task Force did not examine policies and authorities related to rules of engagement, use of cyber offensive capabilities, and inter-agency issues such as the protection of civilian infrastructure. These, nevertheless, are also crucial to the DoD.

2.0. UNDERSTANDING THE CYBER THREAT

U.S. military forces are critically dependent on networks and information systems to execute missions. They are thus highly vulnerable if threats to those networks and information systems are not sufficiently addressed. This chapter describes that threat – first, by defining it; then discussing its realization; and finally considering the impacts of this realization.

2.1. Definition of the Cyber Threat

The cyber threat is characterized in terms of three classes of increasing sophistication: those practitioners who rely on others to develop the malicious code, those who can develop their own tools to exploit publically known vulnerabilities as well as discovering new vulnerabilities, and those who have significant resources and can dedicate them to creating vulnerabilities in systems. The definition adopted by the Task Force enables a more detailed discussion of the characteristics of threat actors, mechanisms that can be used to protect or harden cyberspace components and operations dependent on those components, the impacts that threat actors pose if they are successful in their malevolent behavior, and recovery or response actions commensurate with the specific threat actions.

The taxonomy developed by the Task Force is summarized in Figure 2.1 Cyber Threat Taxonomy. As shown, the threat is divided into three levels of increasing sophistication, each composed of two tiers.

Dollar figures specified for each tier indicate the nominal investment required to participate at the given tier. The width of the figure at the given tiers suggests the decreasing number of practitioners as one ascends the pyramid to higher tiers. There are a vast number of parties with Tier I and II capabilities, while only a few state actors possess Tier V and VI capabilities.

Table 2.1 provides definitions of the tiers. Tier I practitioners, using malicious code developed by others, are commonly referred to as "script kiddies" and are driven as much by the desire to brag about their success in executing an "attack" as they are to cause specific damage. Tier II actors have some ability to develop their own malicious code and their actions may be characterized by pursuit of specific objectives such as the theft of business or financial data. Low-tier actors can employ some very sophisticated tools and techniques developed and exposed by others. Tier III and IV actors employ a broad range of software capabilities to penetrate cyber systems and effect exploits through Internet access. A major distinction between Tiers III and IV is scale – Tier IV is characterized by larger, well-organized teams, either state or criminal. Tiers V and VI encompass actors who can go beyond malicious software inserted through Internet access, and instead, create vulnerabilities in otherwise well-protected systems. Tier V actors are able to insert malicious software or modified hardware into computer and network systems at various points during their lifecycle for later exploit (e.g., a "cyber time bomb"). Tier VI organizations employ full-spectrum techniques, including humans (e.g., spies engaged in bribery and blackmail) and close-access means (physical or electronic) to gain system penetration, and have the resources to conduct many operations concurrently.

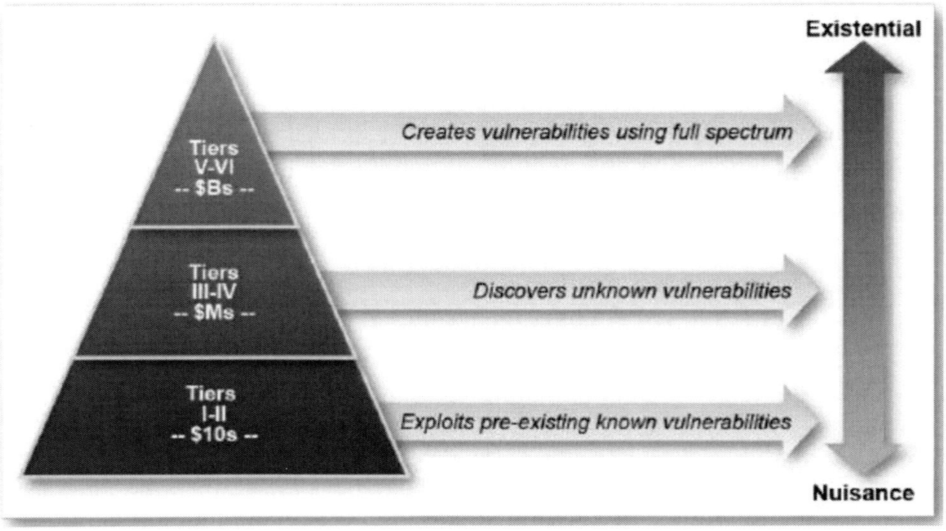

Figure 2.1. Cyber Threat Taxonomy.

Table 2.1. Description of Threat Tiers

Tier	Description
I	Practitioners who rely on others to develop the malicious code, delivery mechanisms, and executionstrategy (use known exploits).
II	Practitioners with a greater depth of experience, with the ability to develop their own tools (from publically known vulnerabilities).
III	Practitionerswho focus on the discovery and use of unknown malicious code, are adept at installing user and kernel mode root kits10, frequently use data mining tools, target corporate executives and key users (government and industry) for the purpose of stealing personal and corporate data with the expressed purpose of selling the information to other criminal elements.
IV	Criminal or state actors who are organized, highly technical, proficient, well funded professionals working in teams to discover new vulnerabilities and develop exploits.
V	State actors who create vulnerabilities through an active program to "influence" commercial products and services during design, development or manufacturing, or with the ability to impact products while in the supply chain to enable exploitation of networks and systems of interest.
VI	States with the ability to successfully execute full spectrum (cyber capabilities in combination with all of their military and intelligence capabilities) operations to achieve a specific outcome in political, military, economic, etc. domains and apply at scale.

Three comments about higher-tier actors should be made. First, while capable of operating at the higher levels, higher-tier actors will use the methods and techniques at the lowest level necessary to accomplish their objectives. They "hide" in the larger set of activity at lower levels to avoid exposing their more sophisticated techniques. Second, states might employ non-state actors as proxies. In such situations, middle-tier organizations gain access to higher-tier capabilities. This is especially true in states that are not as aggressive (passionate) as the United States is about separating the state from commercial and social society, which then blurs distinctions that this Task Force adopted. Third, the scale at which an organization can operate is one of the major discriminators between Tiers V and VI. Operations at scale is particularly challenging at Tier VI because of the complexity and potentially long times required to effect an operation using full-spectrum methods. While one might argue that "most any target" could be penetrated using Tier VI methods and sufficient time, to do so is expensive and resource intensive. The discriminator of a Tier VI actor is funding, people and equipment to conduct many such operations concurrently.

The following examples illustrate the threat-hierarchy tiers. Phishing, wherein malicious code is contained in an email from an unknown source, is an example of a Tier I threat. Spear-phishing, wherein malicious code is contained in an email attachment supposedly from a known party, is an example of a Tier II threat. The most sophisticated Spear-phishing attacks will impersonate a highly trusted source (e.g. close friend, co-worker, boss, etc), and less-sophisticated attacks use broader relationships as the known source (e.g. social network, organization, etc). The recently disclosed Flame virus[11] is an example of a Tier IV threat. It is highly complex software and most likely required a well-funded professional team to develop it. The software complexity and sophistication of OPERATION BUCKSHOT YANKEE[12] are those of Tier IV.

Examples of a Tier V-VI threat include hardware modifications followed by insertion of the hardware into a target system. A recently declassified example of a [then] high-tier exploitation is a Soviet Union operation against the United States during the Cold War designated by the United States as Project GUNMAN.[13] In the 1970s and early '80s, the IBM Selectric typewriter was considered an advanced electromechanical "computer" of its day. Soviet "cyber warriors" managed to replace the comb support bar (Figure 2.2) of the typewriter with a device that externally looked the same but was cleverly modified to enable the transmission in plain text of nearly every typed key to a nearby Soviet listening post. Between 1976 and 1984, sixteen of these typewriters found their way into the U.S. Embassy in Moscow and the U.S. Mission in Leningrad.

The level of sophistication employed by the Soviets made U.S. discovery unlikely without a tipoff from a liaison service exposed to a similar attack. Technical modifications included integrated circuit design technology never before seen by National Security Agency (NSA) engineers, burst transmission techniques designed to defeat U.S. technical security countermeasure equipment, and designs that employed parts of the typewriter as an antenna to transmit the information and provide power, and finally, foretelling later awareness of the field of human factors engineering, a design that allowed easy insertion and maintenance of the modified equipment. Additional non-technical exploitations included Soviet use of unfettered access permitted at customs checkpoints to insert the devices and hiding in the noise of its traditional technical espionage techniques. The Soviets had a longstanding proclivity to employ audio devices against the U.S. Embassy and diplomatic missions that created a U.S. mindset that assumed the Soviets only employed audio devices (e.g. the new

U.S. Moscow embassy that began construction in 1979 was so riddled with implanted listening devices that the United States eventually rejected the building). Even after the tipoff from the liaison service, the U.S. effort to recover the modified equipment and discover the vulnerability required several months. Discovering the modification required an NSA team of approximately 25 engineers working six days a week and the use of X-ray techniques. Even though integrated circuits were relatively simple compared to today's designs, the NSA engineers initially debated whether the anomaly discovered by X-rays was caused by a Soviet modification or was caused by IBM introducing memory circuits into the Selectric. Once the location of the modification was discovered, reverse engineering took additional time and resources to discover how the device worked.

Figure 2.2. Example of a Cold-War era Tier VI Cyber Exploitation.

The complexity of modern integrated circuit processors makes a modern version of the GUNMAN Tier VI capability very feasible (Figure 2.3). Removal of an integrated circuit from its packaging and replacement with a subversive die into the same package can be used to modify processor behavior under trigger conditions determined by the attacker.

The subversive die would not affect system performance through testing qualification or operation until a triggering mechanism was activated (e.g. the reading of specific input by the chip, geographic coordinates or aircraft velocity value, or through external connectivity like software patching mechanisms). This would make it very difficult to find the compromised chip in our systems through inspection or operation - just as it was in the Gunman operation. This chip could be inserted into a specific system through surreptitious means or inserted into a larger batch of systems during "normal" manufacturing in some foreign nation. The subversive die's effects could destroy the processor and disable the system by simply shunting power to ground, change the processor output to incorrect results for specified inputs, or allow information leakage to the attackers. To address the seriousness of the threat, DoD launched a number of supply chain initiatives, including the Trusted Foundry Program in 2004 to help ensure the integrity of hardware and software components in its critical systems.

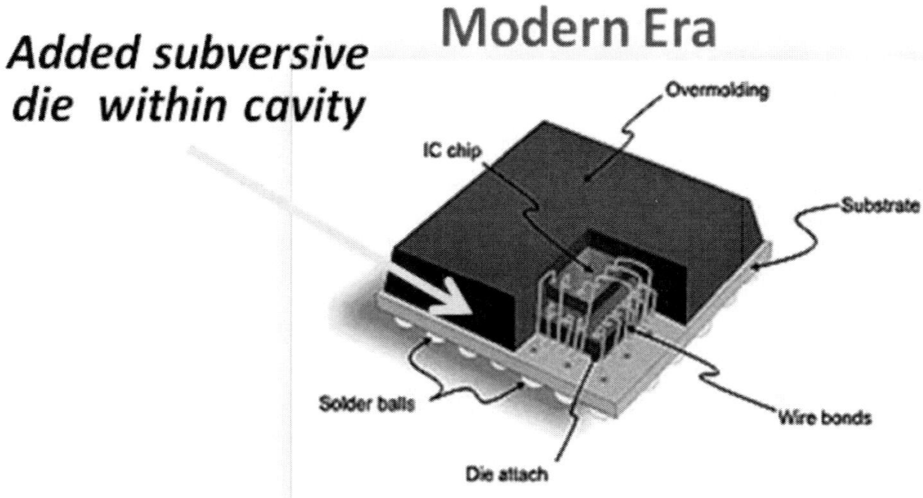

Figure 2.3. A Notional Modified Integrated Circuit.

2.2. Impact of the Cyber Threat

Many factors make modern computing and networking systems vulnerable to the above threats – for example:

- The original Internet design precepts that presumed trusted users, and promised a high degree of user anonymity, yielded an inherently vulnerable system with barriers to attribution
- The complexity of modern software and hardware makes it difficult, if notimpossible to develop components without flaws or to detect malicious insertions
- Many building blocks are created and maintained by third-party sources (e.g. open-source)
- The widespread use of commercial software and hardware (COTS) produced for markets that have low concerns about security
- The offshore development of software and hardware by parties of unknown trust

Figure 2.4 and Figure 2.5 illustrate the complexity issue. The source lines of code (SLOC) of com mercial operating systems have grown to nearly 50 million. Government programs depict simil ar growth trends over several decades.[14,15] On the hardware side, complex integrated circuits n ow have over 2 billion transistors. It is impossible to comprehensively test such software (anyb ody who uses a software product is very familiar with the concept of software updates) and har dware products (the Pentium floating point flaw discovered in 1994 shortly after the processor went to market is an example) completely for vulnerabilities.[16] Attempting to fully test systems of these complexities would take years per operating system or device using state of the art eq uipment. In addition, the design, development and production processes are highly automated and dispersed, relying on libraries for hardware functions and source code.

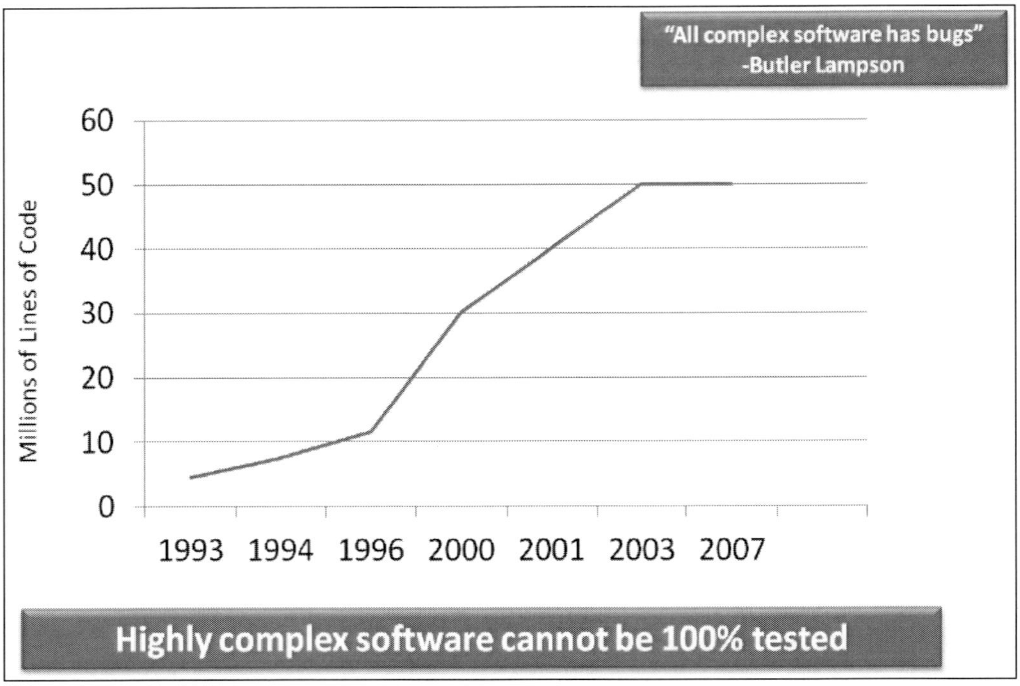

Figure 2.4. Commercial Operating System SLOC Growth.

The realization and exploitation of vulnerabilities is clearly and abundantly illustrated in reports by the government and private security firms, and in the public press.[17, 18, 19, 20] The loss of U.S. intellectual property through cyber exploits has been estimated to be in the hundreds of millions of dollars, if not billions.[21]

The vulnerability of the supervisory control and data acquisition (SCADA) systems controlling public utilities has been demonstrated[22,23,24] raising wide-spread concern that the Internet connectivity of these systems could lead to significant disruption of utility services (especially electricity) by malicious parties. Criminal organizations routinely substitute altered devices (e.g. fake ATMs and card readers) to intercept transaction data.

Of particular concern to this Task Force is the theft of data from the government and defense contractors.

Another manifestation of potential threat actions receiving high-level DoD attention is seen in U.S. military exercises.[25] DoD red teams invariably penetrate DoD networks using Tier I and II threats.

Such penetrations could seriously impede the operation of U.S. forces by degrading network connectivity, corrupting data, and gaining intelligence. Cleary, if U.S. red teams achieve adverse effects using lower level techniques, a sophisticated adversary could achieve even greater effects.

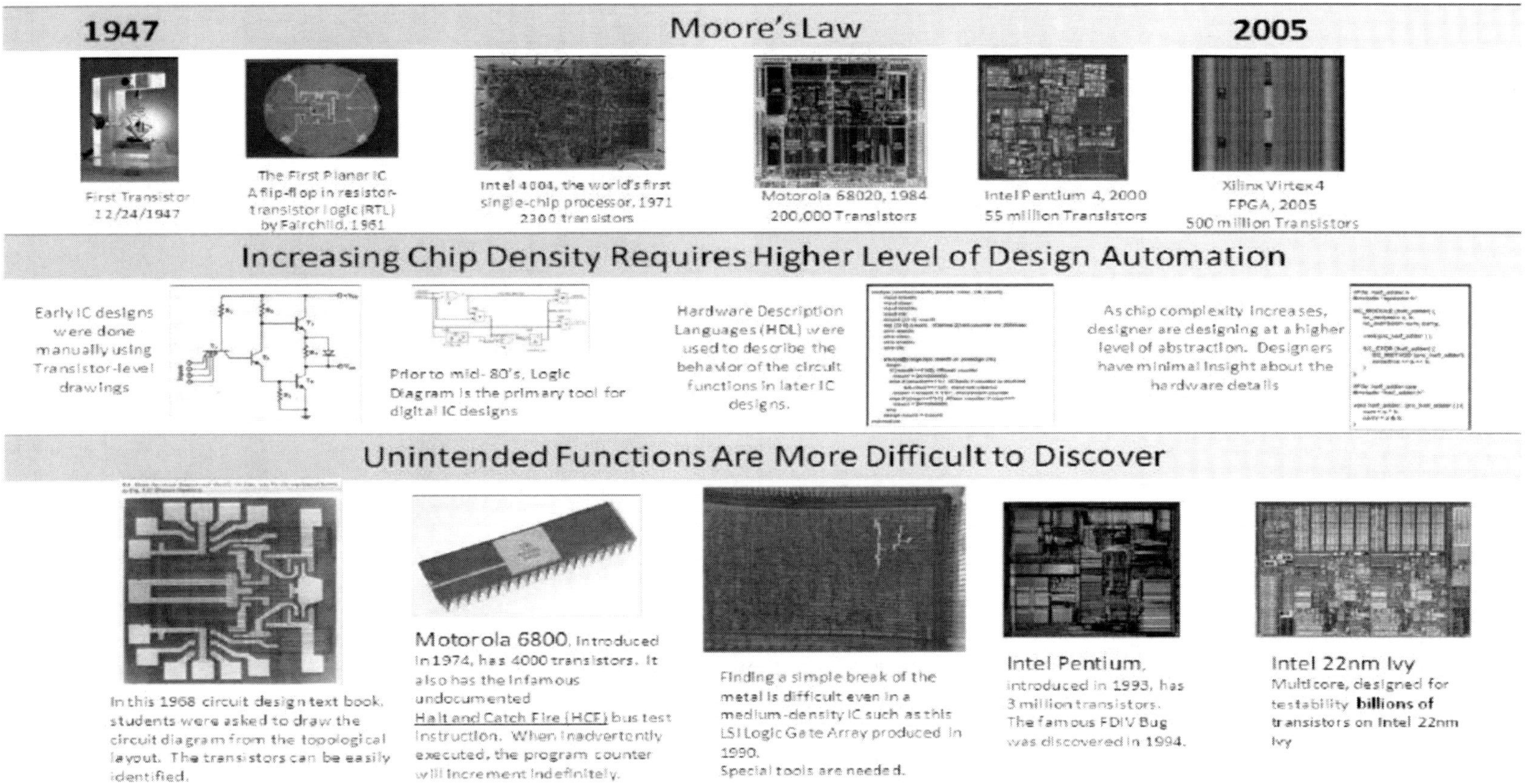

Figure 2.5. Representative Growth in Hardware Complexity.

2.3. Consequences of and Reaction to the Threat

The accomplishment of U.S. military missions is critically dependent on networks and information systems. The threats described in the previous section may impose severe consequences for U.S. forces engaged in combat:

- Degradation or severing of communication links critical to the operation of U.S. forces, thereby denying the receipt of command directions and sensor data
- Data manipulation or corruption may cause misdirected U.S. operations and lead to lack of trust of all information
- Weapons and weapon systems may fail to operate as intended, to include operating in ways harmful to U.S. forces
- Potential destruction of U.S. systems (e.g. crashing a plane, satellite, unmanned aerial vehicles, etc.).

At the national level, one could posit a large-scale attack on the U.S. critical infrastructure (e.g., power, water, or financial systems). An attack of sufficient size could impose gradual wide-scale loss of life and control of the country and produce existential consequences. For such an attack to occur there must be an adversary with both the capability and intent to conduct the attack. A prudent course of action demands that the United States prepare for the possibility of such an attack given the uncertainties about how the future will evolve. Given the severe consequences of the threat, the issue now is how to mitigate it, which is the subject of much of the remainder of this report.

3.0. Defining a Resilience Strategy for DoD Systems

To address the broad level of threats with a unified strategy, it was necessary to think through the threat, vulnerabilities, and consequences associated with these potential attacks. Figure 3.1 describes how the Task Force thought through this challenge. Risk is a function of the threat, the vulnerabilities of the systems to be protected, and consequences of compromise of the systems. The threat broke into two categories: intent of the adversary and their capabilities. Vulnerabilities are described as either inherent or operationally introduced and consequences, either fixable or fatal to the impacted systems.

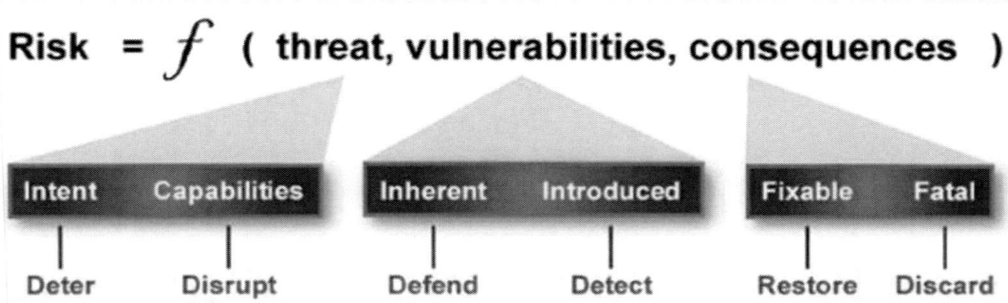

Figure 3.1. Risk Management Parameters.

It is important to understand that the Task Force could not discover a credible mechanism to reduce the value of any of the three parameters (Figure 3.1), alone or in conjunction with the other parameters, to zero. Therefore, the threat, vulnerability and consequence parameters cannot be managed in isolation. A systems solution is required. Today much of DoD's money and effort are spent trying to defend against just the inherent vulnerabilities which exist in all complex systems. Defense only is a failed strategy.

DARPA produced Figure 3.2 that shows the growing gap between defensive and offensive software size. The complexity of the software defending our networks continues to increase exponentially over time due to increased complexity of the systems they attempt to protect, yet the size of software code used for the average successful attack remains nearly constant. This challenge is as old as the ages: the defense must protect against all possible offenses and the offense can mass all its resources against the weakest point of the defense. To address cyber risk, DoD needs a balanced approach across all three major parameters.

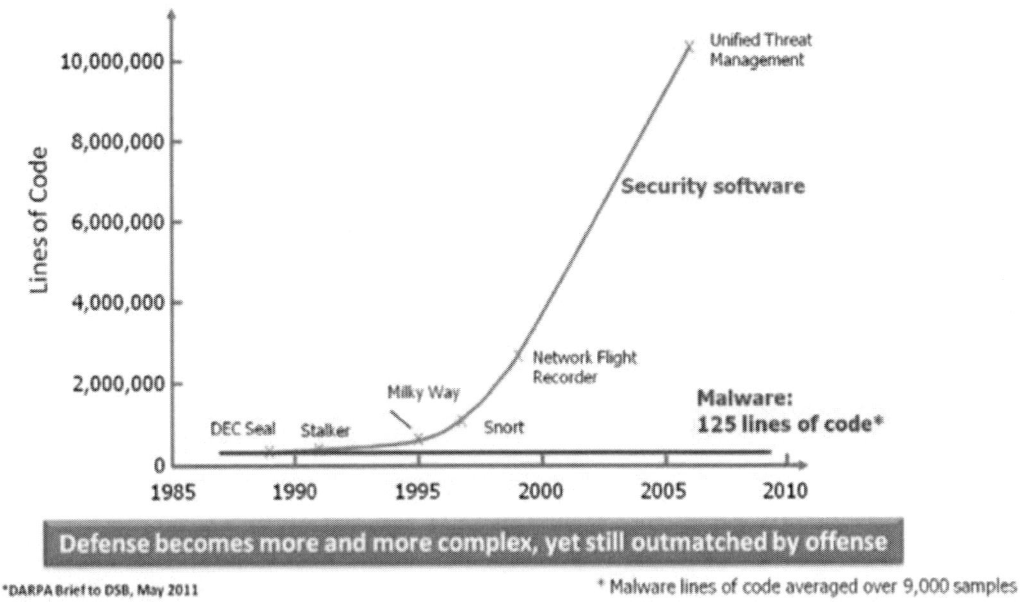

Figure 3.2. Graphic Illustration of the Complexity of Software Required to Defend and Attack our Systems. Very Small Changes (Even Single Bits) Can Cause Major Impacts to the Operation of a System.

There is no single silver bullet to solve the threat posed by cyber-attack or warfare. Solving this problem is analogous to previous complex national security and military strategy developments including counter U-boat strategy in WWII, nuclear deterrence in the Cold War, commercial air travel safety and countering IEDs in the Global War on Terrorism. The risks involved with these challenges were never driven to zero, but through broad systems engineering of a spectrum of techniques, the challenges were successfully contained and managed.

There are several characteristics of the cyber challenge that collectively thwart our attempts to discover a closed-form solution to this national security issue. First, DoD's comprehensive dependence on this vulnerable technology is a magnet to U.S. opponents. DoD's dependency is not going to be reduced and will continue to grow. Thus, the adversary is not going away and their attraction to this weakness will increase. This adversarial persistence yields a **never-ending challenge**.

Secondly, there are no technical approaches that will comprehensively protect DoD against a determined adversary. DoD's diligent work over decades attempting to drive inherent vulnerability out of these systems and components has resulted in some progress, although DoD has barely begun to address the daunting problem of operationally introduced vulnerabilities into systems which is compounded by the large dependence on the global supply chain. In the face of the evolving cyber threat, DoD must recognize the limits to vulnerability reduction and the effectiveness of protection mechanisms and move to employ the threshold of "**good enough**" and work to reduce overall risk by managing all three risk parameters from a **systems perspective**.

Third, while there are many tests to demonstrate the vulnerability or weakness in a system, there will **never be a test** that demonstrates or proves the security of a system. This fact reinforces the need to seek "good enough" and the enduring existence of residual uncertainty.

Finally, because the opponent's advantage in exploiting/compromising/attacking DoD's information technology is substantial (game-changing), they will be highly motivated in their pursuit, innovative in their approach, and adaptive to U.S. strategy. The **adversary gets a vote** and this brings us back to the never-ending challenge. (However, they have many of the same risks to their systems).

The combination of these factors forces the United States to manage risk in this domain through a balanced systems approach.

This Task Force finds that without an urgently implemented and comprehensive strategy to offset the cyber security threat, U.S. national objectives will be nearly impossible to achieve in times of crisis. Additionally, the long term loss of so much intellectual property and capability will result in ***a serious competitive disadvantage*** to the U.S. economy.

Key findings of the study include:

- The cyber threat is serious, with potential consequences similar in some ways to the nuclear threat of the Cold War
- The cyber threat is also insidious allowing adversaries to access vast new channels of intelligence about critical U.S. enablers (operational and technical; military and industrial) that can threaten our national and economic security
- Current DoD actions, though numerous, are fragmented. Thus, DoD is not prepared to defend against this threat
- DoD red teams, using cyber attack tools, which can be downloaded from the Internet, are very successful at defeating our systems
- U.S. networks are built on inherently insecure architectures with increasing use of foreign-built components
- U.S. intelligence against peer threats targeting DoD systems is inadequate
- With present capabilities and technology, it is not possible to defend with confidence against the most sophisticated cyber attacks
- It will take years for the Department to build an effective response to the cyber threat to include elements of deterrence, mission assurance and offensive cyber capabilities.

The Task Force developed a set of recommendations that, when taken in whole, create a strategy for DoD to address this broad and pervasive threat to improve the resilience of DoD systems.

Cyber is a complicated domain and must be managed across threat vectors to successfully address the challenges it presents. The cyber risk elements cannot be reduced to zero. While the problem cannot be eliminated, resilience capabilities can and must be determinedly managed by the Department. Cyber risk can be managed through the combination of deterrence (up to a nuclear response in the most extreme case) and improved cyber defense.

This strategy removes the requirement to protect all of military systems from the most advanced cyber threats, which the Task Force believes is neither feasible nor affordable. It will take time to build the capabilities necessary to prepare and protect our country from the cyber threat. **We must start now!**

3.1. Cyber Strategy for DoD

The following is the Task Force's recommended strategic approach to improving the resilience of DoD systems. The Task Force believes that these actions are in support of the published DoD Cyber Strategy.[26]

- Deter the Tier V-VI threat (raise confidence level that selected systems are protected from cyber attack and therefore available for deterrence)
  - Protect Nuclear Deterrent
  - Protect C2 and Continuity Of Government (separation of networks, war reserves)
  - Ensure some conventional strike and cyber attack capabilities to support escalation ladder (for theater operations as well)
- Minimize the impacts of Tier I-IV threats
  - Incrementally raise defenses
    - Instrument networks for intrusion detection and to provide situational awareness
    - Improve DoD cyber culture and personal responsibilities
    - Enforce universal practice of good hygiene
  - Evolve cyber requirements into DoD acquisition and support systems
- Improve critical capabilities important for both
  - Refocus intelligence collection to understand adversary cyber plans and intentions, and to enable counter strategies
  - Build a world-class cyber offensive capability with well-defined authorities and rules
  - Continue ongoing DoD efforts to develop secure system design and development capabilities, and to improve the security of the cyber supply chain

3.2. Table of Recommendations

Table 3.1. Table of Recommendations

Description of Recommendations
1. Protect the Nuclear Strike as a Deterrent (for existing nuclear armed states and existential cyber attack).
2. Determine the Mix of Cyber, Protected-Conventional, and Nuclear Capabilities Necessary for Assured Operation in the Face of a Full-Spectrum Adversary.
3. Refocus Intelligence Collection and Analysis to Understand Adversarial Cyber Capabilities, Plans and Intentions, and to Enable Counterstrategies.
4. Build and Maintain World-Class Cyber Offensive Capabilities (with appropriate authorities).
5. Enhance Defenses to Protect Against Low and Mid-Tier Threats.
6. Change DoD's Culture Regarding Cyber and Cyber Security.
7. Build a Cyber Resilient Force.

The Task Force anticipates that the implementation of the recommendations in Table 3.1 will be an ongoing effort, and establishing measures is an important step toward executing them. Without such tools, it will be difficult to tell whether or not progress is being made.

4.0. Measuring Progress

The Task Force attempted to define metrics that the Department could use to ultimately manage and shape cyber investments. Measures (used interchangeably with metrics for the contents of this report) are a critical part of any organization or business operation. They form a set of tools by which management determines and communicates the organization's highest priorities to the organization's employees. When done well, metrics act as an alignment tool in driving lower levels of an organization to make decisions consistent with strategies of their leaders. Moreover, the metrics become a mechanism to provide benchmarking, drive continuous improvement, and ensure sharing of best practices throughout an organization. Developing a set of cyber measures, which can be used across the Department to allow quantitative comparisons between options when making cyber (IT) investments and drive operational practices, is critical to increasing cyber resilience.

The Task Force set out to ascertain if useful metrics were currently available to determine or predict the cyber security or resilience of a given system. After several months of researching best practices of cyber metrics in commercial, academia and government spaces, the Task Force determined that no metrics are currently available to directly determine or predict the cyber security or resilience of a given system. Measures to predict cyber system resilience are difficult to create, due to the potential for small changes to cause discontinuous effects. A few critical bits manipulated in a weapon fire control system can render that weapon ineffectual. Millions of bits changed in a less critical portion of software may have only limited effect on the system. Even knowing if a system is compromised is very difficult. Often, when successful network exploits are identified, forensic analysis later shows the exploit lay undiscovered in the system for a year or more.

While difficult to measure cyber resiliency directly, the Task Force did find measures that could be implemented to improve the Department's defense posture and therefore indirectly improve its cyber resilience. To implement these measures however, the Department will have to develop common language and definitions, collection methods, and tools for collating data across the enterprise, and then use those results to drive decisions concerning future operations and personnel performance. This information will form the foundation for an education program that must be spread across the entire enterprise, to establish a common understanding. As experience is gained with these measures, and as more people understand the objectives and techniques, the metrics will evolve to become even more useful for the Department, providing a basis for measuring the effectiveness of future investments.

In a perfect world, DoD operational systems would be able to tell a commander when and if they were compromised, whether the system is still usable in full or degraded mode, identify alternatives to aid the commander in completing the mission, and finally, provide the ability to restore the system to a known, trusted state. Today's technology does not allow that level of fidelity and understanding of systems. When properly constructed, measures can guide design implementations and day-to-day operations to potentially fulfill these system goals at some point in the future. Ultimately, a useful set of measures will help DoD leadership understand if they have prepared the Department to engage competitively in a conflict where cyber is a major component.

Measures must be chosen carefully. They must be leadership-owned and driven from the top. The most successful organizations implement a few carefully chosen metrics that balance between desired outcome, quality and delivery speed. There is an old saying that "you will get what you measure". As management puts its full force behind a strategy supported by a set of measures, their personnel will do what it takes to succeed at those measures, sometimes regardless of the end goal. Therefore, DoD management cannot treat cyber resilience measures as a fire and forget weapon.

The cultural aspects of metrics can be frightening to an organization embarking on this new path. Poor performance that may have been masked in the past could now be exposed. Management's tone on how performance issues are handled will determine whether organizations within the Department provide the minimum data required and attempt to hide from the spotlight, or see the measures as an opportunity to learn from others and improve performance at a faster rate. Ultimately, consistent and continuous improvement is much more important in the long run than the performance levels established at first baseline – good or bad. This Task Force defined an initial useful set of measures, based on collectable data that the Department could use to start down this path. It should be understood that to be successful, DoD leadership must take ownership and evolve this list into one of their own, to align the Department around a common strategy and set of agreed-upon measures. As experience is gained, the metrics will evolve. Building a culture of measurement used to drive continuous improvement and influence future designs and operations is a critical part of the process. Building a culture supporting measurement may seem like a trivial action, but from an historical and cultural perspective, this would be very new to the DoD.

Commercial organizations regularly use metrics to drive their strategies through their businesses, but it is nevertheless difficult to get initial metrics in place and operating.

Establishing metrics should be an iterative process. Over time, and with consistent attention, the alignment of the organization to productive metrics provides great value and consistency in operations. The Task Force has developed two proposed metric panels; the first identifies the establishment of metric collection systems to implement Task Force recommendations, and the second defines performance measures that can be used once the systems are in place to give the Department an understanding of its cyber readiness. The goal is to offer the Secretary and his/her staff a couple of relatively simple charts that can be publicized and reviewed on a regular basis to track progress.

4.1. Metric Collection Systems

The Task Force created a notional metric collection system dashboard to monitor progress of strategy implementation. Before performance measures can be effectively implemented across the Department, collection systems must be put in place. The creation of a metric collection system provides a common language, definitions and standards to allow different organizations in the enterprise to effectively communicate. In addition, the collection system develops reporting, tracking, analysis and display mechanisms for the collected data, to be useful to both Department leadership and managers closer to the front lines. This dashboard is a simple stoplight-chart measuring whether the building blocks required to implement the recommendations in this report are in place, useful, and effective. Note that Figure 4.1 does not represent a detailed DSB assessment of the current DoD status, but provides an illustration of how this tool can be used to drive improvement. The concept is to input data collected from relevant portions of the DoD and aggregate into a single block for each action. The ability to "click" on a block and view the background data on which it was based would allow front line supervisors to understand their performance relative to their peers and allow senior leaders to delve into problem areas and ensure adequate resources and attention are provided to improve performance.

The blocks build on each major recommendation area from bottom (the simplest actions) to the top (most complex actions), leading to a maturity-level of accomplishment measure in building the required systems. As the systems come online, the next section outlines performance metrics that can be collected to drive system performance.

The metric collection system for each major recommendation area is crucial. For example, under the general area of defense/cyber hygiene, the metric collection system starts with developing a defined Department Enterprise Architecture. Creating a defined Enterprise Architecture must drive common definitions of security posture and terms. In addition, the metric collection system devoted to Enterprise Architecture must identify reporting and tracking mechanisms that provide leadership the ability to monitor progress toward the intended goal. These mechanisms need not be complicated (e.g. a simple spread sheet will suffice). The next task requires developing a collection system to measure Regular Network Audits. The collection system must create common language as to what an audit is, how the Enterprise Standard will be audited, and the supporting reporting system (e.g. how often will audits be conducted and on what parts of the network etc). The objective of the audit collection system is to enable the Department to determine whether or not audits are conducted against defined standards. Auditing to standard language and terminologies will allow the Department to make comparisons between networks as data is collected. The next collection system builds off the lower blocks. Once a common enterprise is developed and audits can be conducted, a collection system to measure status of each network must be created.

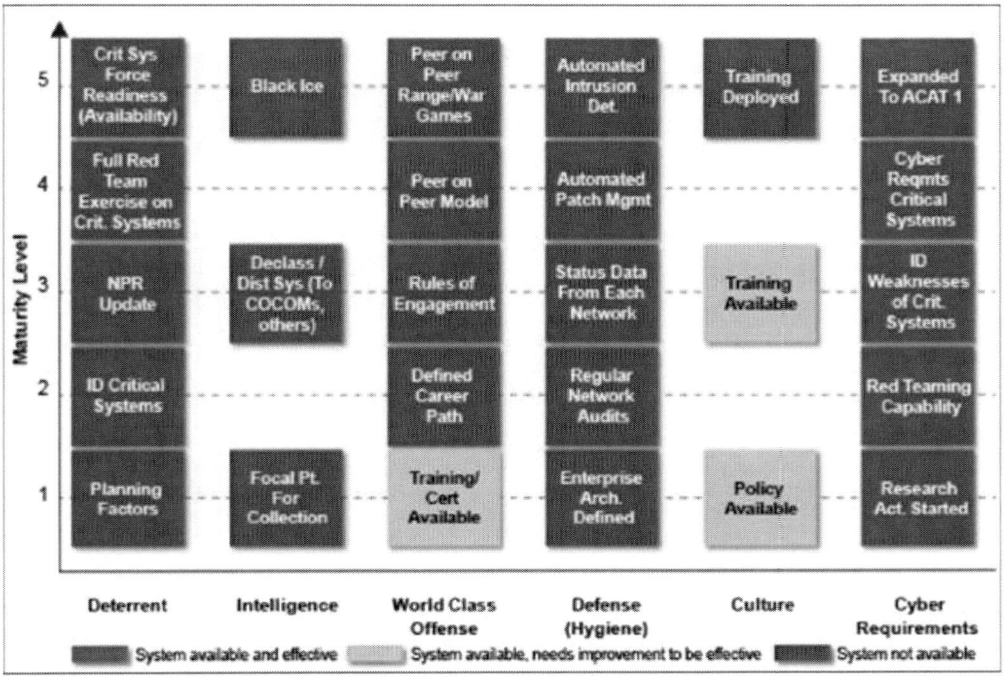

Figure 4.1. Notional Cyber Dashboard for Secretary – Metric Collection Systems.

The collection system needs common terminology encompassing definitions of network and status followed by a reporting mechanism. This provides the foundation for an automated patch management collection system and finally, a metric collection system devoted to Automated Intrusion Detection—to identify how long it takes to find and remove successful intrusions into the network.

Other recommendation areas build similar metric collection systems. A deterrent collection system focuses on defining planning factors that include a cyber component for both strategic nuclear delivery platforms and NC3 (e.g. extension of the current USSTRATCOM planning factors to reflect cyber) and also applied to identification and segmentation of protected conventional capability for assured operation in a contested cyber environment. An intelligence collection system defines and builds out a focal collection point to enable sharing of information between the many communities affected by cyber. A cyber offense collection system should first define training and certification requirements which then will be used to build out a career path capable of providing the United States with offensive dominance. Developing a culture collection system starts with a cyber security policy articulated throughout DoD with clearly defined responsibilities and accountability standards. Finally, the cyber requirements collection system should focus on developing research and also on the development of a standard to address desired cyber resiliency features (e.g. the ability to maintain or return to a known trusted state, network and component awareness, etc) and then to track the incorporation of the standard into requirements and acquisition programs (acquisition category (ACAT) 1 programs first).

4.2. System Performance Metrics

Once collection systems are in place to execute the cyber strategy, the Department can begin collecting performance metrics. To jump to the end (outcome) metrics without the common enterprise standards, audit definitions, and an understanding of what the metrics mean, would generate little value. As an example, immediately gathering the number of cyber violations might appear to provide an indication of personnel compliance. However, if a cyber violation in organization A is not defined the same as a cyber violation in organization B then little is gained from such activity. Ultimately, the Department desires to measure outcomes, such as the average time it takes to detect a successful attack that breaches the network perimeter defenses, and the amount of time it takes to recover a system that is lost as a result of a cyber attack.

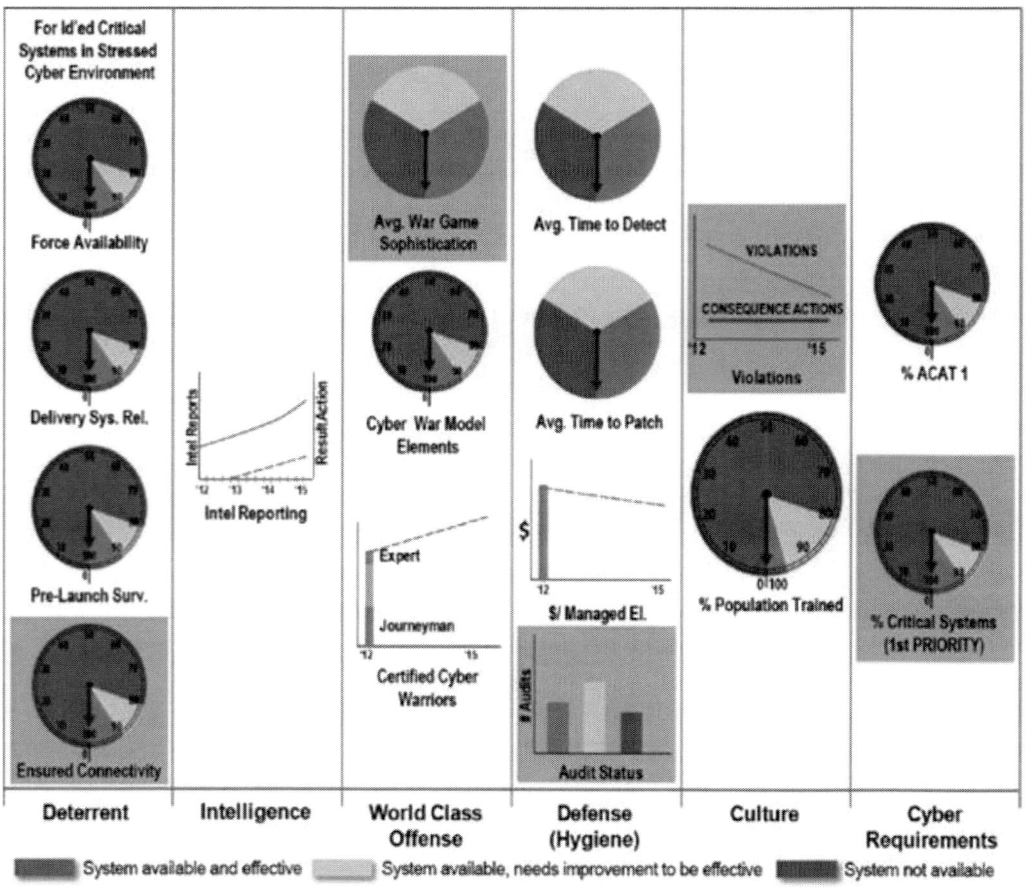

Figure 4.2. Notional Dashboard of System Performance Metrics.

The Task Force estimates that within two years of gathering data, the DoD would have an experience base with the proposed metrics that would begin to allow comparisons of architectures, networks, and system elements for their contribution to cyber resilience and cost to operate. That data would provide DoD insight to inform predictions of performance of various architectures and elements versus available budgets.

The initial set of performance metrics should be kept small until sufficient enterprise experience is established to exercise quantitative assessment of progress. Once an initial set of performance metrics start to identify progress, additional performance metrics may be created. For example, an initial set of performance metrics addressing cyber culture simply measure the number of violations and personnel actions. Once the collection system is capable of accurately capturing this information, follow on performance metrics could be built to measure training responsiveness to new or specific attack vectors or measure training effectiveness by conducting unannounced testing. Training costs could then be assessed by number of violations to both training events and real events.

Performance metrics in other areas should also yield useful information. The following suggested performance metrics identify specific knowledge the Department would use to address its cyber resiliency status. An initial defense hygiene performance metric focusing on the number of audits conducted to a known standard should support comparison of network architectures and operating costs. This is in stark contrast to the current state of auditing which, if done at all, is conducted across an assortment of standards and networks, resulting in the inability to derive enterprise knowledge. Performance measures to track offensive cyber can start simply with focus on the number of certified individuals against time. As baseline data becomes available, the Department will better understand its cyber posture and capabilities and can add more sophisticated measures to accelerate insight and drive progress.

5.0. Maintaining Deterrence in the Cyber Era

In the process of conducting this study, it became apparent that the full spectrum cyber threat represented by a Tier V-VI capability is of such magnitude and sophistication that it could not be defended against. As such, a defense-only strategy against this threat is insufficient to protect U.S. national interests and is impossible to execute. **Therefore, a successful DoD cyber strategy must include a deterrence component.** One key element of deterrence is the believable military capability to either defeat an attack or to provide a survivable response that holds at risk something the adversary highly values (i.e. the adversary's cost exceeds the adversary's gains). The top of that escalation ladder is the present U.S. nuclear deterrent.

The cyber threat highlights another key element of deterrence theory--attribution. Providing attribution against an isolated cyber attack can be slow and difficult. However the Task Force believes that attribution can be accomplished for attacks that would reach the level of really harming the country, because attacks of that scale require planning and multiple attack vectors--which usually leave clues. The Task Force believes attribution can be achieved for a sustained attack over a lengthy time period--whose integrative effects become catastrophic, as well as for a massive large-scale attack. In the former case, U.S. intelligence gathering is proficient at attribution when presented with sufficient time. In the latter case, large-scale attacks leave clues that provide attribution and even warning.

The ultimate goal is to protect the country and provide global stability. A deterrence strategy that encompasses cyber requires that the United States be viewed as a credible cyber force by those who may wish to present a challenge. The strategy will require an escalation framework with associated signaling and red thin-line strategies, and credible survivable military capabilities. The specific force-level and mix of military capabilities for this deterrence strategy requires further study that is beyond the scope of this report. However the Task Force believes a comprehensive deterrence strategy that addresses the cyber threat would certainly include offensive cyber and selected conventional military capabilities that are survivable and support a deliberate escalation ladder.

5.1. Background

The Nuclear Posture Review (NPR), published in April, 2010, provided the Obama Administration's roadmap for nuclear policy. It placed nuclear terrorism and proliferation as top priorities, along with reducing the role and numbers of nuclear weapons. One of the key conclusions from the 2010 NPR is given as follows:[27]

"The United States will continue to strengthen conventional capabilities and reduce the role of nuclear weapons in deterring non-nuclear attacks, with the objective ***of making deterrence of nuclear attack on the United States ...the sole purpose of U.S. nuclear weapons" (emphasis added).***

The United States would only consider the use of nuclear weapons in "extreme circumstances." The United States would not use or threaten to use nuclear weapons against non-nuclear states who are parties to the nuclear proliferation treaty.

The 2010 NPR did not refer to the "New Triad" (nuclear and conventional global strike, defensive systems, and responsive infrastructure) of the 2002 NPR, and instead called for continuation of the traditional Nuclear Triad (e.g. bombers, ICBMs, SLBMs), albeit with reduced warheads and delivery vehicles per the START Follow-On treaty between the United States and Russia. It is important in the context of this report that the 2010 NPR was essentially silent on relationship between the U.S. nuclear deterrent, indeed the U.S. strategic deterrence posture, and the domain of cyber and cyber warfare. Presumably one would characterize a catastrophic Tier V-VI adversary cyber attack on the United States as "extreme circumstances" in the public language of the 2010 NPR, so that is not precluded in the stated policy, but it is not explicitly mentioned.

Over the past decade, policy advocacy grew for a conventional global strike capability (2002 NPR, 2006 QDR). In these cases, there were essentially two arguments justifying a conventional strike capability:

1. To reduce the overall number and reliance on nuclear weapons by now holding nuclear targets at risk with precision conventional (non-nuclear) strike capabilities28,29
2. To offer non-nuclear global strike alternatives to national leadership in time-critical scenarios[30]

The Task Force concluded that the severity of the Type V-VI cyber threat resulted in adding a third reason for a non-nuclear conventional and cyber survivable strike capability with a special emphasis on "survivability":

3. To provide a non-nuclear but cyber survivable escalation ladder between conventional conflict and the nuclear threshold – that is to increase stability and build a new sub-nuclear red line in this emerging era of a cyber peer competitor delivering a catastrophic attack.

Despite the past decade of policy deliberations on new conventional global strike capabilities as part of a deterrence strategy, the situation today is such that the ultimate U.S. deterrent, including response against a catastrophic full spectrum cyber attack, is the nuclear triad– intercontinental ballistic missiles (ICBMs), submarine-launched ballistic missiles (SLBMs), and nuclear-capable heavy bombers. The nuclear command and control (NC2) of the nuclear forces is comprised of systems, communication paths, and procedures associated with National Security Presidential Directive (NSPD)-28, which provides guidance to the Military Departments on the nature of redundant survivable communication paths to each nuclear delivery platform.

Importantly, the definition of "survivability" in the traditional context of Nuclear C2 and forces usually referred to their credible ability to withstand a massive nuclear strike, with all of its attendant effects (including Electromagnetic Pulse (EMP)), and then provide a counter value retaliatory response. The Task Force expands the definition of survivability to include credible capability to withstand a Type V-VI cyber attack.

5.2. Recommendation: Protect the Nuclear Strike As a Deterrent (for Existing Nuclear Armed States and Existential Cyber Attack).

- SECDEF assign USSTRATCOM the task to ensure the availability of Nuclear C3 and the Triad delivery platforms in the face of a full-spectrum Tier V-VI attack – including cyber (supply chain, insiders, communications, etc.)

This Task Force recommends immediate action to assess and assure national leadership that the current U.S. nuclear deterrent is also survivable against the full-spectrum cyber Tier V-VI threat described in the taxonomy of this report. Note that a survivable nuclear triad within a full-spectrum, cyber-stressed environment is required regardless of whether or not one believes U.S. *retaliatory response with our nuclear forces* is a credible response *to a major cyber attack.*

In other words, the basic characteristics of the traditional U.S. nuclear deterrent incorporates survivability as a basic precept; now the U.S. must add survivability in the event of a catastrophic cyber attack on the country as a basic precept.

5.3. Recommendation: Determine the Mix of Cyber, Protected-Conventional, and Nuclear Capabilities Necessary for Assured Operation in the Face of a Full-Spectrum Adversary

- SECDEF and Chairman, Joint Chiefs of Staff (12 months)

The Task Force is confident in the need for assured operation to all three – cyber, protected-conventional, and nuclear – capabilities, including their required C3I infrastructures, against advanced cyber threats. Further analysis is necessary to determine the optimal mix of these capabilities, especially the role of offensive cyber and protected-conventional to form the rungs of an escalation ladder designed to introduce elements of deterrence against Tier V-VI attackers. Recommendation 5.2 addresses the assured availability of the nuclear capability. Similar to the prior argument regarding the cyber resiliency of the nuclear deterrent, DoD must ensure some portion of its conventional capability is able to provide assured operations for theater and regional operations within a full-spectrum, cyber-stressed environment.

The Task Force addresses full spectrum cyber portion later (Chapters 7 and 8). However, the use of offensive cyber as part of an escalation ladder needs further study to determine where and how it can be effectively used. In particular, cyber's inherent stealth nature makes signaling difficult and deliberate signaling may divulge capabilities that then could be easily countered.

The Task Force identified the fundamental attributes of a survivable conventional strike capability comprising the protected-conventional rungs of the escalation ladder:

- Credible counter value effects on target(s) – globally and promptly
- Unambiguous signaling, as part of an escalation ladder, non-nuclear options, capabilities and intentions
- Reliable, safe, and secure; (High confidence of operation in a cyber contested environment)
- Treaty compliant
- Affordable – maximize use of existing systems and infrastructure
- Redundant and cyber survivable command and control (C2)

Because the expected cost of implementing cyber resiliency against V-VI threats is significant, the protected-conventional capability must support a very limited number of cyber- critical, survivable missions. Overextending cyber resiliency for all conventional capability will overwhelm DoD resources (technical, managerial, and financial). DoD must discipline itself to identify sufficient protected-conventional capability for assured operations. Furthermore, cyber resiliency can only be achieved by segmenting and isolating forces from general purpose forces. In the absence of a cyber threat, segmented forces are likely to possess slightly less capability than their non-segmented counterparts due to the isolation from every part of the supporting infrastructure which generates so much advantage to DoD. However, in the face of an adversary employing cyber, the segmented forces will provide far more capability than their non-segmented counterparts.

5.3.1. Segment Sufficient Forces to Assure Mission Execution in a Cyber Environment

Segmentation must differentiate only sufficient forces required to assure mission execution; it is not required across an entire capability. For example, if long range strike is a component of the protected-conventional capability, the DoD should segment a quantity sufficient to provide mission assurance in a hostile cyber environment (notionally, 20 aircraft designated by tail number, out of a fleet of hundreds, segregated and treated as part of the cyber critical survivable mission force). Segmented forces must remain separate and isolated from the general purpose forces with no dual purpose missions (e.g. the current B-52 conventional/nuclear mission). As a starting point, the Task Force proposes the basic force elements comprising a protected-conventional capability take the form of a survivable second strike conventional mission described in Table 5.1 and listed below:

- Long Range Bombers with precision cruise missiles – currently operational with varying force mix options and numbers
- SSGN with long-range precision cruise missiles – currently operational with capability up through Tomahawk Block IV (offering an upper limit of greater than 600 weapons assuming four SSGNs at sea)
- Conventional ballistic missiles or ballistic/glide hybrids - none currently operational; experimental concepts being tested
- Survivable national and CCMD C2 leveraging nuclear thin line

The above supported by:

- Build "true" Out-of-Band Command and Control for the most sensitive systems
- War reserve simplified operating systems

5.3.1.1. SECDEF Assign Unified Command Plan (UCP) Mission of Protected - Conventional

Strike to USSTRATCOM.

- USSTRATCOM given target for initial operating capability (IOC) (24 months)
- USSTRATCOM provide desired planning factors (pre-"launch" survivability, Communications and C2 reliability, targeting/damage expectancy, etc) (6 months)
- USD(AT&L), in coordination with CIO, perform a system of systems (SoS) analysis on selected conventional strike capabilities to determine risk and define an acquisition plan to ensure an enduring survivable capability (6 months)
- Under Secretary of Defense for Policy (USD(P)) engage multi-agency counterparts for an updated Strategic Deterrence Strategy in 2014 NPR – cyber escalation scenarios on both sides (12 months) USSTRATCOM integrate offensive cyber capabilities, as described in Chapter 7, with protected-conventional UCP mission.

Table 5.1. Notional Elements of Protected-Conventional Strike Capability

Precision Strike Platforms	C3
Submarines with Long Range (1000+ nmi) Cruise Missiles	Advanced EHF, ELF/VLF, Dedicated Fiber
Penetrating Bombers	CCMD & Senior Leader Decision Tools & Displays
Long- Range Conventional Missiles	Emergency Action Messages (EAMs) for Conventional Strike ("CAMs")

5.4. Conventional Deterrent Measures

Figure 5.1 shows measures proposed to support the creation of a conventional deterrent as an escalation path to our nuclear deterrent. The establishment of the system performance measures in the previous Chapter called for (starting at the bottom of figure 4.2) the establishment of planning factors, the selection of the "critical systems" that would be included as part of the conventional deterrent, and acquisition plans to bring those capabilities online. As the identified critical systems are modified and built, they would be measured for availability in a stressed cyber environment. Since this is expected to be a relatively small number of systems, each would be measured through analysis, testing or war games for:

- Connectivity to leadership C2 (President of the United States (POTUS)/USSTRATCOM)
- Prelaunch survivability of the system
- Reliability of delivering payload to target

Figure 5.1. Conventional Deterrent Measures.

It's envisioned that each measurement would be in the form of a calculated availability from test and analysis results. The "rolled up" average across systems would be displayed on a dial chart, with red, yellow and green portions as availability is increased. The calculated combination of these three measures provides a force availability measurement of our conventional deterrent capability in a stressed cyber environment. While it may take several years to build the maturity in the systems to be able to populate the force availability metric, the experience gained producing the connectivity, survivability and delivery metrics build to that ultimate Force Availability result.

6.0. Collecting Intelligence on Peer Adversaries' Cyber Capabilities

6.1. Background: Scope of Higher-Tier Threats

The Task Force received briefings on widespread intrusions and the theft of significant amounts of technical information from government and U.S. industrial base networks. There is ample open source evidence to indicate that adversaries are planning high-end attacks. Chinese doctrinal writings[31] on cyber and asymmetric warfare portend that country's use of cyberbased means to disconnect and disable U.S. Command, Control, Communications, Computers, Intelligence, Surveillance, and Reconnaissance (C4ISR) and DoD fighting elements in the event of a conflict.

The widespread theft of intellectual property (IP) from the DoD and U.S. industrial base, could position prospective adversaries with the knowledge needed to employ countermeasures to advanced U.S. military systems, and also shorten a given adversary's research and development timelines for such countermeasures. The Task Force was briefed on Internet-based threats to information systems that originate abroad as well as within CONUS, using "hop points" to avoid some U.S. countermeasures that can only be used against foreign-based threats. These cyber-based capabilities provide a baseline from which to develop and field offensive cyber tools aimed at denying U.S. access to systems and networks.

While the cyber realm presents asymmetric vulnerabilities to networked systems today, high end threats have been around for a long time, and are not confined to software and network operations.

During the Cold War, for example, the United States knew of widespread Soviet theft of US intellectual property, and implemented a program to counter the theft.[32]

The importance of countering cyber threats to U.S. National Security is increasingly recognized by U.S. leadership. In a recent hearing before the Senate Select Committee on Intelligence, FBI Director Mueller said "I do not think today it [cyber] is necessarily the number one threat, but it will be tomorrow. Counterterrorism and stopping terrorist attacks, for the FBI, is a present number one priority. But down the road, the cyber threat, which cuts across all programs, will be the number one threat to the country."[33]

6.2. Recommendation: Refocus Intelligence Collection and Analysis to Understand Adversarial Cyber Capabilities, Plans and Intentions, and to Enable Counterstrategies

- SECDEF, in coordination with the Directors of the Central Intelligence Agency (CIA), Federal Bureau of Investigation (FBI), and the Department of Homeland Security (DHS), should require the DNI to enhance intelligence collection and analysis on high-end cyber threats. Request the creation of an Intelligence Community-wide implementation plan that defines implementable enhancements, and their resource impact on DoD, DHS elements CIA and FBI. (12 months)

Subversions of sophisticated hardware and software systems are extraordinarily difficult to detect through testing and inspection. This led the DSB Task Force to conclude that deeper intelligence about adversaries' offensive software and hardware tools is essential to counter high-end, state-sponsored cyber threats, because it can help focus U.S. efforts on likely targets of compromise.

This intelligence must include the following:

- Identification and understanding of adversarial cyber weapon development organizations, tools, partnerships (e.g., supply chain), leadership, and intentions;
- Development of targeting information to support initiatives to counter cyber weaponization;
- Accurate assessment of adversarial plans and capabilities for policy makers.

Previous DSB reports have addressed both the importance of intelligence and the associated challenges of meeting these intelligence requirements. Based upon the impossibility of sufficiently mitigating a Tier V-VI threat without filling these intelligence gaps and the national security impact of not effectively addressing this threat, the Intelligence Community must increase the priority of its intelligence collection and reporting requirements in this domain.

6.2.1. In Response to State Sponsored Threats, the Task Force Recommends the Creation of a Counterintelligence Capability to Directly Address the Most Sophisticated Threats Using Tools and Techniques Derived from Both Defensive and Offensive U.S. Cyber Programs

6.3. Intelligence Performance Measures

It is essential that organizations throughout the Department (and the United States Government) understand what impact cyber attacks are having on government systems, and what is being done to counter such attacks.

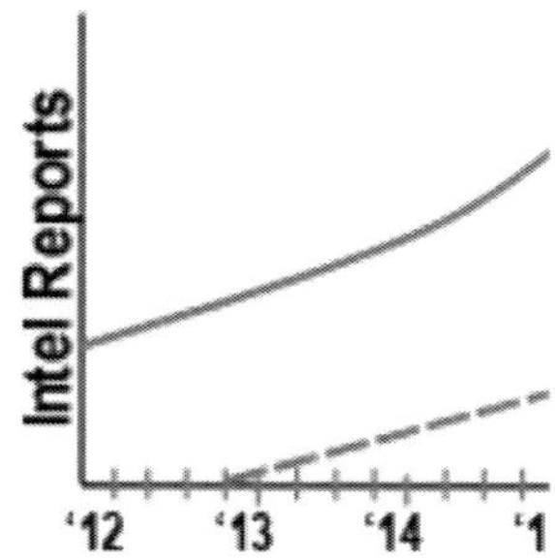

Figure 6.1. Intelligence.

Organizations in the Department today, however, do not generally share details about cyber attacks that have compromised their systems. Instead, system compromises are often classified, keeping people in the dark who must be aware so they can anticipate similar attacks. Consequently, DoD organizations are trying to field defenses based only on partial knowledge of what kind of vulnerabilities are being exploited.

Early performance metrics in intelligence, as illustrated in Figure 6.1 would track the number of reports generated, and the number of those reports that actually generated changes to our systems to better protect them. Further refinement could include a feedback mechanism to track adversary reaction to the initial changes enabled by intelligence.

7.0. Developing World-Class Cyber Offensive Capabilities

7.1. Background

To prevent the threat of cyber attack from limiting U.S. freedom of action in the global economic and political system, no strategic competitor or adversary can be allowed to gain (or mistakenly believe that they have gained) offensive cyber superiority. The U.S. must be a superior competitor in the cyber domain. Current trends, however, could lead some of our country's adversaries to believe that their offensive cyber capabilities, together with their mission-critical defensive postures, are sufficient to neutralize current U.S. conventional or nuclear force capabilities, and thereby hold at risk critical U.S. infrastructures vital to the Nation's economic, political and military operations. Cyber offense is both an enabler for military operations and, as argued in previous chapters, is a critical rung in the escalation ladder for U.S. deterrence strategy.

Offensive cyber operations require *sustained privileged access* to a target system or network. Gaining such privileged access is challenging for most targets of military interest. One must discover or create useful vulnerabilities to gain access, and escalate privilege. Moreover, the existence of this avenue must remain undiscovered by the target for significant periods of time. Target system or network configurations are subject to unexpected changes and upgrades, so an avenue of access that worked one day might not work the next. The adversary can also be expected to employ highly-trained system and network administrators, and this operational staff will be equipped with continuously improving network defensive tools and techniques (the same tools we advocate to improve our defenses). Should an adversary discover an implant, it is usually relatively simple to remove or disable. ***For this reason, offensive cyber will always be a fragile capability.***

Cyber offensive weapons also add a new complexity to warfare. Unlike a conventional bomb, where once it detonates has no further military value, a cyber weapon, if not carefully designed, can be potentially reused by the enemy or "bounce back" and potentially threaten our own systems.

Discovering which of an adversary's system and network components are useful targets requires full-spectrum intelligence support. Intelligence support assets are almost always in short supply and, in the case of those needed to support offensive cyber planning, the shortage is even more acute. In some cases, a component of the system or network of interest may already have been fitted with some level of access arising from non-offensive cyber intelligence priorities. Such access may be helpful but still not offer the granularity needed for precise military targeting. For example, an intelligence agency may have access on a network used for intelligence exploitation and USCYBERCOM[34] may desire to develop an order of battle plan against that target. Intelligence interest may stop at a server or router in the network, to conduct intelligence operations at those points. USCYBERCOM's mission requires situational awareness and access down to the terminal or device level in order to support attack plans. USCYBERCOM would need to work with intelligence agencies to ensure the portions of the system they disable don't disable critical intelligence assets. In other cases, no pre-existing access will be in place and the access effort must start from scratch. History shows that such situations can take a long time (i.e., months or years) to achieve results.

Given the potential stealth (e.g. widespread deployment of relatively undetectable "sleeper malware") and much more compressed time scales likely to be associated with cyber conflicts, a much better understanding of the dimensions and escalatory consequences of such conflicts is needed. Of special significance is the possibility that a well-orchestrated, pre-emptive cyber strike by an adversary, who is able to fully integrate multiple cyber and non-cyber capabilities, could render the U.S. incapable of using any of its own offensive capabilities for a retaliatory strike. The time-honored principles of Initiative and Offense will undoubtedly remain paramount in cyber conflict strategy and doctrine.

U.S. policy must clearly indicate that offensive cyber capabilities will be utilized (preemptively or in reaction; covertly or overtly), in combination with other instruments of national power, whenever the National Command Authority decides that it is appropriate. The recent DoD Cyber Strategy leaves this option open and discusses potential U.S. responses to cyber attack. The appropriate authorities must exist with those responsible to protect U.S. interests.

The intellectual and empirical underpinnings for strategy and doctrine for kinetic, nuclear, counterterrorism, counterinsurgency, and other missions have been extensively documented and debated for decades. Most modern militaries have adapted these underpinnings to their own situations and have implemented them within their own contexts. In contrast, relatively little has been documented or extensively debated concerning offensive cyber operations. This is especially true with respect to the use of offensive capability as a component of a larger strategic deterrence that, to be effective, must achieve visible results against the adversary but not reveal enough about the capability for an adversary to create a defense. DoD should expect cyber attacks to be part of all conflicts in the future, and DoD should not expect adversaries to play by U.S. versions of the rules (e.g. should expect that they will use surrogates for exploitation and offensive operations, share IP with local industries for economic gain, etc.)

USCYBERCOM, and its supporting Service Component Commands, must be the driving force to surface the doctrine, organization, training, materiel, leadership and education, personnel and facilities (DOTMLPF) /Unity-of-Effort gaps and advocate for requisite gap-closure actions. The Intelligence Community and other United States Government Departments and Agencies, with distinct and overlapping authorities, also have key supporting responsibilities. Given the nation's cyber defensive posture, time is of the essence in developing a broader offensive cyber capability.

7.2. Recommendation: Build and Maintain World-Class Cyber Offensive Capabilities (with Appropriate Authorities)

7.2.1. Commander USCYBERCOM Develop a Capability to Model, War Game, Red Team and Eventually Train for Full Scale Peer-on-Peer Cyber Warfare

- Select an FFRDC-like Center of Excellence. (within 6 months)
- Develop capability to model peer-on-peer (red & blue with supporting situation awareness tools and techniques) full scale conflict, similar to nuclear exchange models (trigger uncertainties, deliver link probabilities, blow-back risk, recovery abilities and timelines, etc.) (IOC within 18 months of contract award)
- Develop model and validate—evolve through red team and cyber range/war game exercises. Move beyond tabletop level of sophistication. (IOC within 18 months of modeling capability)

Planning for and successfully executing a single offensive cyber operation requires a significant set of competencies (e.g. computer science, engineering, encryption, linguistics, geo-political context, military planning and targeting, and more). Given peer and near-peer adversaries who may wish to challenge the United States via cyber aggression, the DoD must develop the capacity to conduct many (potentially hundreds or more) simultaneous, synchronized offensive cyber operations, while defending against a like number of cyber attacks. Today, U.S. activities are focused on individual targets in relatively static environments. Understanding interactions and dependencies involved in large scale cyber battle will be required to plan the battle, determine the scale of forces required, and conduct operations at time of conflict.

This situation is similar to when the United States was at the end of WWII, with the newly developed nuclear bomb. It took decades to develop an understanding of how to best use the weapon, and the strategies to achieve stability with the Soviet Union (based on mutually assured destruction). Much of that work started at The RAND Corporation, an FFRDC, with toy rocket surrogates and table top exercises, growing over time into sophisticated simulations and tests that led to strategies for protecting the country. The United States should expect that a similar kind and level of effort will be necessary to mature its understanding and strategies for the use of cyber offensive capabilities. Unfortunately, the Task Force could find no evidence of modeling or experimentation being undertaken to better understand the large-scale cyber war. NSA's recent "red flag war game" is one of the few exceptions that have begun to explore the implications of large-scale cyber operations during the fog of war.

Modeling and understanding a peer-on-peer conflict, with many sorties taking place at once, triggering mechanisms for our own attacks coming and going as networks go offline, addressing blowback of attacks onto its own assets, etc., will be a very complicated undertaking. Even more challenging is that, unlike use of a nuclear weapon (presumably under only extraordinary conditions or threat), cyber attacks are expected in every future conflict, and as discussed earlier in the report, the most significant vulnerability is in the U.S. critical infrastructure on which both the military capabilities and civilian populations depend. To determine the scale of forces needed and the optimal strategies to defend our country, a robust understanding of large scale cyber offense is required. Moreover, the adversary gets a vote. Cyber war is unlikely to be fought as the United States might like to assume it will be. The United States must be ready to adapt to an adversary that is willing to create its own rules.

7.2.2. USD(P) Should Establish a Policy Framework for Offensive Cyber Actions to Include Who Has What Authority (for Specific Actions), under What Circumstances, under What Controls

- Completion Date: 18 Months

The appropriate authorities must exist with those responsible to protect U.S. interests. Cyber actions can take place in very short time periods and those responsible to protect the country must understand their roles and authorities. This Task Force has not extensively studied or made recommendations about the definition of "appropriate authorities." Several other efforts are underway in the administration to address this issue and DoD is only one of many players in the broad protection of the United States against cyber attack.

7.2.3. Commander, USCYBERCOM to Increase the Number of Qualified Cyber Warriors, and Enlarge the Cyber Infrastructure Commensurate with the Size of the Threat

- Completion Date: 18 Months

The DoD has qualified cyber warriors on the job today, supported by robust training programs and cyber toolsets. However there appears to be a "burnout factor" beginning to exhibit itself among these elite people. The Department must scale up efforts to recruit, provide facilities and training, and use these critical people effectively. The Task Force believes there is general agreement today that more cyber warriors are needed, however, no conclusion on the ultimate size for which the department should plan has been reached. Executing this recommendation will generate a requirement for the cyber warrior force size.

7.2.4. USD(P&R), in Collaboration with the Commander, USCYBERCOM and the Service Chiefs Establish a Formal Career Path for Dod Civilian and Military Personnel Engaged in "Offensive Cyber Actions"

- Address training and certification requirements
- Define career designations
- Define incentives for personnel achieving higher levels of certification

- Ensure that there is a cadre of high-end practitioners
- Completion: 18 Months with quarterly reviews with the DEPSECDEF

"Cyber Warrior" is a new domain for the Department, and this new class of job will require career paths, training expectations and incentives to attract and develop the needed expertise. It is not clear that high-end cyber practitioners can be found in sufficient numbers within typical recruitment pools. The DoD has the ability to define what it needs and adjust its personnel policies to enable achievement of that goal.

7.3. World-Class Offense Measures

Building a world-class cyber offense is already well on its way within the Department. The elements needed to ensure a successful capability are:

- A sufficient number of trained cyber warriors
- A formal career path to allow cyber expertise to be rewarded
- The ability to model and simulate peer-on-peer cyber conflict at scale
- The ability to conduct war games against Tier VI capable adversaries

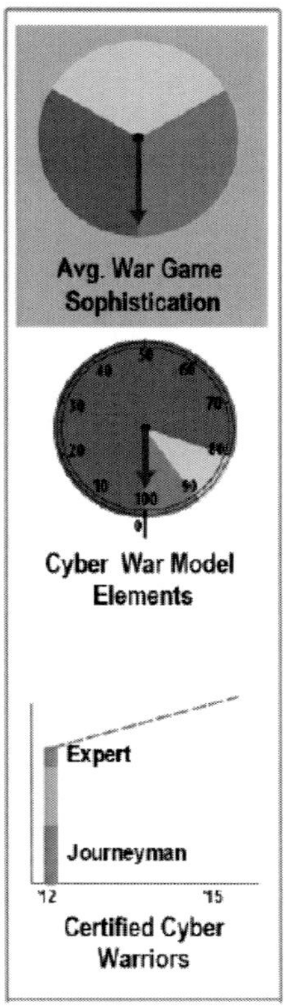

Figure 7.1. World-Class Offense Metrics.

Notional system performance metrics are depicted in Figure 7.1. The first proposed metric is the simple measure of the number of certified cyber warriors over time. The measure would also include a breakdown of the levels of capability comprised within the total number. By tracking the number over time, the Department can ensure it is growing the number of cyber warriors. As modeling and simulation capabilities are further developed, the DoD will be able to project the needed levels of cyber warriors to conduct potential expected operations. At that point a target would be added to the metric.

The second metric focuses on the ability to model and better understand peer-on-peer cyber warfare. The proposed metric is a dial scale building from today's limited understanding of single and small numbers of attacks based on a few network elements up through developing the ability to model and simulate conflicts with hundreds or even thousands of simultaneous events.

The final metric is a measure of war game sophistication. Today most war games and red teams are conducted using low and mid-Tier attack capabilities only. The NSA's recent Red Flag exercise was one of the first attempts at measuring systems against more advanced attack capabilities. DoD must build cyber ranges that can be isolated and controlled, yet still operated at a reasonable scale to continue to develop understanding of the vulnerabilities of operational systems against attacks up to Tier VI sophistication. This measure would take an average of all red teams and war games conducted in any period by the level of sophistication of the threat used in each exercise.

8.0. Enhancing Defenses to Thwart Low- and Mid-Tier Threats

8.1. Background

For more than 15 years, the Department has invested significant resources (people and funding) in an effort to prevent, detect and respond to a full range of cyber threats. Recognizing the interdependency of DoD systems and networks, there has been an attempt to put in place a formal framework and integration capability (Defense-Wide Information Assurance Program and Global Information Grid Information Assurance Program) to provide coherency to the individual Service and Agency programs. The Information Assurance (IA) Component of the DoD Global Information Grid, approved in 2005 provided a broad architectural baseline for implementation of IA and network defense measures.[35] Strong authentication based on the Common Access Card (CAC) and Public Key Infrastructure (PKI) capabilities and other Defense in Depth mechanisms added to the overall “assurance” of the networks.

Then, based on a significant infection of the Unclassified but Sensitive Internet Protocol (IP) Router Network (NIPRNet) and the Secret Internet Protocol Router Network (SIPRNet)in 2008, deployment of additional technologies, e.g., Host Based Security System (HBSS) and other hardening and situational awareness tools were accelerated.

While well-intentioned and strongly supported, these and subsequent initiatives have not had the desired impact on the overall IA posture of the Department. Defensive measures implemented at the boundaries between the NIPRNet and the Internet proved to be only marginally effective in blocking successful intrusions or reducing the overall attack surface of DoD networks and systems. Mobile platforms (smart phones, tablets, etc.) exacerbate this already challenging problem. Red teams, conducting operations during military exercises or at the request of Military Department and Agency officials, continue to have a nearly perfect success rate breaking into the systems.

Within classified networks, once thought to be safe for military command and control traffic, our adversary has successfully penetrated vulnerabilities created by poor user practices and a lack of discipline at all levels of the command structure. Operation BUCKSHOT YANKEE was clearly a wake-up call, suggesting that *every* system relied on for the conduct of war fighting operations is at risk of exploitation by an increasingly sophisticated adversary; an adversary ready and able to exploit any technical or human weakness to achieve their objectives.

After-action reports, long after the detection and mitigation of this serious infection of a classified network, continue to point at residual weaknesses. Heightened awareness, enhanced detection capabilities, and greater accountability of everyone concerned with activities involving the network have not fully eliminated the threat vector originally leveraged in BUCKSHOT YANKEE.

The complexity of systems and networks, connectivity and interdependence (with other DoD, contractor and commercial provider networks); inadequately trained (and overworked) system administrator and maintenance personnel; lack of comprehensive automation capabilities that would free trained personnel to focus on the most serious problems; lack of broad visibility into situational awareness of systems and networks and inadequate or non-existent Mission Assurance Strategies and Plans all contribute to a "Readiness" level that is well below what is appropriate or needed for the Department to project power in the face of the asymmetric threat facing the Nation today. These issues have been the subject of numerous studies, reports, briefings and discussions between all levels of the Department, yet forward progress remains slow while the threat continues to grow rapidly.

The DoD CIO's IT Modernization and Joint Information Enterprise initiative recognizes and addresses many of the existing shortcomings. This effort focused on:

- Collapsing networks
- Providing for a single authoritative source for Directory and Access
- Consolidation of Datacenters
- Common Enterprise Services
- Effective Enterprise governance to achieve compliance
- Adequate funding

The effort to date is not measurably different than previous attempts (implemented through the Defense Information Assurance Program (DIAP) and the Global Information Assurance Portfolio (GIAP) to achieve similar ends. This effort must be expanded to include a specific Enterprise Architecture (EA) that becomes ***THE*** target architecture for every Military Department and Agency within the DoD.

8.2. Recommendation: Enhance Defenses to Protect Against Low and Mid-Tier Threats

8.2.1. Establish an Enterprise Security Architecture, Including Appropriate "Building Codes and Standards", That Ensure the Availability of Enabling Enterprise Missions. The Architecture Should Allow for the Ability to:

- Segment the network
- Provide continuous monitoring and situational awareness
- Automate patch and threat management functions
- Audit to the enterprise standard
- Recover to a known (trusted) state
- Provide out-of-band command and control for most sensitive systems

- Responsibility: DoD Chief Information Officer (in collaboration with Military Departments and Agencies). (6 months)

While the Department's size (about 6 million devices connected to the networks) makes this problem challenging, DoD is made up of individual network segments that are connected together, just like everyone else's networks. Examples of similar (but smaller) network structures from the larger contractors in the defense industrial base offer valuable lessons for the DoD.

In 2005, a number of DoD contractors were the victims of advanced cyber attacks. Then Deputy Defense Secretary, Gordon England, held a meeting with the CEOs of the Department's biggest suppliers and laid out a plan for what became the Defense Industrial Base (DIB) Cyber Security/Information Assurance (CSIA) Pilot program, which enabled these suppliers to share information on cyber attacks and work with the government to protect its networks. A side benefit from the DIB-CSIA pilot was the education of the CEOs about the risk and the importance of deploying a strong defense across their organizations.

The result of the focus on securing their corporate networks drove the development of network security teams, led by a Chief Information Security Officer (CISO), chartered to develop and publish network standards (typically based on National Institute on Standards and Technology (NIST) network standards) that are used by the operating divisions of the company. Networks are segmented and managed separately within the larger organization structure, but under the monitoring and influence of the CISO. Employees are trained and held accountable for their actions, networks are monitored around the clock and threat vectors are shared across network segments. Most importantly, each network segment is audited (including, penetration testing as well as compliance checks) on a regular basis, and segment organizations failing these audits must report to the CEO and Board of Directors on plans to correct the weaknesses. The Board of Director's Audit Committee tracks progress through completion. This commitment and follow-through by the CEOs have made cyber security a high priority within these companies.

While these companies are not able to block all mid and high tier attacks, and still are not perfect against lower-tier attacks, they have made it much harder (more expensive) for attackers to succeed, reduced the "noise level" on their systems, and freed resources to focus on hunting intruders within the network (anomaly investigations).

DoD represents a larger target and must also deal with operating military systems in addition to the IT structure, but the same concepts are useful. DoD has already put in place some of the pieces, but establishing an enterprise level architecture and achieving consistent compliance is still missing.

Finally, DoD has a history of providing network waivers too readily for new systems coming online. While waivers are occasionally necessary, they almost always weaken the network's security status. Waivers that deal with out-of-date legacy equipment should be eliminated by the creation of enclaves and installation of firewalls. And, generally, DoD needs to be considerably less liberal about issuing waivers. The discipline of avoiding waivers for new systems will have a strong impact on the ultimate security posture of DoD networks.

The goal of a consistently applied and managed architecture across the Department is to take the low-tier threats off the table, thereby reducing the noise level on DoD networks. More effective mitigation of mid and high tier threats then becomes feasible.

8.2.1.1. Segment the Network

The Department already operates a mesh of networks that can be controlled independently. That concept should be extended through all operational war fighting systems, and tests/trials/red teams should be conducted to understand the capabilities and impacts of disconnecting an infected network to prevent infection of other, interconnected networks.

8.2.1.2. Provide Continuous Monitoring and Situational Awareness

An additional challenge for DoD is understanding who is "on" and what is the operational status of their network(s). Sensor deployment has begun at Internet access points to monitor and control access and network traffic flow. These Einstein sensors provide monitoring of network ingress and egress through a system of mostly COTS network monitoring tools driven by the NSA-provided signature set. This is a good start, but commercial tools have advanced to include capabilities to operate behind firewalls and to track anomalous activity throughout the components of a network. It is essential to provide continuous monitoring of all networks against cyber attack (see State Department example in Figure 8.1).

The information assurance of operational systems is typically achieved through encryption of data during network transport (and occasionally at rest - while stored) or multi-level security solutions geared toward the safe handling of multiple security levels of data on the same computer (processor). Data must be decrypted prior to processing, and advanced attacks being used today access the data at that point, thereby circumventing the encryption.

Little consideration goes into military system design today on providing test points that can report system health and operation (sensors). Are checksums overflowing in the processor? Is the processor conducting unexpected computations? There are many "tells" (symptoms) that could be detected and reported. Although such test points and their data transmission would also become targets for cyber attack, an adversary must now have a more detailed understanding of system internals to design a successful attack. The adversary would also be required to break into two systems (the main mission and test/sensor system) and change both correctly without setting off alarms to successfully infiltrate the system – a much more difficult task.

In the recent wars, DoD once again learned the value of timely, detailed situational awareness on the battlefield and invested heavily in Intelligence, Surveillance and Reconnaissance (ISR) assets. The United States must now build the same level of understanding into its networks and weapon systems.

8.2.1.3. Automate Patch and Threat Management Functions

Much of network management in the DoD relies on manual tasks performed by overworked network technicians and administrators. The scale of manual efforts is largely driven by legacy systems using unsupported software operating systems and the lack of consistency in network technology implementation across the Department. The recommendation to isolate systems utilizing older software (no longer maintained by commercial industry) means those systems are removed from the group of components that is regularly updated for malware and other software attacks and then assuming that those systems are likely compromised. The larger GIG is then protected from those systems through strong interface firewalls and detection software. The remaining "compliant" systems can then utilize modern COTS network management software and automate much of the effort required to detect intrusions and push software patches across the network.

Over time, fewer staff should be needed to maintain software patches and network configurations, allowing a shift in effort toward hunting adversaries who have penetrated our networks. Most of the COTS technologies available today have user interfaces that allow high levels of flexibility for determining what is deemed unusual network behavior, allowing system administrators to adjust and adapt the monitoring systems as threats evolve.

8.2.1.4. Audit to the Enterprise Standard

Conduct audits and in-process reviews to develop migration and mitigation strategies (systems that cannot be maintained in a timely matter should be restructured into enclaves and isolated from the GIG through firewalls).

The most important part of the recommendation concerns accountability and consistency that must come from senior leadership support and enforcement. Without this management imperative, an attempt at cultural change to improve cyber security will not be taken seriously within the Department.

A useful example of management proactively supporting a cyber standard and driving organizational acceptance is found within the Department of State (DOS). Several years ago the DOS CIO undertook an effort to improve the cyber security of their 100,000 desktop computer network. They focused on three areas: putting in place continual monitoring of their networks, developing a template and collecting audit data for building risk measures for each network, and publishing the results across the DOS to allow the sharing of best practices and using peer pressure to drive low performing network owners toward improvement.

While the DOS system is certainly simpler than DoD's, many of the barriers they had to overcome: culture, use of technology, and the development of standards and templates to create a common language used to address issues across the department, were very similar.

DOS started with five objectives:

- Scan every 36 to 72 hours
- Focus on attack readiness
- Find-fix top issues daily
- Grade personal results
- Hold managers responsible

Figure 8.1 below shows an example scorecard for a network segment from the DOS network assessment process.

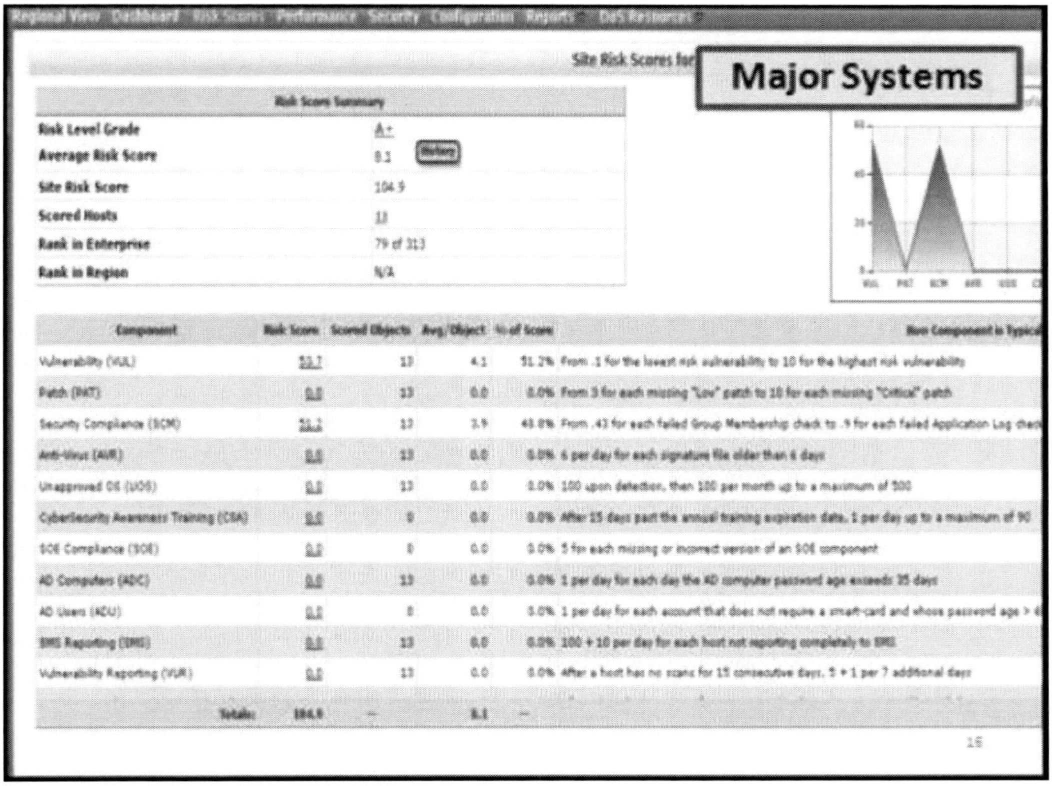

Figure 8.1. DOS System Risk Scorecard.

The data from the scorecards for each network segment are then aggregated into an enterprise view as shown in Figure 8.2. This level of data aggregation allowed DOS senior management to identify risky portions of their broader networks and to focus resources on those areas. While the DoD should develop its own methods and processes to deal with its enterprise, the DOS example is a good reference point.

As a minimum for DoD, continuous monitoring of networks should be expanded to touch all elements with continuous scanning. Audits should be conducted on a regular basis (every 12 to 18 months) on each network segment. The output from the audits should be used by the Secretary of Defense and DoD CIO to improve weak performers toward "green" status and to identify and share best practices across the DoD. ***The results of the audits should become part of a commander's readiness assessment for their operational systems.***

One particular challenge for the DoD is the number of networks and systems that contain technologies no longer supported by the commercial sector. Those systems must be identified and either updated and brought into compliance (preferred, but may not be affordable), or re-positioned in separated enclaves from the broader GIG; connection to these systems should pass through strong firewalls and sensors at CIO controlled points. Permitting out-of-date systems to remain connected to the broader network without the strong controls at access points will only continue to offer attractive vulnerabilities for attackers to exploit.

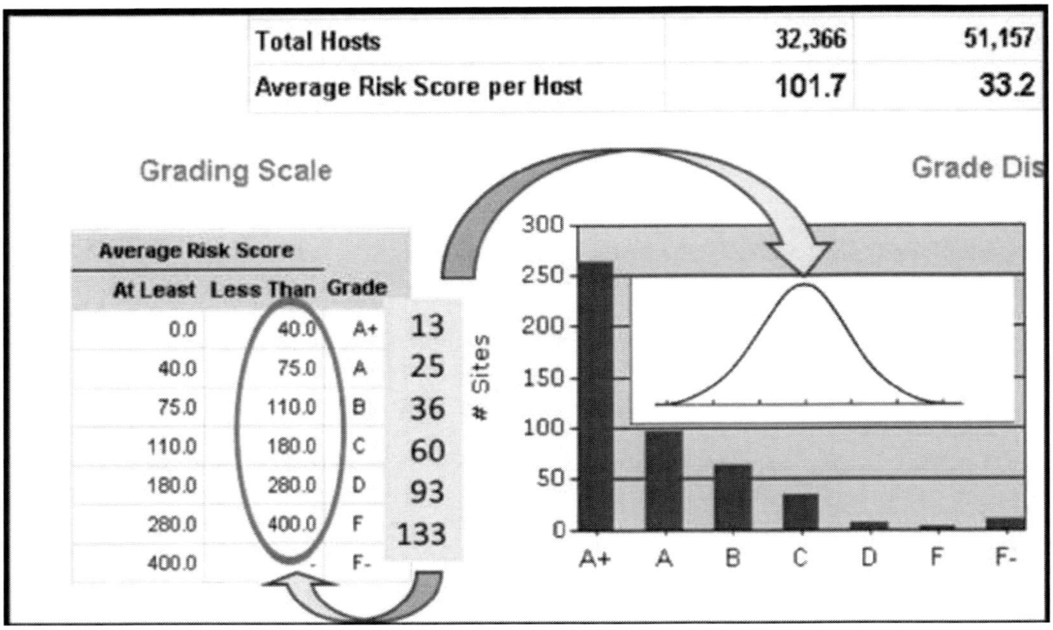

Figure 8.2. DOS Risk Score Indicator for Enterprise.

8.2.1.5. Build Network Recovery Capability

It is not unusual for a sophisticated adversary, who has infiltrated a network, to monitor in real time as the network owners try to kick them out. Frequently, the adversary then implements a counter to the network owner's defensive actions and can be back in the network in a matter of minutes or hours. To fight and win in a war that includes cyber capabilities, DoD can't afford to have the enemy inside its control loops. If DoD is in that situation, then it needs backup (war reserve) mechanisms for C2. Less critical systems need the ability to communicate over an alternative system to address network intrusions, forcing an adversary to penetrate multiple systems and be able to operate both in an integrated, real time fashion to track DoD counterattacks as we try to regain control of our network or system. Having the ability to gracefully degrade and maintain the most critical functions of the systems at an operational level is highly desired, and can usually be achieved with lower bandwidth links.

8.2.1.6. Recover to a Known (Trusted) State

The goal for DoD operational systems should be to:

- Develop the ability to know (and report) if the network or system has been penetrated,
- Gracefully degrade or have provision for alternate mechanisms to continue the most critical mission functions and
- Recover eventually to a known (trusted) state.

Earlier recommendations addressed the first two goals. The last goal is perhaps the most challenging. While maintaining a "gold copy" of system operating software (including firmware, etc.) seems straightforward, a sophisticated adversary will implant an attack into the system via stealthy means. If the adversary has enough patience, as operating systems are updated and gold copies evolve, the adversary's implant will migrate and become part of the trusted baseline. Should a future attack be executed and disable the system, restoring the gold copy software would only reinsert the adversary's original implant.

The Department must develop methods to evolve trusted copies of operating software for systems that ensure only the desired changes are made in the gold copy. Tools exist to perform code checks and are currently used in some important systems (e.g., strategic fire control systems). However, these tools require substantial amounts of human interaction and thus would be difficult to employ broadly across DoD systems. The Department should continue to search the commercial and contractor space to develop tools with higher levels of automation for this function.

Note that these efforts may still be insufficient to protect against an opponent that has operationally introduced vulnerabilities at the hardware level. However, for low- and mid-tier threats, properly executing these measures would significantly enhance DoD's defensive posture.

8.2.2. The Dod Should Leverage Commercial Technologies to Automate Portions of Network Maintenance and "Real-Time" Mitigation of Detected Malware

- Build on existing tools and capabilities currently in use
- Automate response to threat conditions
- Leverage cyber ranges to test emerging technology and develop tactics, techniques and procedures (TTPs) and guide investment strategies.
- Develop mitigation/transition plans for legacy systems
- Responsibility: DoD Chief Information Officer, with support from NSA-IAD, IOC: 6 months, with enhancements released on a quarterly basis

As discussed above, modern COTS software has dramatically improved and can provide automation of several key network management functions. The software products sit at the firewall and behind the firewall which is particularly important to find and track advanced persistent threats. Table 8.1 below includes examples of technologies currently available in the commercial markets and highlights benefits that they offer. The Task Force has been careful to not recommend any products by name or endorse any specific vendors.

Table 8.1. COTS Technology to Automate Portions of Network Management

Technologies Available as COTS	Benefit	Threat LevelAddressed
Enhanced server and network device configuration management.	Automated detection of the status of servers and communications equipment has been refined to a science. New tools are available to dramatically enhance system hygiene through monitoring state and automating patch management. Benefit is enhanced resiliency and better ability to rapidly recover to known best state.	Tiers I, II

Table 8.1. (Continued)

Technologies Available as COTS	Benefit	Threat LevelAddressed
Mobile device configuration management	Enhances ability to manage mobile devices through enterprise tools.	Tiers I, II
Mobile device sandboxing of enterprise data and apps, including virtualization of enterprise desktops	Key to preventing information loss via lost or compromised mobile devices.	Tiers I, II, III
Cloud server security platforms with file integrity monitoring, dynamic firewall automation, configuration monitoring/management, vulnerabilities assessments all optimized for cloud capabilities	Establishes a means to test configuration and manage capabilities provided by public clouds and even internal private clouds shared by internal organizations.	Tiers I - IV
Automation of content distribution and control of content enabling fine-grain tracking of who is authorized to receive and read content.	Mitigates some information disclosures.	Tiers I - IV
Advanced log and event sense-making solutions including analytic approaches for bringing all the data	New Hadoop-based capabilities are enabling enhanced information fusion including sense-making over incredibly large data sets, providing	Tiers I - IV
together for analysis.	benefits of enhanced knowledge of adversary activities.	
Enhanced browser sandboxing to prevent hostile code from entry into the enterprise via the browser.	Significantly reduces the ability of adversaries to trick users to download hostile content or to click on a link that points to a site with malicious code on it.	Tiers I - II
Enhanced configuration management enabling tracking all known state variables to determine device compliance and normality and in real time return systems to known state.	Support to automated hygiene, enhanced defense and more rapid restoration after attack.	Tiers I - IV
Enhance network analysis and real time rule based decisions over traffic at line rates.	Assessment of damage from attacks and continuous hygiene monitoring. Ability to create and update millions of rules on a single device will provide dramatic flexibility in creating new enclaves, blocking communication with hostile sites and preventing malicious code from entering. Will also mitigate key data exfiltration threats.	Tiers I - IV

While these technologies do not address Tier V-VI threats directly, when properly deployed, they make an attacker's task of moving data throughout the systems, while remaining undetected, much more difficult. Our goal is to raise the costs for the Tier V-VI attackers to succeed, limiting the number of operations they can afford to attempt.

8.2.3. USD(P&R), in Collaboration with the DoD CIO and the Service Chiefs Establish a Formal Career Path for DoD Civilian and Military Personnel Engaged in Cyber Defense

- Address training and certification requirements
- Define career designations
- Define incentives for personnel achieving higher levels of certification
- Ensure that there is a cadre of high end practitioners
- Completion: 18 Months with quarterly reviews with the DEPSECDEF

The Task Force expects cyber-focused personnel to move between offensive and defensive focused posts throughout their career. The best defenders will be those who understand what can be accomplished from an offensive point of view (the reverse is also true).

Creating cyber warriors with expertise in offensive and defensive cyber skills should be encouraged. In fact, the Task Force anticipates a greater use of our offensive capabilities to support defensive objectives.

8.3. Cyber Defense (Hygiene) Performance Measures

How DoD defends its systems is perhaps the most straightforward area in cyber to apply useful measures. Most successful attacks reaching DoD networks today result from a personnel failure or out-of-date software in firewalls and detection systems. Most of these attacks are understood and preventable through known signature management (patching), yet DoD defensive systems don't keep up, and attacks continue to penetrate DoD's networks. The architecture and standards to be defined by the DoD CIO in the earlier recommendation provide a starting point toward improving the Department's cyber network defensive posture. A key element for success is driving compliance through the Department. The independence taught to DoD military commanders that provides such significant benefit on the battlefield is a risk to the Departments networks as systems become more and more inter-connected. Relative to cyber, the impact of risk decisions the commanders make in the field is no longer contained within the local environment. To drive the needed behavior, audit results from the CIO must be published and consequences imparted on those consistently out of compliance.

Notional cyber defense hygiene performance measures are depicted in Figure 8.3. The first proposed measure is of the number of audits conducted. The results of these audits can be illustrated on a red-yellowgreen scorecard.

Corporate examples of this practice allow an organization time to move a yellow audit to green by the next audit cycle (typically annually). Red audits require a plan to move the network to green status in a shortened timeframe and are reported to the CEO and the audit committee of the Board of Directors. The same level of leadership attention is required to ensure the importance of compliance to cyber security standards is understood throughout the DoD.

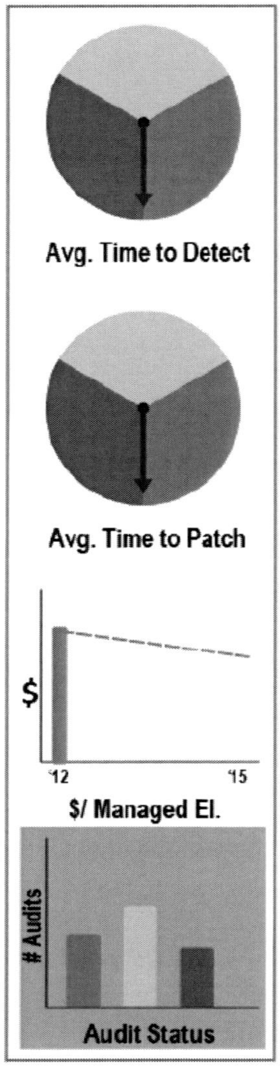

Figure 8.3. Cyber Defense Hygiene Performance Measures.

One of the benefits to each network operating organization conducting CIO-directed audits, will be achieving a higher fidelity inventory of the types and quantities of devices connected to its network. Once those inventories are available, along with the budgets to operate the networks, DoD can produce metrics on the cost to manage a "network element". Collecting this data across DoD networks will provide a basis for comparing network architectures and the actual cost to operate them. This information can be used to identify best-in-class performance within the DoD structure and to drive greater efficiency over time across the broader structure.

The Department would ultimately like to know "who" is in its systems, how they got in, and how long it took DoD to get them out and restore the systems to full operation. To prepare the Department to gather these measures in the future, DoD needs to first understand more about the basic components that drive system vulnerability and develop an ability to detect attacks. Therefore, the next proposed measure is a rollup of the average time to patch a system from the time a software update for a specific attack (signature) becomes available. This report recommends relocating this activity away from manual interaction by network operators to more automated capabilities. As automation levels are increased, the time-to-patch duration should drop precipitously, speeding protection against some (known) attack. The final measure is the average time to detect an attack that has successfully penetrated the network. As successful attacks are found in networks, forensics should be conducted to understand how the attack penetrated and propagated through the network. Gathering information to understand how attacks entered the network and how long they have been sitting in DoD networks marks the beginning toward an understanding of the Department's ability to actually detect and remove successful attacks. It also becomes a measure of how advanced its cyber hunting skills on the network have become as more of the mundane functions are automated and more resources are turned toward ferreting out anomalies within network logs and operations. As more advanced log management tools are deployed on the network and more resources dedicated toward hunting on the network, the time that an attack resides within the network should drop. This data would provide a basis to understand how attacks get into the network, how well we find them and how long it takes to reestablish trust in our systems.

9.0. CHANGING DOD'S CYBER CULTURE TO TAKE SECURITY MORE SERIOUSLY

9.1. Background

DoD's Cyber Culture: Operational Necessity and Personal Culture-Leadership faces an immense challenge to change DoD's culture regarding cyber and cyber capability. Individual and organizational cyber practices result in so many cyber security breaches that many experts believe that DoD networks can never be secure with the current cyber culture. The individual's immersion in the civil sector cyber culture and the military's focus on mission objective are the two most important contributors to DoD's poor cyber culture. In the face of a threat that routinely exploits organizational and personal flaws, DoD leadership must develop a clear vision for the Department's cyber culture.

Most DoD employees, both military and civilian, learned to use the Internet and network capabilities long before they became DoD employees. The naive acceptance of trust in their personal Internet use, and increasing expectation of 24/7 access establishes the baseline for the individual's experience with IT. Little to no thought is given regarding the implications of the vulnerabilities of these personal computing platforms (e.g. smart phones, cameras, printers, etc.). While there is an increasing awareness of personal cyber vulnerability (e.g. identity theft, stolen passwords, etc) and a slowly evolving corresponding acknowledgement of the need for increased security requirements, most problems have not resulted in repercussions serious enough to change behavior. There is very little personal accountability maintained in the civil cyber environment and the consequences of risky behavior is generally marginalized (e.g. the majority of individuals still use predictable and/or easy to crack passwords). Returning to the simpler, more secure non-networked days to solve this problem is an unreasonable expectation and the individual's ability to undermine effective defensive measures cannot be over stated. Since personal cyber practice will potentially trump any rules DoD attempts to impose on its workforce, DoD leadership must take significant steps to educate and impose accountability on individual cyber behavior.

Military culture thrives on overcoming barriers to achieve mission objectives, leaving cyber security, at best, a second thought for even knowledgeable commanders. A common refrain from operational commanders is "Better to be judged by twelve than carried by six." While mission objectives can and should take primacy, commanders must realize the implications of cyber security compromise. A simple tactical expedient in the most remote theater of operations can, under certain circumstances, create a strategic vulnerability elsewhere in the world. However, this is not the first time commanders and political leaders were forced to make disciplined decisions trading tactical objectives against strategic capability. The United States and UK exploitation of ULTRA in World War II often traded short term gains for long term strategic objectives. ULTRA exploitation was so sensitive that it was not officially disclosed until 1974, almost 30 years after the end of WW II.

Additionally, few commanders know or understand the intricate network of devices, hardware, and software that provide them the combat capabilities they depend on to accomplish their missions (e.g. Deputy Secretary Lynn's article "Defending a New Domain"), nor the tools and techniques that are required to infiltrate their systems some as simple as access control. For example the Task Force received a briefing that provided an account of the same individual providing red team member's access via the same known vulnerability two years in a row. Especially worrisome, the individual in question complained to the testing team in year two about the lapse in year one. The individual's failure to address personal shortcomings and the Command's failure to hold its individuals responsible for cyber security in the most routine tasks creates untold vulnerabilities easily exploited by any tier threat.

Communicating Change: Absent strong leadership, individual and organizational behavior are unlikely to change from the permissive and open environment we experience in our personal lives. Senior DoD leadership must communicate a new vision of cyber excellence to the entire Department. This challenge is not new. The U.S. military is one of the best organizations in the world at driving culture and compliance when it chooses. DoD possesses robust cultures impacting physical fitness, weapon control, and handling of classified material-- all communicated by leadership and supported by policy, processes and procedures, training, and breach response actions that strongly reinforce policy to include penalties and loss of privilege that result in loss of employment or prison. In some of the programs mentioned above, achieving compliance required removing the local commander's discretion (e.g. continued failing of weight standards or the physical readiness test will result in dismissal no matter how well the individual performs in all other aspects of their job). Clear expectations of the consequences and mandatory reporting of objective measurements created the environment to drive behavior in the desired direction.

To implement the Department's leadership vision, DoD must develop and apply similar disciplined approaches of personal and command accountability for cyber actions. Leadership must establish policies, standards, and expectations for secure use of DoD networks and systems. While implementation of some cultural practices allow for local command discretion, the cyber threat is too serious. Policies, standards, and expectations must be consistent and not be optional.

To support culture change, leadership focus must provide effective, consistent and sustainable training and education programs. Too much of DoD's required cyber training is a static, checkthe-box drill. DoD needs to develop training programs with evolving content that reflects the changing threat, increases individual knowledge, and continually reinforces policy. Training and education programs should include innovative and effective testing mechanisms to monitor and catch an individual's breach of cyber policy. For example, DoD could conduct random, unannounced phishing attacks against DoD employees similar to one conducted in April of 2011 by a high tech organization to test the cyber security awareness of its workforce. Within a one week period the organization's CIO sent a fake email to about 2000 of its employees. The fake email appeared to originate from the organization's Chief Financial Officer and warned the employees that the organization had incorrectly reported information to the Internal Revenue Service that could result in an audit of their tax return. To determine if they were affected, they were asked to go to (click) to a particular website. Almost 50% of the sample clicked on the link and discovered that this had been a cyber security test. Each of them had failed. Had this been a real phishing attack, every one of these employees not only would have compromised their machines but would have put the entire organization at risk.

Following an initial education period, failures must have consequences to the person exhibiting unacceptable behavior. At a minimum the consequences should include removal of access to network devices until successful retraining is accomplished. Multiple failures should become grounds for dismissal. An effective training program should contribute to a decrease in the number of cyber security violations.

Exercises provide another mechanism to increase effectiveness in an increasingly diverse and hostile cyber environment. Numerous DoD components use realistic exercise programs to increase operational proficiency. Similar techniques must be developed and applied to DoD components and enterprise. Exercise realism should grow from year to year to ensure the DoD closes the cyber threat vulnerability gap.

Today, information assurance and mission assurance are inseparable – as such, command readiness should assess and include cyber policy compliance. Established in 1999, the Defense Readiness Reporting System provides a broad assessment of personnel and systems related to the successful execution of DoD missions. The current DoD Directive (DoDD 7730.65, certified current as of April 23, 2007) provides readiness criteria for virtually every element of war fighting capability, including personnel education, training, and proficiency testing. There are measures to assess Commanders on unit fitness to execute assigned missions and penalties for failure to meet specific standards. Nowhere in the readiness structure are there criteria that specifically addresses the performance of IT components critical to the successful execution of the mission. Reflecting on BUCKSHOT YANKEE, the infection was (likely) caused by a well-intentioned service member who violated policy by moving a flash media device between the unclassified and classified domains. This action resulted in severe impacts on operations and literally months of recovery by individuals already overextended with their normal duties. While this was one of the most egregious examples, any Tier II Computer Network Defense Service Provider (CNDSP) will readily admit that infection of the classified networks due to the inappropriate use of media devices occurs on an all too regular basis. Absent accountability, the situation will never change. Today's permissive cyber culture allows personnel to violate cyber policy in order to get the local job done. These local decisions frequently put the enterprise at risk and as a consequence, mission assurance at risk.

9.2. Recommendation: Change DoD's Culture Regarding Cyber and Cyber Security

9.2.1. Establish a Dod-Wide Policy, Communication, and Education Program to Change the Culture Regarding Cyber and Cyber Security

Secretary of Defense, Chairman, Joint Chiefs of Staff and their direct reports communicate a vision of DoD Cyber Security for 2020. Secretary of Defense and CJCS provide direct communication to all organizational elements explaining the threat and consequences of cyber actions is essential to change DoD's cyber culture. Leadership must change the current culture which is focused on an overwhelming emphasis on operational objectives and shaped by daily exposure in civil cyberspace that imposes little cost to risky behavior.

- Commander, USCYBERCOM and the DoD CIO establish a plan with measureable milestones and flow down to all organization elements. The plan must comprise:
  - The policy, operational rules, and expectations for secure use of DoD networks & systems
  - The training program and follow on continual reinforcement of the policy
  - A small "tiger team" of experts to monitor, test, and catch breaches in policy
  - Clear punitive consequences for breaches of policy

DoD must develop training that evolves with the threat and increases individual knowledge. Training failures must bring consequences, including removal of access to network devices until successful retraining is accomplished. Multiple failures should become grounds for dismissal.

Commanders should use exercises as opportunities to test cyber-hygiene. Realism in exercises should grow over time to ensure operational forces are resilient in the face of an evolving cyber threat.

- Following the education period and a short grace period, penalties should be imposed similar to the breach of policy for classified material
- Command readiness should assess and report cyber policy compliance. SECDEF should require the policy to be communicated within 60 days and the education and roll out to every DoD and contractor employee in 9 months.

The current DoD Directive (DoDD 7730.65, certified current as of April 23, 2007) must be modified to include readiness criteria for cyber capability. Specific performance measures related to the IT components critical to the successful execution of the mission must be used to assess Commanders on unit fitness to execute assigned missions and the readiness system must incorporate penalties for failure to meet specific standards.

9.3. Cyber Culture Performance Measures

The cultural aspect of developing an understanding of the importance of proper cyber hygiene and conduct will probably be the most difficult to achieve activity recommended in this report. It requires changing perceptions and history of how military and civilian personnel are taught to operate. Cyber culture must become as important as weapons handling or physical fitness to our military service members and DoD personnel (and the contractors who support them). Only two performance measures are proposed in this section (Figure 9.1). Each is very simple and consists of easily gathered data. The first is the percentage of the total population to complete the DoD Cyber education program. The green level for the measure should be set very high (above 99%) and the Secretary and his/her direct reports need to take an active ownership role and participate in this education program to ensure ***every*** DoD person has the mandatory training.

The second measure is cyber security violations, rolled up across the Department, and on the same chart the number of punitive actions that have been taken as a result of those violations. Until there are well understood and supported consequences for violating cyber security policies, cyber security will never be viewed as important across the Department.

Figure 9.1. Cyber Culture Performance Measures.

10.0. BUILDING A CYBER RESILIENT FORCE

10.1. Background

Creating a cyber-resilient force in a cost effective manner will challenge DoD. The cyber threat's pernicious intrusion into every aspect of DoD, and its support community, create a global exploitation opportunity for any adversary willing and able to discover or create vulnerability. Fortunately, DoD's experience in building its nuclear deterrent forces provides a proven model to achieve a cyber resilient force (segregation, inspection, trusted suppliers, etc.).

10.1.1. Building a Cyber Resilient Force

The fundamental purpose of building a cyber resilient force is to achieve mission assurance in the cyber environment. Achieving affordable mission assurance, especially against high tier threats (V-VI), requires discipline to first identify protected-conventional capabilities that the United States can rely upon in a cyber attack and then to segment specific forces that will be used to accomplish desired missions. Only these forces receive the highest degree of cyber resilience necessary for assured operation in the face of a full spectrum adversary. This protected-conventional capability, combined with offensive cyber discussed in Chapter 7, form the rungs of an escalation ladder with nuclear forces at the top. To achieve a high degree of cyber resilience at an affordable cost, the Department must segment and segregate the force structure that deliver the desired capability in response to a cyber threat.

As mentioned previously, segmentation must differentiate only those forces required to achieve the desired mission and is not required across an entire capability. This will require a different way of managing the capability. (For example, designating 20 aircraft by tail number as cyber resilient, out of a fleet of hundreds, segregated and treated as part of the cyber critical survivable mission force.) Segmented forces must remain separate and isolated from the general forces, with no dual purpose missions (e.g. the current B-52 conventional nuclear mission). Segmented forces can be used in regional and theater cyber conflicts as a standalone cyber-resilient capability.

Once specific systems are identified, they must be brought to a known cyber resiliency standard which can be used to design, build and measure capability against. The standard must evolve as the cyber threat changes but the Task Force identified a set of attributes for consideration:

- Return to a TRUSTED, known state. The known state must be time invariant. Failing this, components must be controlled throughout their lifecycle and segregated from general purpose forces, including use of and connection to general force networks;
- Maintain component awareness/control (e.g. sensing and reporting of buffer overflow conditions and bit parity checks, reporting and control of update/file transfer points (e.g. USB ports), real time or near real time monitoring at the component level to ensure installation of authentic components/software);
- Maintain network awareness/control (e.g. installation of sensing points to measure network performance and patterns, trusted log audit capability, and trusted and automated patch/update capabilities);
- Provide operational environment support (e.g. identify conditions under which a system can be connected to specified network, conditions under which it must be disconnected or operate in a degraded mode such as use of an out of band path that supplies x% of the unfettered capability, and recovery mechanisms).

Once developed, the standard should inform the requirements process which would allow the operational community to know what it is asking for and also what it is receiving. In addition, a subset of the resiliency standard should be applied to the rest of the force structure at every opportunity to incrementally raise the overall cyber resiliency of DoD. Development and application of a resiliency standard will help tell what DoD is building, but DoD must also focus on how it will accomplish mission assurance.

10.1.2. Subject Defined "Cyber Critical Systems" to More Stringent Mission Assurance Activities

The bottom line objective of system resiliency is assuring mission execution. Therefore, the designated systems must be subjected to a mission assurance assessment process depicted in Figure 10.1 that is structured around a knowledgeable workforce, incorporates feedback from every available means, conducts research and develops new technology addressing cyber resiliency issues, and manages life cycle integrity.

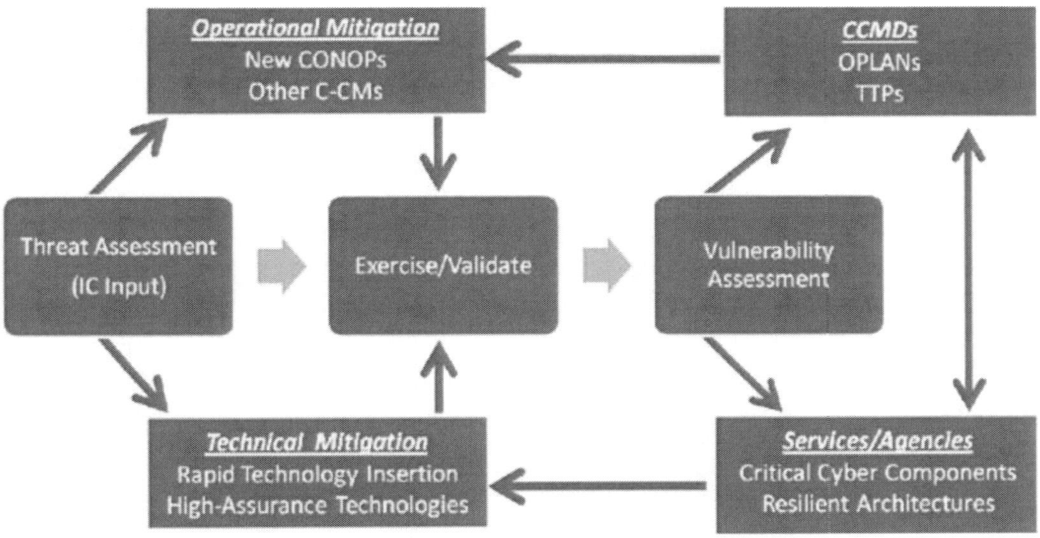

Figure 10.1. Mission Assurance Assessment Process.

The study team could not identify any instances where mission-based analyses were being routinely and systematically used to enhance cyber resiliency. However, there is recognition within DoD of the need for such assessments; for example, the working group under the DoD Cyber Integration Group charged with the task "develop and implement resilient, defensible cyber environment" is promoting activities that would lead to such assessments.

Enhancing Operational Feedback: As mentioned above, success will require operational know-how. While the current level of cyber activity develops a cache of experience and operational know-how that can be applied to the workforce, there are gaps at all levels (tactical, operational, and strategic) due to the newness and current compartmentalization of cyber operations. Lacking a full scale cyber war, the development of U.S. nuclear deterrent forces again provides a good model for obtaining operational knowledge in the cyber environment. Specifically, the Department should develop/expand opportunities, including enhanced ability to feed to/from operational exercises (e.g. CCMDs, Services, joint operations) and the testing community, developing sophisticated modeling and simulation capabilities, utilizing inputs from the intelligence community, and building partnerships with the private sector that provide information of the operational cyber environment to be applied to building cyber critical survivable mission force components.

The Department is moving in this direction. For example, in February 2011, Chairman, Joint Chiefs of Staff issued an instruction[36] to incorporate realistic cyberspace conditions in major DoD exercises. In response to the Instruction, exercise planning has begun to address these realistic conditions and most notably to understand and redress the shortcomings.[37] While these efforts offer promise, they need to be developed into a more comprehensive and systematic approach to fully address the mission assurance limitations and meet the intent of the Instruction.

10.1.3. Developing the Cyber Work Force

Developing and meeting standards and requirements will require a technologically competent cyber workforce. The workforce must be capable of providing disciplined system architecture, engineering expertise and operational knowhow capable of specifying buildable, measureable, and testable systems that support the overall realization of cyber resiliency. Developing an ability to correct known (Tier I-II) vulnerabilities in complex, interconnected systems requires both a global perspective (not typically present at the Program Manager level) and technical expertise at the Component level.

Developing a capability to rapidly respond to the discovery of new vulnerabilities (Tier III-IV) requires implementation of new concepts in the requirements, acquisition, testing and operational communities. Success against the Tier V-VI threats (causing frustration and additional cost for the attackers) will require informed decisions balancing operational objectives and technical performance--to include out-of-band communication capacity and degraded modes of operation in the cyber environment.

The technical cyber workforce must work across the capability lifecycle. Standards and requirements are addressed above but the Acquisition Community (e.g. Development Centers, Depots and industrial partners) bears a significant responsibility in this endeavor. DoD systems are acquired through development centers with responsibility for specific mission areas (e.g. space systems, aircraft, ships, C2 systems, etc.). Since virtually all DoD systems use cyber components in increasingly critical roles, all development centers must engage the cyber security challenge. Depots are charged with maintenance and updating of substantial components of the DoD infrastructure and will be targeted by those seeking to compromise the DoD cyber capability, just as are the other elements of the system lifecycle infrastructure. Industrial partners that produce DoD systems must also address the cyber threat.

10.1.4. Development of Secure System Technology

In addition to failures in cyber hygiene and in tepid response to exposed cyber shortcomings and transgressions, it is clear that the DoD and its community do not possess tools to produce and operate systems at a high enough level of cyber integrity. One potential architectural solution is identified by the other component of the DSB Cyber initiative, the *DSB Task Force on Cybersecurity and Reliability in a Digital Cloud.* That Task Force examined the applicability of cloud architecture to DoD uses. That study determined that a well-architected cloud significantly enhances the ability to deal with known Tier I-II vulnerabilities and could provide advanced analytic capability to mitigate Tier III-IV threats. However, the study acknowledges that today's cloud architectures are not applicable to all DoD systems (e.g. nuclear command and control) and will not address legacy systems, therefore other solutions are required.

The DoD science, technology and engineering community must engage with those in academia, government laboratories, and industry working innovative cyber technologies, processes and disciplines needed to raise the level of our national competency and capability in secure systems. System security engineering is a discipline that needs particular attention, and can be a bridge between the engineering and IT communities. Areas to be pursued in the longer term include: development of special purpose system architectures with inherent resilience, systematic analysis of potential modes of cyber vulnerability of systems, use of emerging technology developments for system resilience, such as trust anchors, minimal functionality components, simplified operating systems, developing a means to verify compromise of fielded systems contributing to critical missions, creating trust in systems built with un-trusted components, and restoring to a known state ("gold standard").

Addressing Infrastructure Vulnerabilities: Although not specifically tasked to examine infrastructure vulnerability, it became readily apparent to the Task Force that infrastructure is vulnerable to the cyber threat. The Task Force identified some areas of technology for rapid development that potentially increase the cyber security of critical infrastructure systems.

Similar to previous DSB work[38] involving infrastructure vulnerability, DoD's primary interest in critical infrastructure is associated with its force projection capability. However, as discussed in previous chapters, the Task Force finds that a catastrophic cyber attack on the infrastructure poses an existential threat to the nation. Fortunately a number of infrastructure systems (e.g. power systems, water systems, air traffic control systems) share characteristics that could allow better protection from cyber attacks (e.g. relatively few in number, can be operated with modest bandwidth, and can tolerate decision time cycles in seconds instead of microseconds). Potential areas of consideration which need to be addressed to mitigate infrastructure vulnerabilities include:

- Trusted hardware coprocessors with appropriately validated software;
- Techniques to monitor and verify tampering;
- Encryption;
- Reset mechanism through parallel processor;
- Insider protection schemes (e.g. 2-person rule for critical system override).

As long as DoD mission success relies upon infrastructure, it must actively engage in and encourage efforts to reduce infrastructure vulnerability.

10.1.5. Component Sourcing- Intelligence Community Initiate Supply Chain Collection Activity

DoD is in the process of institutionalizing a Supply Chain Risk Management (SCRM) strategy. The strategy prioritizes scarce security resources on critical mission systems and components, provides supply chain intelligence analysis to acquisition programs, and incorporates vulnerability risk mitigation requirements into system designs via engineering and acquisition practices. Component sourcing is an increasingly important contributor to cyber resiliency. An increasingly globalized development and production system supplies the electronic components (hardware, software and firmware) of DoD systems. Production of these "parts", sometimes including customized parts, external to the United States comprises a serious threat vector to the U.S. DoD architecture and systems. If DoD is to improve cyber defense and resiliency of DoD systems, it must better understand the implications of the supply chain for the components of U.S. systems, including the substantial amounts of custom hardware and software developed, deployed, operated and maintained in systems by and for the DoD.

Several approaches exist to address untrustworthy or unprotected sources. Supply chain assessment is an essential component of an overall cyber resiliency approach. However, many tiers in the supply chain (designers, producers, brokers, subsystem suppliers, major system integrators, etc.) limit visibility and make the origins of components difficult to track and certify. DoD's previous use of a trusted foundry program addresses both untrustworthy source issues and also missions requiring such limited number of parts (e.g. radiation hardened components) as to be economically unviable for commercial chip manufacturers. However, trusted foundries are capital intensive and present challenges with ensuring the broad spectrum of DoD microelectronics needs, which span generations of technology as well as leading edge. Fortunately, market forces provide an economic incentive to some companies to pursue cyber integrity of their products. DoD will need to share best practices with these same companies as part of its resilient force buildup.

10.2. Recommendation: Build a Cyber Resilient Force

10.2.1. DEPSECDEF Should Direct Specific Actions to Introduce Cyber Resiliency Requirements throughout DoD Force Structure

10.2.1.1. The DoD CIO, in Coordination with USD(AT&L) Should Establish a Resiliency Standard Which Can Be Used to Design, Build and Measure Capability against. The Joint Staff Will Use the Standard to Inform the Requirements Process

Realizing that the standards are likely to evolve as the cyber threat evolves, the Task Force identified certain characteristics that the Department should address as it develops the standards and requirements for cyber resiliency to apply to key conventional force capabilities designated as components of the escalation ladder described in Chapter Five. These include:

- Until a return to a TRUSTED, known state capability is developed, the forces and capability components providing a cyber critical survivable mission must be controlled throughout their lifecycle and segregated from general purpose forces, including use of and connection to general force networks. Segregation must provide sufficient capability to provide a credible component of the escalation ladder yet not be so large as to create a resource black hole.
- Maintaining component awareness/control is an important feature of resiliency. Desired awareness measures include sensing and reporting of buffer overflow conditions and bit parity checks, reporting and control of update/file transfer points (e.g. USB ports), and in the future--real time or near real time monitoring at the component level to ensure authentic components/software are installed.
- Maintain network awareness/control. Install sensing points to measure network performance and patterns, develop and maintain trusted log audit capability, and incorporate trusted and automated patch/update capabilities.
- Support the operational environment such as the conditions under which a system can be connected to specified network, conditions under which it must be disconnected or operate in a degraded mode (e.g. using an out-of-band path that supplies x% of the unfettered capability), and recovery mechanisms.

The Department must write achievable and testable requirements. For example, establishing a requirement that "System X" must be protected against a Tier III-IV threat will force the test community to engage in an infeasible activity as they are forced to certify a system against undiscovered vulnerabilities. The Task Force is wary of the efficacy of establishing a resilience "ility" to work in the same trade space as other "ilities". This approach tends to be bureaucratic and prior to adoption, must demonstrate real effectiveness against the cyber threat.

10.2.1.2. Apply the Cyber Resiliency Standard to the Segmented Force Identified As Part of the Escalation Ladder Described in Chapter Five

In the absence of a cyber threat, the segmented forces are likely to possess slightly less capability than their non-segmented counterparts due to the isolation from every part of the supporting infrastructure which generates so much advantage to DoD. However, in the face of an adversary employing cyber, the segmented forces will provide far more capability than the non-segmented counterparts.

Subsets of the cyber resiliency requirements for cyber critical survivable missions should be incorporated into the rest of the force structure to defend against Tiers I/II, mitigate the effects of Tier III-IV attacks, and drive up the costs for Tier V-VI attacks.

10.2.1.3. Increase Feedback from Testing, Red Teaming, Intelligence Community, and Modeling and Simulation As a Development Mechanism to Build out DoD's Cyber Resilient Force (USD(AT&L), USD(I), DOT&E, Saes, CJCS)

DoD must ensure feedback from these exercises impacts system designs, upgrades, CONOPs and TTPs. Lacking a full-scale cyber conflict, DoD will struggle to understand the full implications and effects of the cyber threat. DoD must fight through compartmentalization, understand a nascent but significant capability with limited real operational experience, and avoid typical first adopter mistakes to maximize its resiliency while retaining the huge advantage gained through the networking. The feedback mechanism will also aid the creation of processes to inform development efforts for new and evolved cyber threat vectors.

10.2.1.4. For Programs Not Part of the Segmented Force, Provide a Cyber Standard Set of Requirements (Expected to Be a Subset of the Critical Program Requirements List) to Be Applied to All DoD Programs (USD(AT&L), DoD CIO, Saes))

The DoD CIO, in coordination with USD(AT&L) should establish a subset of the resiliency standard developed above which can be applied to the rest of the force structure. The subset should be applied at every available opportunity (e.g. new starts, refurbishment, and repair). Legacy systems unable to meet the standard should be isolated or replaced.

The Department must still discipline itself in its application of the subset of resiliency standard to the rest of the non-escalation ladder components. Not every capability must protect against a Tier III-IV threat but all must defend against a Tier I-II threat.

In addition, initial incorporation of the subset of the resiliency standard is likely to require dedicated management to identify and overcome the issues with implementation. The Task Force urges the Department to apply the initial subset of resiliency standards to ACAT 1 programs. Once experience is gained, the resiliency standard can be applied across the Department.

10.2.1.5. Develop DoD-Wide Cyber Technical Workforce to Support the Build out of the Cyber Critical Survivable Mission Capability and Rolled out to DoD Force Structure (USD(AT&L), CIO, SAEs, DOT&E, USD(I), USD(P&R))

The technical cyber workforce must function across the capability lifecycle. Similar to the requirements to develop and attract the correct level of cyber talent for DoD's offensive and defensive missions, USD(P&R) must develop supporting policies to build the cyber workforce. The Acquisition Community (e.g. Development Centers, Depots and industrial partners) bears a significant responsibility in this endeavor along with the operational forces, test community, and scientific and engineering community. Historically, security functional responsibilities were assigned to security specialists who typically do not possess an engineering background. While not all participants need to be qualified to work at the highest levels, DoD must ensure that sufficient workforce capability exists. Programs for training and certification must be developed or enhanced so that qualifications can be measured and used in personnel and acquisition decisions. Equal attention must be applied to develop expertise to address system security during design, manufacturing, and sustainment phases of the lifecycle, with particular attention paid to controlling and limiting opportunity for malicious manipulation of components.

10.2.1.6. The Science and Technology Community Should Establish a Secure System Design Project with Ffrdcs, Uarcs, Academia, Commercial and , Defense Industry (ASD R&E, Initiate in FY13; Four-Year Research Activity)

The DoD science, technology and engineering community must engage with those in academia, government laboratories, and industry working innovative cyber technologies, processes and disciplines needed to raise the level of our national competency and capability in secure systems. Areas to be pursued in the longer term include: development of special purpose system architectures with inherent resilience, systematic analysis of potential modes of cyber vulnerability of systems, use of emerging technology developments for system resilience, such as trust anchors, minimal functionality components, simplified operating systems, developing a means to verify compromise of fielded systems contributing to critical missions, creating trust in systems built with un-trusted components, and restoring to a known state ("gold standard").

10.2.1.7. The Intelligence Community Should Initiate a Supply Chain Collection Activity (USD(I), 18 Months)

The DoD should assess the end-to-end process by which electronic "parts" and systems are produced by select companies to determine if what is known of the cyber threat vectors, including those in Tier V-VI, is appropriately reflected in the efforts of the suppliers. In addition, there is a nexus between cyber threat and relabeled and counterfeit hardware in DoD systems. Both DoD and industry counterfeit mitigation efforts should be developed further in conjunction with DoD cyber defense efforts.

The DoD must similarly assess the software supply chain to gain an understanding of the cyber threat vectors and to understand where mitigation might be possible, practical and affordable. In the parallel DSB study on Cyber Security in Cloud Computing, presentations were received from COTS software suppliers detailing their efforts to create processes for producing high(er) cyber integrity software. DoD should assess best practices in industry for threat mitigation and resiliency engineering, and where appropriate incorporate them into DoD processes and encourage their use in the broader supply chain.

The Acquisition Community must develop partnerships for select capabilities that will enhance the Department's cyber posture. It is generally accepted that the U.S. Intelligence Community possesses the best understanding of the Cyber threat vectors facing the United States. The Intelligence Community must be tasked with specific collection, analysis and reporting requirements on the cyber threat vectors, priorities and activities of U.S. adversaries. Although the Defense Intelligence Agency (DIA) has initiated efforts to provide supplier threat information to the Major Defense Acquisition Program (MDAP) acquisition community, it is not sufficiently broad or mature to serve the needs of critical mission systems. Mechanisms must be developed to share the resulting intelligence assessments, as appropriate, among the significant players in the DoD supply chain and broader national industries.

10.3. Integrated Cyber Requirements Measures

As response to the cyber threat becomes a mainstream component of how DoD operates, it must be reflected in the acquisition cycle used to purchase equipment and systems. Notional performance metrics are depicted in Figure 10.2. The first measure proposed is a simple measure of whether cyber requirements have been included in the acquisition plans and requirements for those systems defined as most critical as part of the conventional deterrent capability.

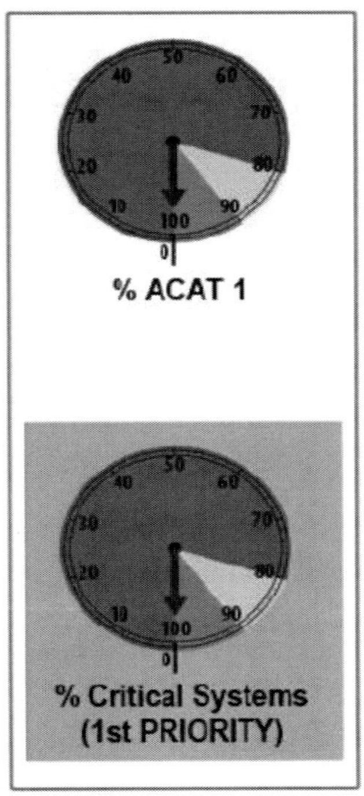

Figure 10.2. Integrated Cyber Requirement Measures.

Exactly what is meant by cyber requirements is left to the discretion of the Department. The Task Force envisions such requirements going beyond encryption, storage, and multilevel security, and including requirements to provide sensor points and reporting to better understand if a system has been compromised. For example, if the processor of a system executing activities is not consistent with the expected activities associated with that mission or if buffer register overflows are occurring, etc.

We would expect the same level of requirements, once understood and trialed on the most critical systems, to evolve into the remaining DoD systems, starting first with ACAT 1 programs.

11.0. ORDER OF MAGNITUDE COST ESTIMATES

The Task Force did not prepare detailed cost estimates for the recommendations in this report. However, due to the fiscal constraints expected in U.S. budgets for the next several years, estimates to the rough magnitude of investment are shown in Table 11.1.

Table 11.1. Estimated Investment Requirements for Study Recommendations

		ROM	**Timeframe**
1 & 2	Protect the Nuclear Strike as a Deterrent (for existing nuclear armed states and existential cyber attack). Determine the Mix of Cyber, Protected-Conventional, and Nuclear Capabilities Necessary for Assured Operation in the Face of a Full-Spectrum Adversary.	$$$$	36-60 mo.
3	Refocus Intelligence Collection and Analysis to Understand Adversarial Cyber Capabilities, Plans and Intentions, and to Enable Counterstrategies.	$	12-24 mo.
4	Build and Maintain World-Class Cyber Offensive Capabilities (with appropriate authorities).	$$	12-24 mo.
5	Enhance Defenses to Protect Against Low and Mid-Tier Threats.	$	6-18 mo.
6	Change DoD's Culture Regarding Cyber and Cyber Security.	$	12-48 mo.
7	Build a Cyber Resilient Force.	$$	12-24 mo.
ROM Costs $ <$50M/yr, $$ $50M-$100M/yr, $$$ $100M-$500M/yr, $$$$ >$500M/yr			

Even within a difficult budget environment, much can be done to address challenges faced in the cyber domain. The Task Force believes it is essential that the Department move quickly to better understand the cyber threat and how it relates to national defense and issues of deterrence and escalation. The only recommendations expected to require a large amount of resources are those to ensure the U.S. strategic deterrent is protected to a high degree of confidence and those that build out a protected set of conventional capabilities. While the basic capabilities and components of these systems exist today, understanding and remedying their cyber vulnerabilities, separating their C2 systems and providing backup or war reserve capabilities to ensure available operation in the face of an aggressive attack by a sophisticated adversary, will require time and resources.

11.1. Recommendation: Protect Nuclear Strike, Ensure Availability of Conventional Capabilities

U.S. nuclear capabilities are well isolated and go through regular evaluations of risk against outside forces. Adding analysis and testing against Tier V-VI adversaries is needed to maintain a high level of confidence in the availability of the systems. As the Department considers which systems would make up the ensured conventional strike, there is a range of approaches available to improve the availability of those systems against the cyber threat. Completely isolating systems, redesigning with components from trusted foundries, adding additional modes for navigation, and fire controls could very quickly lead to costs of billions of dollars. The Task Force feels there are logical compromises that could be made to greatly improve the confidence of system availability during a cyber attack without requiring a total redesign of systems. For instance, focusing some of the capabilities into the submarine force where isolation is already designed into how they operate and fight. U.S. strategic bombers currently use the same air platforms for nuclear and nonnuclear missions. There is a risk due to the broader personnel access allowed during the nonnuclear missions that could impact nuclear missions. Dedicating a number of the bombers to only conduct nuclear or critical conventional missions (as defined in Recommendation 2), and not letting those platforms be utilized for other missions could substantially reduce the risk of cyber compromise of the systems.

11.1.1. Recommendation: Refocus Intelligence

The recommendations around refocusing our intelligence effort are viewed by the Task force as a shifting of priorities and reallocation of a portion of our counterterrorism capabilities toward the advanced cyber threat and therefore not expected to drive significant cost growth.

11.1.2. Recommendation: Build/Maintain World-Class Cyber Offense

While the United States needs to scale up its cyber offensive capabilities, the size of force to support cyber offense is not expected to be as large-scale as that to defend its systems. The development of modeling and test capabilities are very important to understand this new domain. The overall investment is expected to be moderate.

11.1.3. Recommendation: Enhance Cyber Defenses

The Department already spends significant resources attempting to defend our networks and protect our data. The enterprise architecture recommendation, coupled with the automation recommendations, should actually reduce some of the effort DoD spends today. Gains in efficiency by eliminating many of the mundane tasks through automation can be used to expand Department's efforts toward hunting for intruders within DoD's networks. The Task Force expects the overall cost to remain about the same as today, but the performance results and efficiencies should improve dramatically.

11.1.4. Recommendation: Change DoD Cyber Culture

While a huge challenge for the Department, money is not a limiting factor. The price to execute this recommendation is measured in the will and determination of DoD leadership.

Training expense, which is a time cost only for people already paid for through department budgets, is not expected to impact budgets.

11.1.5. Recommendation: Incorporate of Cyber Requirements into System Lifecycle

The Task Force focused on the expense of introducing cyber requirements to acquisition programs. If done carefully, rolling cyber requirements into new programs throughout the lifecycle should drive only moderate costs into those programs. The alternative is to continue building systems that have little chance of performing as expected in the face of a peer adversary. Developing and gaining experience in building testable cyber requirements will take time and require developing the workforce to manage through the Department. The DoD must avoid the trap of trying to require a system to be defendable against all comers, thereby putting an ever-evolving (and un-testable) requirement onto the acquisition community and the development contractor(s). The focus must be on architectures and techniques that allow the systems to be adapted as cyber threats evolve, and can be tested along the way. (We can test an alternate communications path, a degraded operations mode, overflow buffers in a processor, etc.)

The Task Force recommends beta testing new requirements on the defined critical systems first, then using that experience to impact ACAT 1 programs, and continuing to smaller efforts.

12.0. Summary of Study Recommendations

12.1. Recommendation: Protect the Nuclear Strike As a Deterrent (for Existing Nuclear Armed States and Existential Cyber Attack)

- SECDEF assign USSTRATCOM the task to ensure the availability of Nuclear C3 and the Triad delivery platforms in the face of a full-spectrum Tier VI attack – including cyber (supply chain, insiders, communications, etc.)

This Task Force recommends immediate action to assess and assure to national leadership that the current U.S. nuclear deterrent is also survivable against the full-spectrum cyber Tier V-VI threat described in the taxonomy of this report. Note that a survivable nuclear triad within a full-spectrum, cyber-stressed environment is required regardless of whether or not one believes U.S. *retaliatory response with our nuclear forces* is a credible response *to a major cyber attack.* In other words, the basic characteristics of the traditional U.S. nuclear deterrent incorporates survivability as a basic precept; now the U.S. must add survivability in the event of a catastrophic cyber attack on the country as a basic precept.

12.2. Recommendation: Determine the Mix of Cyber, Protected-Conventional, and Nuclear Capabilities Necessary for Assured Operation in the Face of a Full-Spectrum Adversary

- SECDEF and CJCS (12 months)

The Task Force is confident in the need for assured operation to all three – cyber, protected-conventional, and nuclear – capabilities, including their required C3I infrastructures, against advanced cyber threats. Further analysis is necessary to determine the optimal mix of these capabilities, especially the role of offensive cyber and protected-conventional to form the rungs of an escalation ladder designed to introduce elements of deterrence against V-VI attackers.

As a starting point, the Task Force proposes the basic force elements comprising a protected-conventional capability take the form of a survivable second strike conventional mission listed below:

- Long-Range Bombers with precision cruise missiles – currently operational with varying force mix options and numbers
- SSGN with long-range precision cruise missiles – currently operational with capability up through Tomahawk Block IV (offering an upper limit of greater than 600 weapons assuming four SSGNs at sea)
- Conventional ballistic missiles or ballistic/glide hybrids--none currently operational; experimental concepts being tested.
- Survivable national and CCMD C2 leveraging nuclear thin line
  - Build "true" Out-of-Band Command and Control for the most sensitive systems
  - War reserve simplified operating systems

12.2.1.1. SECDEF Assign UCP Mission of Protected -Conventional Strike to USSTRATCOM

- USSTRATCOM given target for IOC (24 months)
- USSTRATCOM provide desired planning factors (pre-"launch" survivability, Communications and C2 reliability, targeting/damage expectancy, etc) (6 months)
- USD(AT&L), in coordination with CIO, perform an SoS analysis on selected conventional strike capabilities to determine risk and define an acquisition plan to ensure an enduring survivable capability (6 months)

12.2.1.2. DoD Engage Multi-Agency Counterparts for an Updated Strategic Deterrence Strategy in 2014 NPR – Cyber Escalation Scenarios on Both Sides (12 Months)

12.3. Recommendation: Refocus Intelligence Collection and Analysis to Understand Adversarial Cyber Capabilities, Plans and Intentions, and to Enable Counterstrategies

- SECDEF, in coordination with the Directors of CIA, FBI, and DHS, should require the DNI to enhance intelligence collection and analysis on high-end cyber threats. Request the creation of an intelligence community-wide implementation plan that defines implementable enhancements, and their resource impact on DoD and DHS elements, and CIA and FBI. (12 months)

Subversions of sophisticated hardware and software system are extraordinarily difficult to detect through testing and inspection. This led the DSB Task Force to conclude that deeper intelligence about adversaries' offensive software and hardware tools is essential to counter high-end, state-sponsored cyber threats, because it can help focus U.S. efforts on likely targets of compromise.

This intelligence must include:

- Identification and understanding of adversarial cyber weapon development organizations, tools, leadership, and intentions;
- Development of targeting information to support initiatives to counter cyber weaponization;
- Accurate assessment of adversarial plans and capabilities for policy makers.

12.3.1. In Response to State-Sponsored Threats, the Task Force Recommends the Creation of a Counterintelligence Capability to Directly Address the Most Sophisticated Threats Using Tools and Techniques Derived from Both Defensive and Offensive U.S. Cyber Programs.

12.4. Recommendation: Build and Maintain World-Class Cyber Offensive Capabilities (with Appropriate Authorities)

12.4.1. Commander USCYBERCOM Develop a Capability to Model, War Game, Red Team and Eventually Train for Full Scale Peer-on-Peer Cyber Warfare

- Select an FFRDC-like Center of Excellence. (within 6 months)
- Develop capability to model peer-on-peer (red & blue with supporting situation awareness tools and techniques) full-scale conflict, similar to nuclear exchange models (trigger uncertainties, deliver link probabilities, blow-back risk, recovery abilities and timelines, etc.) (IOC within 18 months of contract award)
- Develop model and validate—evolve through red team and cyber range/war game exercises. Move beyond tabletop level of sophistication. (IOC within 18 months of modeling capability)

Planning for and successfully executing a single offensive cyber operation requires a significant broad set of competencies (e.g. computer science, engineering, encryption, linguistics, geopolitical context, military planning and targeting, and more). Given peer and near-peer adversaries who may wish to challenge the United States via cyber aggression, the DoD must develop the capacity to conduct many (potentially hundreds or more) simultaneous, synchronized offensive cyber operations, while defending against a like number of cyber attacks. Understanding interactions and dependencies involved in large scale cyber battle will be required to plan the battle, determine the scale of forces required, and conduct operations at time of conflict.

Moreover, the adversary gets a vote. Cyber war is unlikely to be fought as the United States might like to assume it will be. The United States must be ready to adapt to an adversary that is willing to create its own rules.

12.4.2. USD(P) Should Establish a Policy Framework for Offensive Cyber Actions to Include Who Has What Authority (for Specific Actions), under What Circumstances, under What Controls

- Completion Date: 18 Months

The appropriate authorities must exist with those responsible to protect U.S. interests. Cyber actions can take place in very short time periods and those responsible to protect the country must understand their roles and authorities. This Task Force has not extensively studied or made recommendations about the definition of "appropriate authorities." Several other efforts are underway in the administration to address this issue and DoD is only one of many players in the broad protection of the United States against cyber attack.

12.4.3. Commander, USCYBERCOM to Increase the Number of Qualified Cyber Warriors, and Enlarge the Cyber Infrastructure Commensurate with the Size of the Threat

- Completion Date: 18 Months

The DoD has qualified cyber warriors today, who are supported by robust training programs and cyber toolsets. However there appears to be a "burnout factor" beginning exhibit itself among these elite people. The Department must scale up efforts to recruit, provide facilities and training, and use effectively these critical people.

12.4.4. USD(P&R), in Collaboration with the Commander, USCYBERCOM and the Service Chiefs Establish a Formal Career Path for DoD Civilian and Military Personnel Engaged in "Offensive Cyber Actions"

- Address training and certification requirements
- Define career designations
- Define incentives for personnel achieving higher levels of certification
- Ensure that there is a cadre of high-end practitioners
- Completion: 18 Months with quarterly reviews with the DEPSECDEF

"Cyber Warrior" is a new domain for the Department, and this new class of job will require career paths, training expectations and incentives to attract and develop the needed expertise. It is not clear that high-end cyber practitioners can be found in sufficient numbers within typical recruitment pools. The DoD has the ability to define what it needs and adjust its personnel policies to enable achievement of that goal.

12.5. Recommendation: Enhance Defenses to Protect against Low and Mid-Tier Threats

12.5.1. Recommendation: Establish an Enterprise Security Architecture, Including Appropriate "Building Codes and Standards", That Ensure the Availability of Enabling Enterprise Missions. The Architecture Should Allow for the Ability to

- Segment the network

    - Provide continuous monitoring and situational awareness
    - Automate patch and threat management functions
    - Audit to the enterprise standard
    - Recover to a known (trusted) state
    - Provide out-of-band command and control for most sensitive systems
- Responsibility: DoD CIO (in collaboration with Military Departments and Agencies). Due Date – 6 months

The goal of a consistently applied and managed architecture across the Department is to take the low-tier threats off the table, thereby reducing the noise level on DoD networks. More effective mitigation of mid and high tier threats then becomes feasible.

12.5.1.1. Segment the Network

The Department already operates a mesh of networks that can be controlled independently. That concept should be extended through all operational war fighting systems, and tests/trials/red teams should be conducted to understand the capabilities and impacts of disconnecting an infected network to prevent infection of other, interconnected networks.

12.5.1.2. Provide Continuous Monitoring and Situational Awareness

Sensor deployment has begun at Internet access points to monitor and control access and network traffic flow. Commercial tools have advanced to include capabilities to operate behind firewalls and to track anomalous activity throughout the components of a network. It is essential to provide continuous monitoring of all networks against cyber attack (see State Department example in Figure 8.1).

The information assurance of operational systems is typically achieved through encryption of data during network transport (and occasionally at rest - while stored) or multi-level security solutions geared toward the safe handling of multiple security levels of data on the same computer (processor). Data must be decrypted prior to processing, and advanced attacks being used today access the data at that point, thereby circumventing the encryption.

Little consideration goes into military system design today on providing test points that can report system health and operation (sensors). Are checksums overflowing in the processor? Is the processor conducting unexpected computations? There are many "tells" (symptoms) that could be detected and reported. And although such test points and their data transmission would also become targets for cyber attack, an adversary must now have a more detailed understanding of system internals to design a successful attack.

12.5.1.3. Automate Patch and Threat Management Functions

The scale of manual efforts is largely driven by legacy systems using unsupported software operating systems and the lack of consistency in network technology implementation across the Department. The recommendation to isolate systems utilizing older software (no longer maintained by commercial industry) means those systems are removed from the group of components that is regularly updated for malware and other software attacks and then assuming that those systems are likely compromised. The larger GIG is then protected from those systems through strong interface firewalls and detection software.

Most of the COTS technologies available today have user interfaces that allow high levels of flexibility for determining what is deemed unusual network behavior, allowing system administrators to adjust and adapt the monitoring systems as threats evolve.

12.5.1.4. Audit to the Enterprise Standard

Conduct audits and in-process reviews to develop migration and mitigation strategies (systems that cannot be maintained in a timely matter should be restructured into enclaves and isolated from the GIG through firewalls).

The most important part of the recommendation concerns accountability and consistency that must come from senior leadership support and enforcement. Without this management imperative, an attempt at cultural change to improve cyber security will not be taken seriously within the Department.

12.5.1.5. Build Network Recovery Capability

It is not unusual for a sophisticated adversary, who has infiltrated a network, to monitor in real time as the network owners try to kick them out. Frequently, the adversary then implements a counter to the network owner's defensive actions and can be back in the network in a matter of minutes or hours. To fight and win in a war that includes cyber capabilities, DoD can't afford to have the enemy inside its control loops. If DoD is in that situation, then it needs backup (war reserve) mechanisms for C2. Less critical systems need the ability to communicate over an alternative system to address network intrusions, forcing an adversary to penetrate multiple systems and be able to operate both in an integrated, real time fashion to track DoD counterattacks.

12.5.1.6. Recover to a Known (Trusted) State

The goal DoD for operational systems should be to:

- Develop the ability to know (and report) if the network or system has been penetrated,
- Gracefully degrade or have provision for alternate mechanisms to continue the most critical mission functions and
- Recover eventually to a known (trusted) state.

Earlier recommendations addressed the first two goals. The last goal is perhaps the most challenging.

The Department must develop methods to evolve trusted copies of operating software for systems that ensure only the desired changes are made in the "gold copy". The Department should continue to search the commercial and contractor space to develop tools with higher levels of automation for this function.

12.5.2. Recommendation: The DoD Should Leverage Commercial Technologies to Automate Portions of Network Maintenance and "Real-Time" Mitigation of Detected Malware

- Build on existing tools and capabilities currently in use
- Automate response to threat conditions

    - Leverage cyber ranges to test emerging technology and develop TTPs and guide investment strategies
    - Develop mitigation/transition plans for legacy systems
- Responsibility: DoD CIO, with support from NSA-IAD, IOC: 6 months, with enhancements released on a quarterly basis

As discussed above, modern COTS software has dramatically improved and can provide automation of several key network management functions. The software products sit at the firewall and behind the firewall, which is particularly important to find and track advanced persistent threats.

While these technologies do not address Tier V-VI threats directly, when properly deployed, they make an attacker's task of moving data throughout the systems, while remaining undetected, much more difficult. Our goal is to raise the costs for the Tier V-VI attackers to succeed, limiting the number of operations they can afford to attempt.

12.5.3. Recommendation: USD(P&R) Should, in Collaboration with the DoD CIO and the Service Chiefs, Establish a Formal Career Path for DoD Civilian and Military Personnel Engaged in Cyber Defense

- Address training and certification requirements
- Define career designations
- Define incentives for personnel achieving higher levels of certification
- Ensure that there is a cadre of high-end practitioners
- Completion: 18 Months with quarterly reviews with the DEPSECDEF

The Task Force expects cyber-focused personnel to move between offensive and defensive focused posts throughout their career. The best defenders will be those who understand what can be accomplished from an offensive point of view (the reverse is also true). Creating cyber warriors with expertise in offensive and defensive cyber skills should be encouraged.

12.6. Recommendation: Change DoD's Culture Regarding Cyber and Cyber Security

12.6.1. Establish a DoD-Wide Policy, Communication, and Education Program to Change the Culture Regarding Cyber and Cyber Security

SECDEF, CJCS and their direct reports should communicate a vision of DoD Cyber Security for 2020. The Secretary and Chairman should provide direct communication to all organizational elements explaining the threat and consequences of cyber actions is essential to change DoD's cyber culture. Leadership must change the current culture which is focused on an overwhelming emphasis on operational objectives and shaped by daily exposure in civil cyberspace that imposes little cost to risky behavior.

- Commander, USCYBERCOM and the DoD CIO should establish a plan with measureable milestones and flow-down to all organization elements. The plan must comprise:

    - The policy, operational rules, and expectations for secure use of DoD networks and systems
    - The training program and follow on continual reinforcement of the policy
    - A small "tiger team" of experts to monitor, test, and catch breaches in policy
    - Clear punitive consequences for breaches of policy
- Following the education period and a short grace period, penalties should be imposed similar to the breach of policy for classified material.
- Command readiness should assess and report cyber policy compliance. SECDEF should require the policy to be communicated within 60 days and the education and roll out to every DoD and contractor employee within 9 months.

The current DoD Directive (DoDD 7730.65, dated April 23, 2007) must be modified to include readiness criteria for cyber capability. Specific performance measures related to the IT components critical to the successful execution of the mission must be used to assess Commanders on unit fitness to execute assigned missions and the readiness system must incorporate penalties for failure to meet specific standards.

12.7. Recommendation: Build a Cyber Resilient Force

12.7.1. DEPSECDEF Should Direct Specific Actions to Introduce Cyber Resiliency Requirements throughout DoD Force Structure

12.7.1.1. The DoD CIO, in Coordination with USD(AT&L) Should Establish a Resiliency Standard Which Can Be Used to Design, Build and Measure Capability against. The Joint Staff Will Use the Standard to Inform the Requirements Process

Realizing that the standards are likely to evolve as the cyber threat evolves, the Task Force identified certain characteristics that the Department should address as it develops the standards and requirements for cyber resiliency to apply to key conventional force capabilities designated as components of the escalation ladder described in Chapter Five. These include:

- Until a return to a TRUSTED, known state capability is developed, the forces and capability components providing a cyber-critical, survivable mission must be controlled throughout their lifecycle and segregated from general purpose forces, including use of and connection to general force networks. Segregation must provide sufficient capability to provide a credible component of the escalation ladder, yet not be so large as to create a resource black hole.
- Maintaining component awareness/control is an important feature of resiliency. Desired awareness measures include sensing and reporting of buffer overflow conditions and bit parity checks, reporting and control of update/file transfer points (e.g. USB ports), and in the future-- real time or near real time monitoring at the component level to ensure authentic components/software are installed.
- Maintain network awareness/control. Install sensing points to measure network performance and patterns, develop and maintain trusted log audit capability, and incorporate trusted and automated patch/update capabilities.

- Support the operational environment such as the conditions under which a system can be connected to specified network, conditions under which it must be disconnected or operate in a degraded mode (e.g. using an out-of-band path that supplies x% of the unfettered capability), and recovery mechanisms.

The Department must write achievable and testable requirements. For example, establishing a requirement that "System X" must be protected against a Tier III-IV threat will force the test community to engage in an infeasible activity as they are forced to certify a system against undiscovered vulnerabilities. The Task Force is wary of the efficacy of establishing a resilience "ility" to work in the same trade space as other "ilities". This approach tends to be bureaucratic and prior to adoption, must demonstrate effectiveness against the cyber threat.

12.7.1.2. Apply the Cyber Resiliency Standard to the Segmented Force Identified As Part of the Escalation Ladder Described in Chapter Five

In the absence of a cyber threat the segmented forces are likely to possess slightly less capability than their non-segmented counterparts due to the isolation from every part of the supporting infrastructure which generates so much advantage to DoD. However, in the face of an adversary employing cyber, the segmented forces will provide far more capability than their non-segmented counterparts.

Subsets of the cyber resiliency requirements for cyber critical survivable missions should be incorporated into the rest of the force structure to defend against Tiers I/II, mitigate the effects of Tier III-IV attacks, and drive up the costs for Tier V-VI attacks.

12.7.1.3. Feedback from Testing, Red Teaming, Intelligence Community, and Modeling and Simulation Should Be Increased as a Development Mechanism to Build out DoD's Cyber Resilient Force (USD(AT&L), USD(I), DOT&E, SAEs, CJCS)

DoD must ensure feedback from these exercises impacts system designs, upgrades, CONOPs and TTPs. Lacking a full-scale cyber conflict, DoD will struggle to understand the full implications and effects of the cyber threat. DoD must fight through compartmentalization, understand a nascent but significant capability with limited real operational experience, and avoid typical first adopter mistakes to maximize its resiliency while retaining the huge advantage gained through the networking. The feedback mechanism will also aid the creation of processes to inform development efforts for new and evolved cyber threat vectors.

12.7.1.4. For Programs Not Part of the Segmented Force, a Cyber Standard Set of Requirements (Expected to Be a Subset of the Critical Program Requirements List) Should Be Applied to All Dod Programs (USD(AT&L), DoD CIO, Saes))

The DoD CIO, in coordination with USD(AT&L) should establish a subset of the resiliency standard developed above which can be applied to the rest of the force structure. The subset should be applied at every available opportunity (e.g. new starts, refurbishment, and repair). Legacy systems unable to meet the standard should be isolated or replaced.

The Department must still discipline itself in its application of the subset of resiliency standard to the rest of the non-escalation ladder components. Not every capability must protect against a Tier III-IV threat but all must defend against a Tier I-II threat. In addition, initial incorporation of the subset of the resiliency standard is likely to require dedicated management to identify and overcome the issues with implementation. The Task Force urges the Department to apply the initial subset of resiliency standards to ACAT 1 programs. Once experience is gained, the resiliency standard can be applied across the Department.

Lacking a full-scale cyber conflict, DoD will struggle to understand the full implications and effects of the cyber threat. The feedback mechanism will also aid the creation of processes to inform development efforts for new and evolved cyber threat vectors.

12.7.1.5. A DoD--Wide Cyber Technical Workforce Should Be Developed to Support the Build-out of the Cyber Critical Survivable Mission Capability; It Should Then Be Rolled out to DoD Force Structure (USD(AT&L), CIO, Saes, DOT&E, USD(I) and USD(P&R))

The technical cyber workforce must function across the capability lifecycle. Similar to the requirements to develop and attract the correct level of cyber talent for DoD's offensive and defensive missions, USD(P&R) must develop supporting policies to build the cyber workforce. The Acquisition Community (e.g. Development Centers, Depots and industrial partners) bears a significant responsibility in this endeavor along with the operational forces, test community, and scientific and engineering community.

12.7.1.6. The Science and Technology Community Should Establish a Secure System Design Project with Federally Funded Research and Development Centers (FFRDCs), University Affiliated Research Centers (UARCs), Academia, Commercial and Defense Industry (ASD R&E))

Areas to be pursued in the longer term should include: development of special purpose system architectures with inherent resilience, systematic analysis of potential modes of cyber vulnerability of systems, use of emerging technology developments for system resilience (such as trust anchors), minimal functionality components, simplified operating systems, developing a means to verify compromise of fielded systems contributing to critical missions, creating trust in systems built with untrusted components, and restoring to a known state ("gold standard").

12.7.1.7. The Intelligence Community Should Initiate a Supply Chain Collection Activity (USD(I))

The DoD should assess the end-to-end process by which electronic "parts" and systems are produced by select companies to determine if what is known of the Cyber threat vectors, including those in Tier V-VI, is appropriately reflected in the efforts of the suppliers.

The DoD must similarly assess the software supply chain to gain an understanding of the cyber threat vectors and to understand where mitigation might be possible, practical and affordable.

The Intelligence Community must be tasked with specific collection, analysis and reporting requirements on the cyber threat vectors, priorities and activities of U.S. adversaries. Although DIA has initiated efforts to provide supplier threat information to the MDAP acquisition community, it is not sufficiently broad or mature to serve the needs of critical mission systems. Mechanisms must be developed to share the resulting intelligence assessments, as appropriate, among the significant players in the DoD supply chain and broader national industries.

APPENDIX 1—TERMS OF REFERENCE

DEPUTY SECRETARY OF DEFENSE
1010 DEFENSE PENTAGON
WASHINGTON, DC 20301-1010

MAY 1 9 2011

MEMORANDUM FOR CHAIRMAN, DEFENSE SCIENCE BOARD

SUBJECT: Terms of Reference – Defense Science Board (DSB) Task Force on Resilient Military Systems

You are hereby directed to establish a Task Force to assess issues affecting the resiliency of military systems that rely on information and communication technology (ICT), including through consideration of the following for mission operational systems:

- Identify measures and techniques under development in the ICT space to quantify system vulnerability and the effectiveness of defense measures;
- Dissect the concept of operations (CONOPS) of various potential cyber attacks and describe the opportunities in the system to develop diagnostics relating to detecting and understanding the attack;
- Apply the diagnostics to 2-3 different mission threads to understand the differences in risk among different types of architecture components (e.g., hardware, software, network, and human risks);
- Study tool/modeling opportunities to predict/measure system vulnerabilities.
- Assess techniques/processes to identify the applicability of human suitability and reliability (e.g., the Personnel Reliability Program);
- Define meaningful measures and metrics to evaluate and monitor the level of system resiliency. Survey metrics developed to characterize resilience in other domains (e.g., insurance, financial systems, and security systems); and
- Identify tactics, procedures and design techniques that could improve system resiliency. In addition, identify research opportunities and estimate the level of investment to achieve results consistent with DoD needs.

Innovative use of modern ICT (e.g., networks, software and microelectronics) in military systems plays a key and vital role in making the U.S. military second to none. However, the effectiveness of these military systems is extremely dependent upon the information assurance provided by its ICT underpinnings and on the personnel who operate and maintain the systems. An unintended consequence of the reliance on ICT to sustain superior U.S. capability is that our adversaries can erode or eliminate our advantage by targeting and exploitation at both the system and component level.

Several factors complicate the ability to maintain our advantage. A short, but certainly not comprehensive, list would identify the complex technology involved, the slowness to understand the problem, and the difficulty to develop effective metrics.

OSD 04475-11

Based in part on the complexity of modern software and microelectronic systems, very small and difficult-to-detect defects or subversive modifications introduced at some point in the life cycle of the systems create debilitating effects. As an example, although remote software system upgrades (remote provisioning) provide great flexibility and efficiency, they also introduce a very attractive vector for an enemy to compromise a system. The same complexity amplifies the human factor – whether malicious or innocent. Insertion of an infected flash drive produced the most significant breach of U.S. systems to date; while the intentional downloading of thousands of classified documents to "music"-labeled CDs generated its own set of problems. As a result of the great and growing complexity of DoD systems, cyber resiliency is an extremely broad and difficult attribute to guarantee.

DoD and military officials have long understood our advantage in the utilization of these technologies in military systems. Unfortunately, DoD officials have been slow to develop sufficient understanding of the mission assurance implications of adversary capability to operationally exploit these systems. Although the contest is simple to characterize, it is an extremely complex matter and a difficult one in which to achieve confidence in the desired outcome. To continue to take advantage of modern technology to increase our military effectiveness, we must possess sufficient confidence that these systems are not compromised to such a degree that we lose the benefit. In addition, we want to work actively to decrease the confidence of our adversaries that their clandestine operations targeting our systems are effective enough to eliminate our advantage.

An important step toward designing, implementing, and maintaining more resilient systems is to understand how to measure the resiliency of those systems relative to various cyber attacks and adversaries. Establishing useful measures and metrics is a first step toward quantifying and developing systematic methods and standards to improve both real resiliency and confidence in our process. These tools would allow organizations to apply scarce resources (people and dollars) more effectively in all phases (research, acquisition, and maintenance) of the life cycle of these systems to improve our confidence in the resiliency of these capabilities, and to enhance the ability of those systems to perform as expected in a hostile environment.

Prior efforts to develop useful measures and metrics have largely failed due to the difficulty of the subject. There is no guarantee that this effort will fare better. However, if fully adequate and robust metrics are not developed, the Task Force will describe the weaknesses of the proposed metrics and describe an iterative process to obtain improved metrics over time.

Administration support and funding will be provided by the Under Secretary of Defense for Acquisition, Technology, and Logistics. Additional support will be provided by the Assistant Secretary of Defense for Networks and Information Integration/DoD Chief Information Officer, the Director, Operational Test and Evaluation (DOT&E), the Vice Chairman of the Joint Chiefs of Staff, and the Commander, U.S. Cyber Command. All Task Force members, consultants, and supporting personnel will be appointed or designated in accordance with DoD Instruction (DoDI) 5105.04, "Department of Defense Federal Advisory Committee Management Program."

The Task Force will be established and operated in accordance with the provisions of the "Federal Advisory Committee Act" (5 U.S. Code Appendix, as amended), DoDI 5105.04, the DSB Charter, and all applicable laws, policies, and regulations. It is not anticipated that this Task Force will need to go into any "particular matters" within the meaning of section 208 of title 18, U.S. Code, nor will it cause any member to be placed in the position of acting as a procurement official.

APPENDIX 2—TASK FORCE MEMBERSHIP

Co-Chairs

Mr. James R. Gosler	Sandia National Laboratory
Mr. Lewis Von Thaer	General Dynamics

Executive Secretary

Mrs. Kristen Baldwin	OASD(R&E)
Mr. Steve Gates	ODT&E

Members

Dr. Allen Adler	The Boeing Company
Dr. James Babcock	Northrop Grumman
Mr. Dean Clubb	Independent Consultant
Dr. Craig Cook	MITRE
Dr. Donald Duncan	Johns Hopkins University/APL
ADM William J. Fallon, USN (Ret.)	Independent Consultant
Mr. Robert Gourley	Crucial Point, LLC
Dr. Richard Ivanetich	Institute for Defense Analyses
Dr. Ronald L. Kerber	Independent Consultant
Hon. Donald M. Kerr, PhD.	Independent Consultant
Dr. William LaPlante	MITRE
Hon. Judith A. Miller, Esq.	Independent Consultant
Mr. Al Munson	Potomac Institute for Policy Studies
Mr. Richard Schaeffer	Independent Consultant
Dr. Fred B. Schneider	Cornell University
ADM William Studeman, USN (Ret.)	Independent Consultant
Mr. Michael Swetnam	Potomac Institute for Policy Studies
Dr. Peter Weinberger	Google, Inc.
Dr. Robert Wisnieff	IBM

Government Advisors

Mr. Rick Wilson	National Security Agency
Mr. Mitchell Komaroff	CIO-ODA SD (I&IA)
Mr. RC Porter	Defense Intelligence Agency

Senior Advisors

Dr. Craig Fields	Independent Consultant
Dr. Robert Hermann	Independent Consultant
Mr. Robert Stein	Independent Consultant

DSB Secretariat

Mr. Brian Hughes	Defense Science Board
Lt. Col. Michael Warner, USAF	Defense Science Board
CDR Doug Reinbold, USN	Defense Science Board

Support

Mr. Chris Grisafe	SAIC
Ms. Tammy-jean Beatty	SAIC

APPENDIX 3—TASK FORCE MEETING SCHEDULE AND BRIEFINGS

March 16-17 2011		
Title	**Briefer**	**Organization**
AT&T Operations Center Metrics	Mr. Ed Amoroso	AT&T
Cross Sector Information Sharing, Analysis & Collaboration Initiative	Mr. Robert Dix	Juniper Networks
Carnegie Mellon Cyber SOC	Mr. Terry Roberts	Carnegie Mellon University
In-Q-Tel Cyber Measures Research	Mr. Dan Geer	In-Q-Tel
State Department Measures	Mr. John Streufert	Department of State
Why This is So Hard?	Mr. Carl Landwehr	National Science Foundation
Cybersecurity in the Digital Cloud Overview	Dr. Eric Evans	DSB Cybersecurity in the Digital Cloud Task Force
System Security Metrics	Dr. Salvatore J. Stolfo	Columbia University
Metrics, Models, and Analysis of Network Security and Survivability	Mr. Kishor Trivedi	Duke University

April 20-21, 2011		
Title	**Briefer**	**Organization**
DoD Strategy for Operation in Cyberspace	Mr. Robert Butler	OSD Policy
The Supply Chain Threat Assessment Center	Mr. Cal Temple	DIA
Building Resilient Network Architectures	Mr. Kevin Bingham	DoD CIO
Examples of Advanced Cyber Threat Assessments	Ms. Yulin Bingle	DIA
Examples of Cyber Metrics in Use by DoD	Mr. David Aland	DOT&E
Examples of DoD Red Teaming	CAPT Forbes MacVane, USN LCDR John Kaltwasser, USN Mr. Scott Brown	NSA
Examples of Navy Red Teaming Impacts on Military Systems	LT Greg Smith	NIOC

May 17-18, 2011

Title	Briefer	Organization
NCIX	Ms. Margie Gilbert	
NIC	Mr. Sean Kanuck	NIC
TRANSCOM	Mr. Steve Stone CAPT Mike Murray	USTRANSCOM
NCIJTF	Mr. Brad Bleier	NCIJTF
Cyber Analytical Framework	Daniel Kaufman	DARPA
Dynamic Quarantine of Worms Cyber Gnome	Dr. Timothy Fraser	DARPA
TRUST, ISIS (Follow Program)	Dr. Carl McCants	DARPA
National Cyber Range	Dr. Jinendra Ranka	DARPA
Cloud to the Edge	Dr. Keith Gremban	DARPA
Vulnerability Assessment: Virtual Machine	Mr. Tony Sager	NSA/CSS
Terremark	Ms. Jamie DosSantos	Terremark, Inc.
Systems Security Engineering	Ms. Jennifer Bayuk	Independent Consultant
Research Roadmap	Mr. Barry Horowitz	University of Virginia
	June 23-24, 2011	
Title	**Briefer**	**Organization**
Terminal Fury	Mr. David Aland	DOT&E
DIB Cyber Security	Mr. Steven D. Shirley Mr. Jeffrey Stuzman	DoD Cyber Crime Center
NSA High Assurance Platform	Mr. Neil Kittleson	NSA/CSS
Virtual Secure Enclave	Dr. Matt Goda	USPACOM
NSA Gold Standard	Ms. Carol Walters Mr. Mike Escazage Ms. Ann Erickson Mr. John Schuessler	NSA/CSS
Improving Mission Assurance by Using New Techniques in Network Analysis	Dr. Don Snyder	RAND Corporation
Resilience Metrics	Dr. Erik G. Mettala	Battelle
NRO Information Assurance	Ms. Bonnie Paul	NRO
	July 18-19 2011	
Title	**Briefer**	**Organization**
Neural IQ	Mr. Bill Stacia	Neural IQ
Measuring Cyber Vulnerabilities and Response Effectiveness	Mr. Mike Papay	Northrop Grumman
Measuring Security	Mr. Steve Lipner	Microsoft
Security and Resiliency	Mr. Michael Berman	Catbird
Cyber Resilience	Mr. Iven Connary	Q1 Labs
	August 10-11, 2011 (Joint Meeting with Cloud TF, 8/11)	
Title	**Briefer**	**Organization**

DoD CIO Briefing	Ms. Teri Takai	DoD CIO
Cyber Law and Policy	Dr. Catherine Lotrionte	Georgetown University Law Center
Bromium	Mr. Simon Crosby	Bromium Inc.
Cloud Computing: Key Questions	Ms. Melissa Hathaway Mr. G. Gaffney	Hathaway Global Strategies DNI
	September 22-23, 2011	
Title	**Briefer**	**Organization**
IDA Brief	Dr. Margaret Myers	Institute for Defense Analyses
United States Cyber Command	Mr. Mark Young	USCYBERCOM
	October 24-27, 2011 (Offsite Joint Meeting with Cloud TF, 10/27)	
Title	**Briefer**	**Organization**
United States Cyber Command	Mr. Mark Young	USCYBERCOM
	November 17-18, 2011	
Title	**Briefer**	**Organization**
DDR&E Resilient Systems Program	Dr. Steve King	DDR&E
DoD CIO and the Working Group on Network Resilience	Ms. Laura Boehm	DoD CIO
Secure Configuration Management	Mr. Kevin Dulany Ms. Robby Ann Carter	DIAP
	January 19-20, 2012	
Title	**Briefer**	**Organization**
Law and Policy Discussion	Mr. Gary Sharp	DoD
	February 9-10, 2012	
Title	**Briefer**	**Organization**
Cyber Deterrence	Ms. Michelle Markoff	State Department
Conventional Thin Line	Mr. Dave Dick Mr. Carl Prantl	OSD

APPENDIX 4—ACRONYMS USED IN THIS REPORT

ACAT	Acquisition Category
ASD(R&E)	Assistant Secretary of Defense for Research and Engineering
C2	Command and Control
C3	Command, Control, Communications
C4ISR	Command, Control, Communications, Computers, Intelligence, Surveillance, and Reconnaissance
CAC	Common Access Card
CCC	Cyber Conflict College
CCMD	Combatant Command
CCR	Centers for Communication Research
CEO	Chief Executive Officer
CIA	Central Intelligence Agency
CIO	Chief Information Officer

CISO	Chief Information Security Officer
CISSP	Certified Information Systems Security Professional
CJCS	Chairman of the Joint Chiefs of Staff
CNDSP	Computer Network Defense Service Provider
CNE	Computer Network Exploitation
COG	Continuity of Government
CONUS	Continental United States
COTS	Commercial off the Shelf
CPGS	Conventional Prompt Global Strike
CSIA	Cyber Security/Information Assurance
DARPA	Defense Advanced Research Projects Agency
DASD(SE)	Deputy Assistant Secretary of Defense for Systems Engineering
DEPSECDEF	Deputy Secretary of Defense
DHS	Department of Homeland Security
DIA	Defense Intelligence Agency
DIAP	Defense Information Assurance Program
DIB	Defense Industrial Base
DISA	Defense Information Systems Agency
DNI	Director of National Intelligence
DoD	Department of Defense
DOS	Department of State
DOTMLPF	Doctrine, Organization, Training, Materiel, Leadership, Personnel, Facilities
DSB	Defense Science Board
DSP	Defense Service Provider
EA	Enterprise Architecture
EMP	Electromagnetic Pulse
FBI	Federal Bureau of Investigation
FFRDC	Federally Funded Research and Development Center
GIAP	Global Information Assurance Portfolio
GIG	Global Information Grid
GWOT	Global War on Terror
HBSS	Host Based Security System
HUMINT	Human Intelligence
IA	Information Assurance
IC	Intelligence Community
ICBM	Intercontinental Ballistic Missile
ICIECS	International Conference on Information Engineering and Computer Science
ICT	Information and Communications Technology
IED	Improvised Explosive Device
IOC	Initial Operating Capability
IP	Intellectual Property
IPB	Intelligence Preparation of the Battlespace
ISR	Intelligence, Surveillance and Reconnaissance
IT	Information Technology

JPIOE	Joint Intelligence Preparation of the Operational Environment
JROC	Joint Requirements Oversight Council
MDAP	Major Defense Acquisition Program
NC2	Nuclear Command and Control
NDU	National Defense University
NIPRNet	Unclassified but Sensitive Internet Protocol (IP) Router Network
NIST	National Institute of Standards and Technology
NPR	Nuclear Posture Review
NSA	National Security Agency
NSA-IAD	National Security Agency Information Assurance Directorate
ODNI	Office of the Director of National Intelligence
OPLANS	Operational Plans
OSD	Office of the Secretary of Defense
PKI	Public Key Infrastructure
POTUS	President of the United States
PPBS	Planning, Programming and Budgeting System
SAE	Service Acquisition Executives
SCADA	Supervisory Control and Data Acquisition
R&D	Research and Development
SCRM	Supply Chain Risk Management
SCADA	Supervisory Control and Data Acquisition
SECDEF	Secretary of Defense
SIGINT	Signals Intelligence
SIPRNet	Secret Internet Protocol Router Network
SIGINT	Signals Intelligence
SLBM	Submarine-Launched Ballistic Missile
SLOC	Source Lines of Code
SOF	Special Operations Forces
SoS	System of Systems
SSGN	Cruise Missile Submarine
TF	Task Force
TTP	Tactics, Techniques, and Procedures
UARC	University Affiliated Research Center
UCP	Unified Command Plan
USCYBERCOM	United States Cyber Command
USD(AT&L)	Under Secretary of Defense for Acquisition, Technology, and Logistics
USD(I)	Under Secretary for Defense Intelligence
USD(P)	Under Secretary of Defense for Policy
USD(P&R)	Under Secretary of Defense for Personnel and Readiness
USSTRATCOM	United States Strategic Command

End Notes

[1] Office of the National Intelligence Executive; "Foreign Spies Stealing US Economic Secrets in Cyber Space: Report to Congress on Foreign Economic Collection and Industrial Espionage;" 2011

[2] Gen Keith Alexander; testimony to US Senate Armed Services Committee on US Strategic Command and US Cyber Command in Review of the Defense Authorization Request for Fiscal Year 2013; Tuesday, March 27, 2012

[3] Maneki, Sharon; "Learning from the Enemy: The Gunman Project;" Center for Cryptologic History, National Security Agency; 2009

[4] US-Canada Power System Outage Task Force Final Report on the August 14, 2003 Blackout in the United States and Canada: Causes and Recommendations; April 2004; Excerpt from report: "The generation and delivery of electricity has been, and continues to be, a target of malicious groups and individuals intent on disrupting this system. Even attacks that do not directly target the electricity sector can have disruptive effects on electricity system operations. Many malicious code attacks, by their very nature, are unbiased and tend to interfere with operations supported by vulnerable applications. One such incident occurred in January 2003, when the "Slammer" Internet worm took down monitoring computers at FirstEnergy Corporation's idled Davis-Besse nuclear plant. A subsequent report by the North American Electric Reliability Council (NERC) concluded that although the infection caused no outages, it blocked commands that operated other power utilities."

[5] In the Crossfire Critical Infrastructure in the Age of Cyber War; 2010 joint study between McAfee and CSIS

[6] CJCSI 6510.01F: Information Assurance and Support to Computer Network Defense, 9 February 2011

[7] United States Air Force Scientific Advisory Board Defending and Operating in a Contested Cyber Domain; Report on Implications of Cyber Warfare; August 2007; SAB-TR-07-02

[8] DSB Task Force on Time Critical Conventional Strike from Strategic Standoff, March 2009

[9] Internet Security Threat Report, Volume 17; 2011; Symantec

[10] User mode rootkits involve system hooking in the user or application space. Whenever an application makes a system call, the execution of that system call follows a predetermined path and a Windows rootkit can hijack the system call at many points along that path. Kernel mode rootkits involve system hooking or modification in kernel space. Kernel space is generally off-limits to standard authorized (or unauthorized) users. One must have the appropriate rights in order to view or modify kernel memory. The kernel is an ideal place for system hooking because it is at the lowest level and thus, is the most reliable and robust method of system hooking.

[11] "Cyberattacks on Iran—Stuxnet and Flame;" New York Times; June 1, 2012

[12] OPERATION BUCKSHOT YANKEE is the code name of the Pentagon's operation to counter the attack that then Deputy Secretary Lynn described in his 2010 Foreign Affairs article cited in this report's Executive Summary

[13] Maneki, Sharon; "Learning from the Enemy: The Gunman Project;" Center for Cryptologic History, National Security Agency; 2009

[14] Flight Software Complexity (https://acc.dau.mil/adl/en-US/.../FlightSoftwareComplexityBriefing v5.ppt)

[15] DSB Task Force on Defense Software, November 2000; (Figure 3.4a)

[16] Pan, Jiantao; "Software Testing;" Carnegie Mellon University; Spring, 1999

[17] DoD Strategy for Operating in Cyber Space, July 2011

[18] Statement of General Keith Alexander, Commander USCYBERCOM, before the Senate Committee on Armed Services, March 27, 2012

[19] AFP; Sophisticated cyber thieves behind Epsilon attack, April 6, 2011

[20] Wall Street Journal; Hackers Broaden Their Attacks

[21] Dowdy, John; "The Cybersecurity Threat to US Growth and Prosperity;" McKinsey & Company; 2011

[22] Industrial Control Systems Alert: MOXA Device Manager Buffer Overflow; ICSA-10-301-01; October 28, 2010

[23] Industrial Control Systems Alert: SPECVIEW Directory Traversal; ICSA-12-214-01; August 1, 2012

[24] Industrial Control Systems Alert: Increasing Threat to Industrial Control Systems; ICSA-12-046-01; February 15, 2012

[25] Director of Test and Evaluation 2011 Annual Report

[26] See classified (SECRET) version of the May 2011 document titled: Department of Defense Strategy for Operating in Cyberspace

[27] Nuclear Posture Review Report, 2010

[28] 2002 Nuclear Posture Review Report

[29] 2006 Quadrennial Defense Review Report

[30] DSB Task Force on Time Critical Conventional Strike from Strategic Standoff, March 2009

[31] Oakley, John, "Cyber Warfare: China's Strategy to Dominate in Cyber Space," 2011; US Army Command and General Staff College

[32] Weiss, Gus W (1996), "The Farewell Dossier: Duping the Soviets", *Studies in Intelligence* (Central Intelligence Agency)

[33] Transcript, 31 January 2012 Senate Select Intelligence Committee open hearing on worldwide threat

[34] USCYBERCOM is responsible for planning, coordinating, integrating, synchronizing, and directing activities to operate and defend the Department of Defense information networks and when directed, conducts full-spectrum military cyberspace operations (in accordance with all applicable laws and regulations) in order to ensure US and allied freedom of action in cyberspace, while denying the same to our adversaries.

[35] DoD 8570.01-M; Information Assurance Workforce Improvement Program, December 19, 2005

[36] CJCSI 6510.01F: Information Assurance and Support to Computer Network Defense, 9 February 2011

[37] DoD 8570.01-M; Information Assurance Workforce Improvement Program, December 19, 2005

[38] DoD Energy Strategy (published Feb 2008); Critical Homeland Infrastructure Protection (published Jan 2007); DoD Roles and Missions in Homeland Security (November 2003).

In: Cyber Resiliency, Security …
Editor: Jesse A. Flanagan
ISBN: 978-1-62948-868-4

Chapter 2

CYBER SECURITY AND RELIABILITY IN A DIGITAL CLOUD*

Defense Science Board

November 27, 2012

MEMORANDUM FOR UNDER SECRETARY OF DEFENSE FOR ACQUISITION, TECHNOLOGY & LOGISTICS
SUBJECT: Final Report of the Defense Science Board (DSB)
Task Force on Cyber Security and Reliability in a Digital Cloud

I am pleased to forward the final report of the DSB Task Force on Cyber Security and Reliability in a Digital Cloud. This study comprises one part of a DSB Cyber Initiative. A study on Resilient Military Systems is the other component of the initiative.

The Task Force assessed the implications of using cloud computing resources and services for Department of Defense (DoD) mission needs. The report offers important recommendations for the DoD focused on: identification and application of cloud computing resources to DoD mission areas; improving DoD's implementation of cloud computing; enhancing cloud resiliency in degraded operations; and finally, areas requiring further research and development. Particular emphasis is given to improving cloud computing resilience for deployed forces.

I fully endorse all of the Task Force's recommendations contained in this report, and urge their careful consideration and soonest adoption.

Dr. Paul Kaminski
Chairman

* This is an edited, reformatted and augmented version of Defense Science Board; Department of Defense, dated January 2013.

November 27, 2012

MEMORANDUM FOR UNDER SECRETARY OF DEFENSE FOR ACQUISITION, TECHNOLOGY, AND LOGISTICS
Subject: Report of the Defense Science Board Task Force on Cyber Security and Reliability in a Digital Cloud

The final report of the Defense Science Board Task Force on Cyber Security and Reliability in a Digital Cloud is attached. The Task Force conducted an independent assessment of the suitability of cloud computing architectures for DoD applications. Key factors in the assessment included DoD mission enhancements, cyber security benefits and risks, and potential cost savings associated with cloud computing.

The Task Force also investigated the benefits and risks of cloud computing for the needs of deployed forces. Several enhancements in cloud computing architectures and training and operational exercising are recommended to improve the access to important data and computing resources under degraded operational conditions.

The Task Force recommends that for sensitive, classified, or time-critical applications, the DoD should pursue private cloud computing to enhance mission capabilities, provided that strong security measures are in place. This report recommends several improvements in cloud computing implementations to strengthen cyber security and reliability.

Dr. Eric D. Evans
Co-Chairman

Dr. Robert L. Grossman
Co-Chairman

EXECUTIVE SUMMARY

Cloud computing is viewed by many as the next major step in the evolution of computing infrastructure. Very large commercial cloud computing data centers have emerged around the world with petaflops of processing capacity, hundreds of petabytes of data storage, and wideband network access. Services, including electronic mail, data storage, database management, application hosting, very large dataset processing, and high performance computing, are globally available today from many cloud computing data centers. Cloud computing advocates promise on-demand delivery of these massive, warehouse-scale computing resources simply and easily through a network browser.

Much of the technology and computer architecture that enable modern cloud computing has roots in the mainframe, client-server, and early internet computing eras. What has emerged in recent years, however, differs from all of these in many attributes. Cloud computing data centers have different capabilities, risks, and security concerns than conventional networks, as well as different cost and efficiency models.

These differences are substantial, and have resulted in a wide variety of realistic and unrealistic claims for cloud computing, as well as a good deal of hype and confusion. With the proper implementation and operations, cloud computing data centers have demonstrated as good or better cyber security, capabilities, and cost than is currently available in Department of Defense (DoD) data centers. These improvements, however, are by no means guaranteed for every case and very much depend on the specific details of the implementation and operations.

Cloud computing offers the DoD new, agile computational capabilities to support increasingly multifaceted missions. Some DoD missions likely to benefit from cloud computing services will involve varying or unpredictable computing requirements, or the integration of many, high-capacity data feeds from sensor networks and other sources. Other missions may include the analysis of very large data sets or those that require the ability to move computational resources. An additional benefit is the productivity gained from a ubiquitous connection to common cloud-based services, such as email, shared calendars, unclassified training, or document preparation.

This study investigates the suitability of the cloud computing approach for addressing the DoD enterprise and operational computing needs. Over the past few years, DoD has transitioned some of its computing needs to cloud computing data centers. The main factors driving this transition include enhanced mission capabilities, potential reduction in data center costs, and potential improvement in cyber security. This study has investigated these factors in detail and has analyzed the characteristics that should be considered when DoD contemplates moving applications onto cloud computing data centers. The study also investigated ways for the DoD to manage the cyber security risks and benefits associated with cloud computing.

Important Cloud Computing Issues for the Defense Use

Types of Cloud Computing Service Configurations

An important issue is selecting an appropriate configuration of cloud services for DOD cloud computing applications:

- Cloud computing services may be provided by a company that provides similar services to the public, a defense-only contractor, or the DoD itself.
- Cloud computing resources may be shared among a number of customers, or only a single organization.
- The staff that manages the hardware, software, and services may be uncleared employees of a public company, cleared DoD contractors, or DoD employees.
- The cloud computing hardware resources may be located in shared space with other customers, in dedicated space in a building with other customers, at a dedicated facility, or on a military base.
- Cloud computing software resources may be based on a standard or modified software stack used by a public cloud computing services provider, standard or modified open source software stack, proprietary software stack, custom software stack, or some combination of these.

As is clear from this list, multiple dimensions distinguish how cloud computing services may be provisioned. Simply distinguishing between "public clouds"—commercial public companies operating their own data centers that are shared among many external customers using their own custom software and their own staff—and non-public or private clouds can cause confusion. In this report, the task force describes the specific aspects of the cloud computing configuration that are relevant to avoid the simple choice of public or private clouds.

National security concerns clearly preclude putting the computing resources of some sensitive DoD missions and capabilities in public shared clouds operated by non-cleared personnel. In general, however, the decision whether to host a particular application in a particular cloud computing data center depends upon the specific details of the application and the data center.

Detailed Mandates for Enhanced Cyber Security

An issue of importance to DoD is the development of a detailed approach for enhanced cyber security across both its conventional and cloud computing enterprise.

The hardware and software used in cloud computing, like all hardware and software, may have vulnerabilities that can be exploited by adversaries. Cloud computing processes, fortunately, offer the potential for improved cyber security through a number of attributes, primarily better traffic filtering and malware scanning, monitoring of usage patterns and end-device configurations, varying provisioning of data resources, and improved management of systems operations. Whether allocating an existing application to a cloud computing data center increases or decreases cyber security depends upon the specific application, the specific characteristics of the configuration, and the specific implementation.

The cyber security of cloud computing needs additional attention when it is used to support mission-critical DoD applications. The task force found that, in many cases, deploying applications to cloud computing data centers increased cyber security, especially against less sophisticated threats. The task force also found that many risks can be managed with available hardware and software measures, but the DoD needs to carefully implement these measures before transitioning existing applications to cloud computing systems.

Research and development work within the Military Services, the Defense Advanced Research Projects Agency (DARPA), and the intelligence community offers technology that promises significant improvements for cloud computing cyber security in the long term, and this work should be better integrated with acquisition planning for DoD cloud computing data centers. In some DoD cloud computing implementations currently underway, a larger emphasis on cyber security measures is needed.

Control of Cloud Computing Transition and Sustainment Costs

Realizing the potential cost savings associated with cloud computing is important to DoD. The transition of Federal government applications to cloud computing data centers have, in some cases, resulted in cost savings. The task force found the actual cost benefits to be highly case-dependent.

This cost savings for the transition from conventional enterprise computing to cloud computing has been achieved in a number of ways: through staffing, electric power usage, and computing efficiency. Conventional systems typically require one professional staff per tens to hundreds of servers, whereas most cloud computing data centers only require one professional staff for thousands of servers. Electric power is a large component of data center costs, and cloud computing data centers can be located where power is relatively less expensive. Finally, through virtualization and improved processing management, servers in cloud computing data centers can be more efficiently used, often achieving greater than five times the server efficiency as compared with conventional computing.

The required cost to enhance cyber security for any cloud computing implementation will need additional investigation. Some additional hardware and software will be required, and the cost for these components will need to be incorporated into the transition and sustainment costs when contemplating transition to a cloud computing data center.

DoD Cloud Computing Data Centers

Of particular importance to DoD will be finding ways to mitigate risk while achieving the capability benefits and potential cost reductions that cloud computing promises. An important aspect of cloud computing is the ability to operate infrastructure at a warehouse-scale data center and, thus, to provide new capabilities and enable cost savings. But warehouses are, by their nature, highly visible; having only a few, very large DoD data centers may create attractive targets for an adversary to attack. Further, the centralization implied by a "Fort Knox" approach—with a single, very large data center—cannot provide DoD with resilience or low-data transfer latencies required for global operations.

The task force therefore recommends that DoD design, implement, and deploy a set of geographically distributed data centers that could be could be operated as a single system. A few tens of such consolidated cloud computing data centers, established across the United States and around the world, seems like a good start at creating a sensible cloud capability for DoD. If appropriately designed, a collection of modular data centers would provide DoD with robust and elastic computing capacity.

Commercially available data centers, with servers embedded in modular units, offer DoD a relatively low cost and rapid way to develop a defense cloud computing infrastructure. The DoD could situate clusters of these modular data centers in physically secure areas. These may include military bases that have access to low cost and reliable power and wideband networks.

These modular data centers could be designed as a unit and purchased over time. In this way, standard best practices could be applied, such that one-third of the decentralized data center could be refreshed each year to ensure ongoing modernization. Such a design can also provide agility because computing infrastructure could be moved between geographic locations when needed.

Resilient Cloud Computing Resources for Deployed Forces

A final issue of importance for the DoD is to provide resilient cloud computing resources at the warfighter "edge"—locations and times with scarce bandwidth. Deployed forces often execute their missions under degraded conditions and disadvantaged data links, and this limits a warfighter's access to the most current data. In these cases, thick clients—with enhanced data storage and redundant data links— could ensure limited access to data. When low-latency processing is needed, cloud computing data resources could be deployed in close proximity to the data streams.

The availability of secure, modular cloud computing resources could provide DoD with the capability to forward-deploy data and computing resources to meet warfighter needs.

Summary of Key Findings and Recommendations

The Significance and Impact of Cloud Computing

Finding 1: Although cloud computing is an overloaded term, cloud computing providers are offering services that are fundamentally new and useful, typically delivering the:

- ability for massive scale-up of storage and computing
- rapid, agile, elasticity with the ability to increase and decrease storage and computing capacity on-demand, when the community of tenants don't all require that capacity at the same time
- metered services where the user pays only for what is used
- self-service start-up and control

Finding 2: Modular data centers offer an approach to quickly set up cloud computing capacity, to add additional capability to existing cloud computing data centers, and to easily refresh or update existing capability. This concept is illustrated in Figure F-1.

Finding 3: Cloud computing services can scale to data centers or "warehouse-scale" computing. Elastic, warehouse-scale cloud computing is fundamentally new and can provide DoD with important new capabilities.

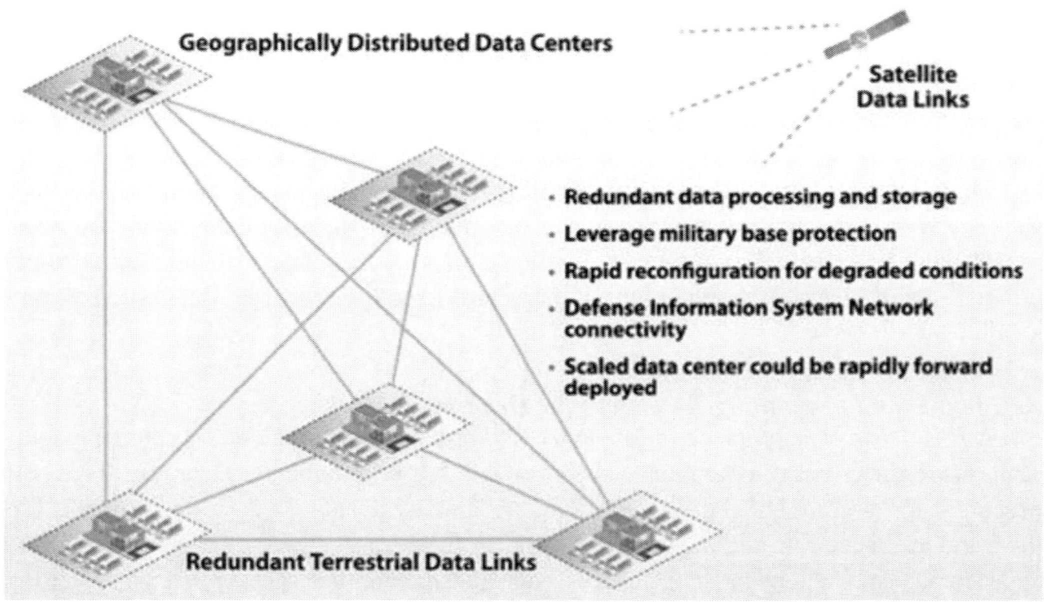

Figure F-1. Concept for a geographic distribution of DoD data centers.

The Security of Cloud Computing

Finding 4: Cloud computing is not intrinsically more secure than other distributed computing approaches, but its scale and uniformity facilitate and enable the wholesale and consistent application of security practices. Secure aspects include large scale monitoring and analysis of data to detect attacks, and automated and persistent provisioning and re-provisioning to foil intrusions. For these reasons, well-operated cloud computing facilities can exhibit better security hygiene than conventional data centers. However, the centralization of resources in a huge data center also encourages more determined attacks, especially on critical components broadly affecting security. This is similar to conventional systems where attacks are observed to focus on central directories.

Finding 5: The scale of cloud computing enables the analysis of packet and log data that provides new capabilities for event forensics and real-time detection of malicious behavior. The ability to manage very large, diverse datasets facilitates a data-centric security model in which users are authorized to work with data based upon their security credentials and the security markings on the data rather than the conventional enclave-centric security model in which users are provided access to an enclave and can access all the data in the enclave.

Finding 6: No cloud computing deployment model is uniformly suitable for hosting all DoD applications. In general, sensitive, classified, and time-critical DoD applications should be deployed only in private clouds or conventional non-cloud approaches.

Finding 7: The case for transitioning a DoD application to a cloud computing data center must include a security assessment detailing the impact of the transition. Whether security will be improved by transitioning an application to a cloud computing data center will depend on factors specific to the application, to the cloud computing data center, and to the transition process.

Finding 8: The DoD has not established effective plans for cloud computing facility backup or for dealing with any anticipated degradation of communications between the cloud computing facilities and the end user.

The Costs Associated with Cloud Computing

Finding 9: Potential cost reductions or increases incurred during the transition to and sustainment of cloud computing infrastructure depend on the specifics of the implementation. Potential cost-reduction factors include a higher utilization of servers, lower professional support staff needs, economies of scale for the physical facility, and the flexibility to locate data centers in areas with lower-cost power.

Research and Development for Cloud Computing Technologies

Finding 10: The DoD has active research and development efforts in technology areas applicable to cloud computing performance and security. Sustained DoD investment in cloud computing security technology is critically important to allow DoD data centers to continue improving their defenses against evolving threats.

Research and development in software stack protection, monitoring, and forensics of very large datasets, secure hypervisors, and advanced encryption offer significant possible security benefits.

Overarching Recommendations

Recommendation 1: For some sensitive, classified, and time-critical applications, the DoD should pursue private cloud computing, provided that strong security measures are in place.

In particular, cloud computing-based solutions should be considered for applications that require the agility, scale-out, and ability to integrate and analyze massive data that cloud computing can provide. Examples of such applications include: big data analysis and all-source intelligence integration; processing, exploitation, and dissemination of data gathered through intelligence, surveillance, and reconnaissance (ISR); large-scale modeling and simulation; open source data collection, storage, and assessment; and advanced decision support systems.

Recommendation 2: The DoD CIO in partnership with the military Services should deploy interconnected, modular cloud computing data centers located at secure locations, such as military bases.

The development of large, private community clouds in DoD will enable greater computing and storage elasticity and the improved ability to operate under degraded conditions. The DoD CIO should guide this development with an eye on both current and future DoD computing needs.

A DoD private community cloud may include in-house, in-sourced, or out-sourced private clouds. Implemented through interconnected, modular cloud computer data centers, this can be operated as an integrated unit to improve the potential reducing costs.

Because large data centers can also be attractive targets, geographically distributed modular data centers are recommended that are operated as a single, large-scale, distributed cloud. The design should include a distributed data center architecture that allows access by multiple Services and Agencies. Cost savings would be achieved through shared development, operations, and maintenance support.

These modular data centers could be located on military bases in order to provide good physical security. The location should also be influenced by the cost and availability of reliable electric power. It is anticipated this will be similar to the National Security Agency private cloud models. Shared cyber security event response and rapid forensics would be an enhanced capability.

By designing and acquiring these data centers as a system, the DoD can achieve the economies of scale typically associated with large data centers.

Recommendation 3: The DoD CIO and DISA should establish clear security mandates for DoD cloud computing.

Security mandates should be aimed at reducing the number of cloud compromises and to mitigate those that occur. Some examples of potential mandates include:

- Hypervisors hosting DoD operating systems should have effective cryptographic sealing, attestation, and strong virtual machine isolation.

- Data at rest should be stored in encrypted form with keys protected using hardware attestation, such as a trusted platform module (TPM).
- Data in transit on communication lines should be encrypted with keys protected using hardware attestation, such as a TPM.
- Access to cloud computing systems should require multifactor authentication.

Recommendation 4: The DoD CIO should establish a central repository to fully document cloud computing transition and sustainment costs and best practices for programs underway or completed.

Because the cost savings to be gained through cloud computing are case-dependent, a central repository documenting DoD cloud computing programs is needed. The goal of this repository is to improve the understanding of the following:

- system costs before the switch to cloud computing, costs during transition, and sustainment costs
- enhanced functionality attributable to cloud computing architectures
- best practices for cloud computing security
- issues surrounding service license agreements
- metrics for availability and reliability

This repository will enable leveraging the lessons learned from several DoD cloud computing initiatives underway, including:

- NSA development and use of private clouds
- DISA Rapid Access Computing Environment (RACE)
- Army Enterprise Email

Recommendations to Improve DoD's Implementation of Cloud Computing

Recommendation 5: The DoD USD AT&L and the DoD CIO should establish a lean, rapid acquisition approach for information technology infrastructure, including cloud computing hardware and software.

Acquisition guidelines for all information technology—not only cloud computing hardware and software—should strive to create a lean, capabilities-based approach with strong, clear security mandates. Rapid certification and accreditation (C&A) and other characteristics to streamline acquisition of cloud computing hardware and software should be developed and implemented quickly.

Recommendation 6: The DoD CIO and DISA should establish standard service level agreements for private and public cloud computing.

Key attributes that should be included in service level agreements include availability, authentication and authorization approaches, data processing and storage locations, software and data back-up approaches, cyber attack event notification, required staff clearances and background checks, software and data disposition, risk disclosure requirements, and contingency plan.

Transparency in all of these aspects for DoD service providers will help set standards for secure cloud computing across the economy.

Recommendation 7: The DoD CIO and DISA should participate in the public development of national and global standards and best practices for cloud computing.

A key outcome of this activity will be to inform the private sector and open source developers about the agility and auditability requirements for DoD cloud computing.

Recommendations to Improve Cloud Computing for Degraded Operations

Recommendation 8: The DoD and the intelligence community leadership should develop a unified approach for training and exercising with degraded information infrastructure, including cloud computing hardware and software.

Degraded operations in a realistic operational exercise must be implemented organically, *i.e.*, beyond simply holding up a white card to introduce a cyber event to an exercise. Advanced cyber security threats should be exercised, including a gradual ramp-up of threat and loss of disadvantaged communication and data links as well as primary capabilities. Enhanced red and blue teaming should be established along with operational exercises incorporating degraded cloud computing infrastructure. Participants should demonstrate a rapid forensics response and effective backup plans.

Recommendation 9: The Joint Chiefs of Staff and Combatant Commands should establish effective back-up plans for operations with degraded information infrastructure, including cloud computing hardware and software.

Candidate plan attributes include implementing thicker clients and forward caching of data as well as backup data networks, processors, and storage. Each organization should also develop operational contingencies for degraded networks. Potential strategies also include using local network connectivity for forward clients and narrowband, analog communication links for situational awareness and warning.

Recommendations for Investment

Recommendation 10: The DoD should continue investing significantly in information security research and development, including research and development for secure cloud computing technology.

To best leverage state-of-the-art cloud computing technologies for DoD, significant investment should continue for technology research and development activities in areas such as: efficient operations of cloud computing data centers; cloud security; secure, lean hypervisors; micro-virtualization; advanced TPMs; homomorphic computing; and cloud situational awareness software.

1. Scope of the Report

1.1. Terms of Reference

Over the past several years, cloud computing has had a major impact on commercial information processing. This report examines the suitability of cloud computing for DoD infrastructure, support applications, and mission applications.

The terms of reference for this study identified the following topics for investigation:

- Characterize the operational properties of clouds and the quality of service that can be delivered to connected users.
- Consider alternative designs and implementations of these technologies and evaluate their use for varied military and intelligence applications.
- Evaluate the vulnerability of a cloud infrastructure to various attacks, compared to alternative infrastructures.
- Determine how to avoid the danger of concentrating data and computation.
- Review and project the consequence of current trends in digital technology on cloud deployments.
- Comment on customer practices and modes of interaction with the cloud that may aid in increasing security.
- Make recommendations on what aspects of these technologies should be considered to increase reliability and to assure security as the military and intelligence communities evolve their digital infrastructure.
- Identify research opportunities and estimate the level of investment to achieve results consistent with DoD needs.

The full terms of reference can be found on page 68 of this report.

1.2. Task Force Approach

As shown in Figure 1, the task force investigated in detail cloud computing definitions, attributes, and service management models, as well as dimensions for implementation. Proposed motivation that were assessed for transitioning to cloud computing architectures included potential DoD mission capability enhancement, security improvements, and cost reductions.

The task force then developed examples for areas where cloud computing would benefit DoD missions. This resulted in a set of findings and recommendations for improving the DoD's ability to use cloud computing architectures effectively, with cost reductions and sufficient levels of security.

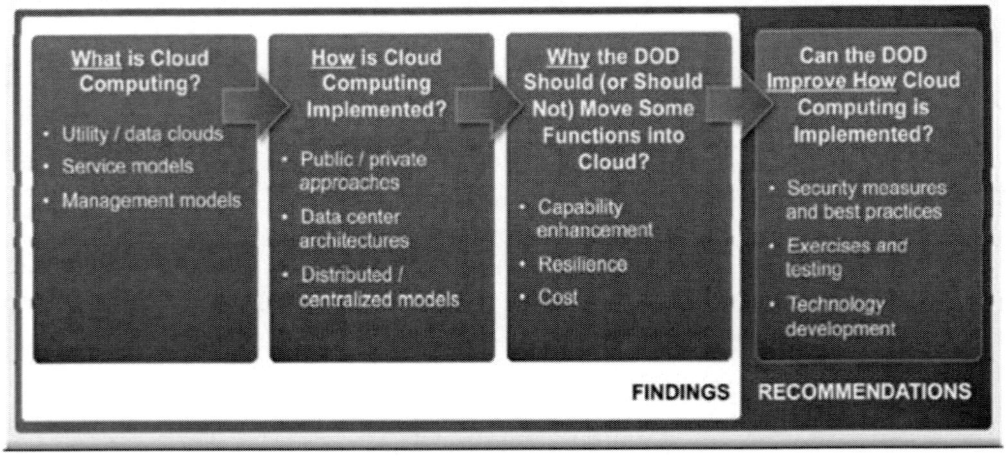

Figure 1. The task force approach.

In a final phase, the task force discussed in several meetings how the DoD could improve the implementation of cloud computing systems for DoD missions and applications.

1.3. Organization of the Report

An overview of cloud computing is presented in Chapter 2. This chapter also defines terms and concepts used throughout the report. The National Institute of Standards and Technology (NIST) provided a consensus definition of cloud computing that was a useful starting point for discussions; however, the task force found places where a broader definition was also useful.

In Chapter 2, a variety of different service models and deployment models for cloud computing are described. The task force found it helpful to view a cloud computing facility as a warehouse-scale computing facility that supports computing applications and services for remote users connected using a network.

Some well-known examples of commercial cloud service providers include Google, Amazon, Yahoo!, and Microsoft, but these services can also be provided by defense agencies or defense-only contractors. Confusion regarding DoD use of cloud computing has arisen, in part, because of unstated assumptions on who provides the service.

Chapter 3 looks in some detail at cloud computing architectures and how cloud computing is implemented. A commercial cloud computing facility can contain hundreds of thousands of servers, with applications and services scaled to employing this capacity. Computing at this scale is a fundamentally new capability.

One way that commercial cloud computing facilities achieve efficiencies is through virtualization. With virtualization, operating systems and applications operate on independent virtual machines that share physical processors. By implementing many virtual machines entirely in software on a large physical machine, the arrangement more efficiently utilizes physical resources while providing computational isolation. Because virtual machines can be migrated between computers located in different geographically distributed data centers, the system experiences improved fault tolerance and load-balancing.

Chapter 4 looks at some of the benefits to DoD's mission that could be enabled by cloud computing. The mobility of computing infrastructure has important implications for DoD. The ability to move collections of virtual machines and the virtual networks that connect them will be critical for future DoD applications and missions.

Today, commercial cloud computing facilities offer an ability to self-provision computing infrastructure on demand and as needed, paying just for what the customer uses. This agility is extremely useful for settings where there is widely varying or unpredictable computing needs. The task force also observed that the wide availability of cloud computing leads to the reasonable assumption that adversaries of the United States may use cloud computing for both defensive and offensive missions.

Chapter 5 discusses security of cloud computing, which has been questioned in a number of strategies and studies.[1,2,3,4] The task force found this to be a complex subject where evolving objectives make analysis particularly difficult. The task force observed several subtleties that affect this analysis. These are highlighted here, and discussed in detail in Chapter 5.

The responsibility for security in most cases is shared between a cloud service provider and a cloud service client. Different cloud computing service and deployment models split this responsibility differently, with many models requiring that two or more parties be involved in managing the computing infrastructure and security measures. Such sharing can be a problem when the provider and client are different organizations without unrestricted two-way communication.

Security cannot be discussed independently of a defined threat. Protecting against high-level threats is extremely difficult; the safest course is to assume that any computing infrastructure might be compromised, to develop mechanisms that operate in the presence of such compromise, and to design in a way that will mitigate the impact of compromises. Cloud computing differs little from conventional computing infrastructures in this regard.

The scale of cloud computing is vastly different from conventional computing systems. Such scale requires automation for provisioning and management of the computing infrastructure with humans out of the loop. For this reason, the security hygiene of cloud computing systems tends to be better than computing systems of comparable size. Thus, cloud computing can offer equivalent or better protection against low level threats that tend to exploit vulnerabilities caused by poor system hygiene.

Chapter 6 considers issues and circumstances in which cloud computing can be expected to lower the costs of computing infrastructure. By leveraging scale, commercial cloud computing suppliers can offer computing services and applications at lower cost than a company or organization can often achieve internally.

For example, because of the scale and the automation of provisioning and management of computing infrastructure, commercial cloud computing data centers generally require far fewer systems administrators. As an example, conventional enterprise-computing might require one system administrator per tens or hundreds of servers, while a commercial cloud service provider might only require one system administrator per thousands of servers.

These advantages must be considered against the higher costs that defense systems may incur. These may include DoD acquisition process requirements or specific certification and accreditation processes.

Chapter 7 suggests areas for research and development of technology that could be important to the DoD's use of cloud computing. An emphasis is placed on research that improves the security and capabilities of cloud computing systems. Payoffs for some investments will be seen in a few years; other problems, however, will be solved only with longer-term sustained research support.

Finally, Chapter 8 presents the study recommendations that flow from the assessments and findings in the first seven chapters. The chapter includes proposed DoD leads to take responsibility for the recommendations, and some additional detail is provided to clarify the intent of the recommendations..

2. Overview of Cloud Computing

The phrase "cloud computing" has evolved to have different meanings for different people. Rather than defining it, this chapter describes some historical background, various types of cloud computing platforms, and different characteristics of cloud computing architectures. The task force believes that, over time, cloud computing models will evolve, and this evolution may not be reflected in today's descriptions. In this report, standard definitions are used where they suffice and are expanded where necessary.

2.1. The Latest Step in an Evolutionary Process

Cloud computing can be viewed as the natural evolution of a variety of computing technologies, including virtualization, client-server architecture, the World Wide Web, and networking. The evolution of some computing platform precursors to cloud computing is shown in Figure 2.

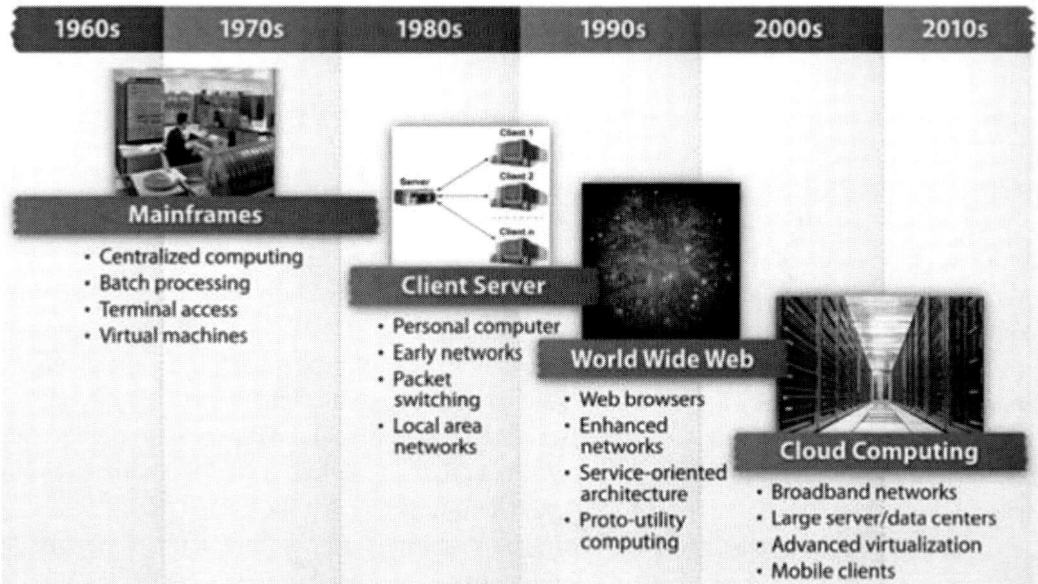

Figure 2. Historical precedents for cloud computing.

As early as the 1960s, mainframe computers were shared among multiple users across an enterprise, while logically isolating their processing and data from each other. In the 1980s, standardized packet network protocols were developed and widely deployed, along with client-server architectures to utilize them. The ability to connect users to computing and data resources via standardized networks is a key enabler of cloud computing.

The development of the World Wide Web in the 1990s, with its standard markup language, transfer protocol, and graphical browsers, made client-server computing ubiquitous. Business began to provide servers to deliver content and services at a truly global scale.

Seen in this historical context, the development of cloud computing is the next logical step in the evolution of computation. It has been enabled by the availability of broadband networks and inexpensive end-user devices, as well as commodity computing nodes that can be simply interconnected and controlled, and virtualization to provide the appearance of isolating processes that share computers.

2.2. What is Cloud Computing?

One well-known definition of cloud computing was provided by NIST.[5] It begins:

> "Cloud computing is a model for enabling ubiquitous, convenient, on-demand network access to a shared pool of configurable computing resources (*i.e.*, networks, servers, storage, applications, and services) that can be rapidly provisioned and released with minimal management effort or service provider interaction."

The definition goes on to identify five essential characteristics of cloud computing. These are as follows:

- **On-demand self-service**. A consumer can unilaterally provision computing capabilities, such as server time and network storage, as needed automatically without requiring human interaction with each service provider.
- **Broad network access**. The cloud's capabilities are available over the network from a wide variety of edge devices, including workstations, laptops, tablets, and mobile phones.
- **Resource pooling**. The cloud computing provider's resources are pooled to serve multiple consumers using a multi-tenant model, with different physical and virtual resources dynamically assigned and reassigned according to consumer demand. The customer (or tenant) generally has no control or knowledge about the exact location of allocated resources, but may be able to specify location at a higher level of abstraction (*e.g.*, country, state, or datacenter). Examples of resources include storage, processing, memory, and network bandwidth.
- **Rapid elasticity**. Cloud computing capabilities allocated to the customer can be elastically provisioned and released as required by demand, in some cases automatically. To the customer, the cloud capabilities available often appear to be unlimited and can be appropriated in any quantity at any time.
- **Measured service**. Cloud computing systems automatically control and optimize resource use by leveraging a metering capability appropriate to the type of service

(*e.g.*, storage, processing, bandwidth, and active user accounts), typically on a pay-per-use basis. Resource usage can be monitored, controlled, and reported, providing transparency for both the provider and consumer of the utilized service.

Two aspects of cloud computing are of particular significance. The scale of processing and storage that becomes available through cloud computing is unprecedented, with up to hundreds of thousands of computers acting in concert. It is this large scale—sometimes called warehouse-scale or internet-scale computing—that enables the design of reliable computing services using less-than-reliable commodity computers. Solving this challenge has provided new capabilities.

Also new is the ease-of-use of cloud computing services. Many cloud computing service providers allow a user to configure a new computing infrastructure through a simple web form with instantaneous payment by credit card. The ability to remotely request hundreds of servers for a few hours and to have them available a few minutes later is another new capability. This capability has transformed the work of many scientists and engineers, as well as their information technology support personnel.

2.2.1. Data, Utility, and Other Cloud Computing Services

Different types of cloud computing are provided from large, remotely located, interconnected data centers—hence, the common use of cloud computing to describe different uses. Cloud computing services are primarily categorized as utility- or data-intensive, and also include storage, high performance computing, and other specialized functions.

Utility computing is a label for cloud service providers that make computing resources available to consumers, much as electric companies and other utilities provide services to consumers. With an electric power utility, a homeowner can, within limits, request electricity simply by flipping a switch on a device, receive that power instantly from a distant generating facility, share the generating facility with thousands of other customers, use more or less power as needed, and pay only for the power actually used.

Utility computing customers include, for example, a retailer who chooses to purchase cloud services to host an internet-facing e-commerce web site. In this way, the retailer gains increased capacity and geographic presence over what could be obtained if the retailer had to buy, operate, maintain, and upgrade their own dedicated computing resources. Another example of a utility computing customer was demonstrated by the *New York Times* in 2008 to process more than a hundred years of digitized archived images, articles, and metadata in order to produce more web-friendly images and more accessible JavaScript data files. By using Amazon Web Services, the *Times* completed this enormous task in less than 36 hours.[6] In these examples, cloud computing service providers enabled customers to perform compute-intensive processes as needed without a large investment in infrastructure.

Utility computing enables a cloud service provider to exploit economies of scale and uncorrelated customer demands to share computing capability among a collection of customers, at an attractive price. Individual consumers perceive that they are accessing an infinite resource on demand. They also perceive that their computing tasks are operating in isolation from those of other consumers.

Data-intensive cloud computing is a type of parallel processing applied to very large datasets. An example of data-intensive computing is the process by which search engines index the data available on the World Wide Web. The underlying computational steps required to index data are simple—sorting, counting, merging, and so on—but the amount of data to be processed is so large that it requires specially-adapted software for data ingestion, analysis, database operations, and file system storage.

Data centers will generally be designed and optimized for different requirements. Utility computing design focuses on sharing resources, lowering the cost of computing to the customer, and providing computing capacity on-demand. The utility computing customer trades capital costs for operating costs. Data-intensive computing focuses on performing rapid analysis of large datasets, and vast amounts of computing resources may be dedicated to a single user or task. A data-intensive architecture will be optimized for large scale parallelization.

2.2.2. Cloud Computing Software Stack and Virtualization

Today, cloud computing infrastructure usually consists of a large number of interconnected, inexpensive, commodity processors. The software running on each processor is modular and layered. Figure 3 shows a typical layered "stack" of software running on a single cloud computing node, with descriptions of each layer in the stack.

The hypervisor provides virtualization by providing an interface to the virtual machines (VMs) that gives each of them the illusion that they have complete, exclusive access to the underlying hardware resources. The ability to run multiple, isolated virtual machines on a single hardware node is fundamental to cloud computing because it enables resource pooling and rapid elasticity. Multiple users can use the same physical node without interfering with each other, and nodes can be rapidly assigned and reassigned as users' computing demands ebb and flow.

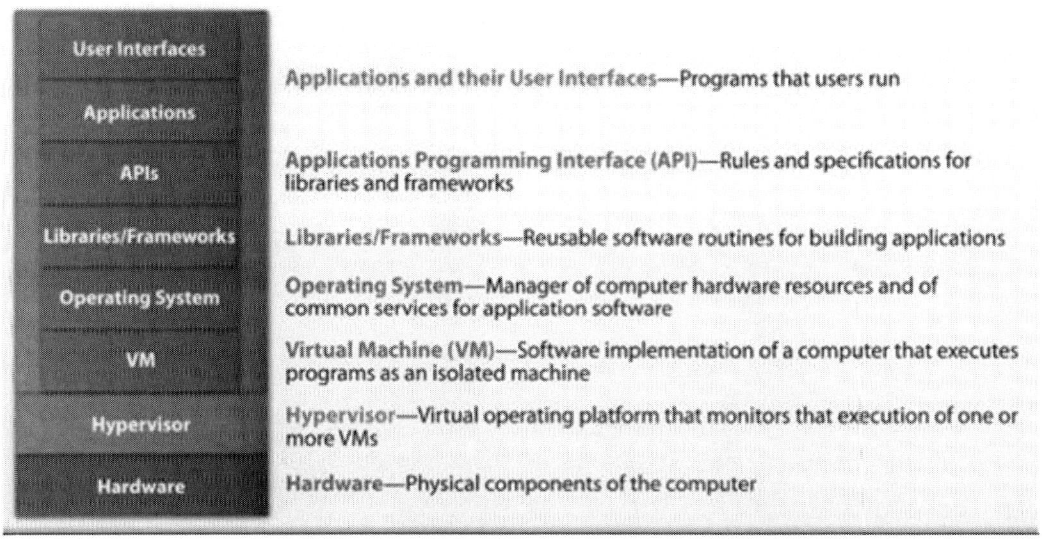

Figure 3. The main components of a cloud computing software stack.

Although virtualization is one of many enablers of cloud computing, cloud computing is more than just virtualization, and there are applications of virtualization that are not instances of cloud computing. For example, a departmental data center may use virtualization to allow a single hardware server to run multiple VMs, with each VM configured to run only one specific service. Such implementations may offer limited resource pooling and no elasticity—the virtualization is used in this case merely as a convenient mechanism for ensuring adequate isolation between services that is more cost-effective than assigning one hardware server per service.

The various cloud software service models assign responsibility for managing the software stack differently. Figure 4 shows that the cloud service provider provides the underlying hardware and the hypervisor in all service models, and that the upper layers of the stack can be provided and managed either by the service provider or by the cloud computing customer.

2.2.3. Cloud Computing Service Models

Different types of service are available to cloud computing customers, depending on how much control a customer requires. The NIST definition of cloud computing describes three service models (as reflected in Figure 4):

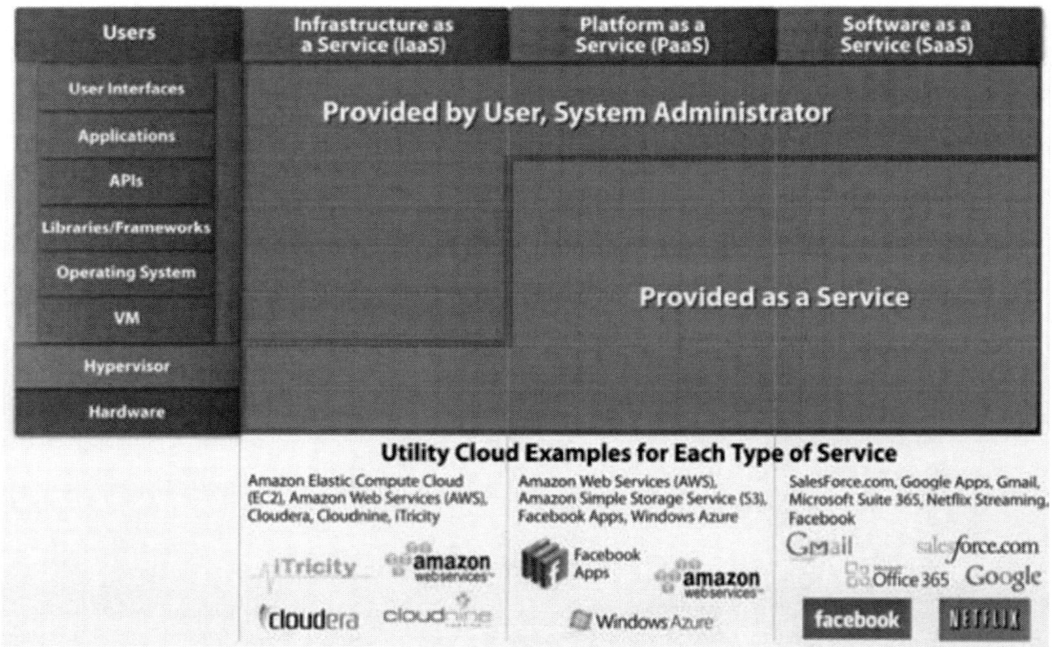

Figure 4. A cloud computing software stack responsibility as a function of service model.

- **Software as a Service (SaaS)**. With SaaS, customers use software applications that are developed, managed, and operated by a provider. The applications are accessible from various client devices through either a thin client interface, such as a web browser (*i.e.*, web-based email), or a specifically developed programmatic interface. The customer does not manage or control the underlying cloud infrastructure, including network elements, servers, operating systems, storage, or even individual application capabilities, with the possible exception of limited user-specific application configuration settings.
- **Platform as a Service (PaaS)**. With PaaS, customers create their applications using standardized programming languages, libraries, services, and tools supported by the

provider. The customer does not manage or control the underlying cloud infrastructure (including networks, servers, operating systems, or storage) that execute the applications, but the customer has control over the deployed applications and possibly over configuration settings for the application-hosting environment.
- **Infrastructure as a Service (IaaS)**. With IaaS, the customer provisions processing, storage, networks, and other low-level computing resources. Also with IaaS, the customer can deploy and run arbitrary software, which can include operating systems and applications. The customer has some control over operating systems, storage, and deployed applications; and possibly limited control of select networking components (*i.e.*, host firewalls or software defined networks).

In SaaS, customers have limited ability to make configuration changes, but cannot modify the application, such as a web-based email system. In PaaS, the consumer is able to build and upload his own software applications for running on the provider's computing resources, but is constrained to use the tools supported by the cloud provider. This gives the PaaS consumer more flexibility than SaaS without all the complexity of managing lower-level components (*i.e.*, the operating system). In IaaS, consumers have maximum control over the software running on the provider's hardware, with responsibility for many of the attendant management and security challenges.

These NIST-defined service models span a single dimension—the level of software control ceded by the provider to the consumer. Another important dimension is how the computing provided by the cloud is used, which leads to phrases like "data as a service" for cloud storage of data, and "security as a service" for security services provided via cloud computing, such as host-based antivirus and firewall software.

2.3. Managing Cloud Computing

The NIST definition lists four deployment models for sharing cloud resources:

- **Private cloud**. Provisioned for exclusive use by a single organization, the cloud infrastructure might be owned, managed, and operated by the organization, a third party, or some combination of them, and it may exist on or off premises.
- **Community cloud**. Provisioned for exclusive use by a specific community of consumers from organizations that have shared concerns (*i.e.*, mission, security requirements, policy, and/or compliance considerations), the cloud infrastructure can be owned, managed, and operated by one or more of the organizations in the community, a third party, or some combination of them, and it might exist on or off premises of one of the organizations.
- **Public cloud**. Provisioned for use by the general public, the cloud infrastructure might be owned, managed, and operated by a business, academic, or government organization, or some combination of them. It exists on the premises of the cloud provider.
- **Hybrid cloud**. The cloud infrastructure is a composition of two or more distinct cloud infrastructures (private, community, or public) that remain unique entities, but

are bound together by standardized or proprietary technology that enables data and application portability (*i.e.*, cloud bursting for load balancing between clouds).

Consumers of services with the least tolerance for sharing resources and relinquishing control usually choose a private cloud deployment, while those with more tolerance will choose a community, hybrid, or public cloud.

2.3.1. Cloud Management Models

NIST defines the four deployment models, but users of cloud computing services face many more choices as they decide who will own, manage, operate, and support the site of the cloud computing infrastructure, who will own, manage, operate, and support the hardware, who will own, manage, operate, and support the various layers of software, and so on. For all cloud computing users, these configuration options must be weighed against economics, security, and other factors. This balance is evolving.

Figure 5 lays out a range of possibilities for management and operating cloud computing infrastructure. The far left of the table suggests that very sensitive applications are not suitable for deployment in cloud computing architectures. Such applications include nuclear weapon security systems, some command and control systems, and weapon system fire control.

Other sensitive applications are best reserved for in-house private cloud computing. For the in-house private approach, the DoD would host the cloud computing infrastructure, control the hardware and software implementation, and use DoDemployed staff support.

For the in-sourced private model, the DoD hosts the cloud computing infrastructure. The hardware and software stack and staff support might be provided by an external contractor. For the out-sourced private model, an external cloud service provider would host hardware to be used exclusively by the DoD. The control of the hardware and software stack and staff support might be provided by both the DoD and an external contractor. Some less sensitive applications may be appropriate for these approaches.

	Not Cloud	In-house Private	In-sourced Private	Out-sourced Private	Public
Hosting	DoD site	DoD site	DoD site	Commercial site	Commercial site
Hardware	DoD owned	DoD owned	DoD or Commercial owned	DoD or Commercial owned	Commercial owned
Software	DoD specialized	DoD stack	DoD or Commercial stack	DoD or Commercial stack	Commercial stack
System Administrator	DoD	DoD	DoD/Commercial	DoD/Commercial	Commercial
	Nuclear security Command and control Weapons fire control Highly classified needs	More Sensitive Geospatial image analysis Moving target radar analysis Geo-location processing Data integration Large simulations		Less Sensitive Email Calendars Logistics Purchasing Finance records	Public released data External web sites Public services Recruiting

Figure 5. Cloud computing management models.

For the public cloud computing model, an external cloud service provider employs hardware at its site. The hardware may not be used exclusively by the DoD, and the cloud service provider controls the software stack and employs the staff support. For some applications, where data or processing has been publicly released and required latency and system availability is consistent with public cloud service providers, public cloud computing could be acceptable for the DoD.

The following cloud data center management models are described in more detail:

- **In-house private design**. DoD privately operates the data center with high physical security. The DoD directly controls the hardware and software configuration, and the IT operational support staff is employed by the DoD. The cloud data center may have as its tenants a single mission or multiple missions.
- **In-sourced private design**. DoD privately operates this data center with high physical security. DoD either directly or through contractors assembles the infrastructure, with the goal of maximizing the use of well-vetted infrastructure components. However, DoD (or its contractors) might themselves build some infrastructure or application components when assurance needs dictate. The cloud data center might have as its tenants a single mission or multiple, shared missions.
- **Out-sourced private design**. A DoD contractor operates the data center. All DoD applications are run in a DoD enclave, physically segregated from non-DoD tenants in the cloud data center. Data center personnel with access to the DoD enclave are U.S. citizens, meeting specified personnel security requirements. All security-critical components in the cloud data center are subject to DoD review. These components are likely to include those concerned with, data integrity, software integrity, key management, and key storage. DoD has access to incident and forensic information concerning all cloud tenants. Individual tenants are responsible for building or integrating applications, but those applications are subject to the data center's security requirements for operation and audit.
- **Public, with user provenance design**. A commercial contractor operates the data center. It provides services under commercially available terms. Security-critical components in the cloud data center are subject to DoD review, including components that affect data security, data integrity, software integrity, key management, and storage. DoD has access to incident and forensic information concerning all cloud tenants. Individual tenants are responsible for building and integrating applications, and those applications are subject to commercially established security requirements for operation and audit.

2.3.2. Cloud Computing Service Providers and Proprietary Networks

Services offered by cloud computing providers may be connected to proprietary networks to provide services that users require. These services might be deployed according to any of the various deployment and management models described above.

A salient example is the Global Information Grid (GIG). The GIG is the DoD's globally interconnected end-to-end set of information capabilities, associated processes, and personnel for collecting, processing, storing, disseminating, and managing information on demand. Users include warfighters, policy makers, and support personnel. The GIG includes DoD-owned and leased communications, computing systems and services, software applications, data, security services, and other associated systems.

Figure 6 is a simplified diagram that shows a notional relationship of cloud computing to some traditional functional components of the GIG. As shown here, cloud computing brings a new capability to the GIG, but it does not replace the GIG.

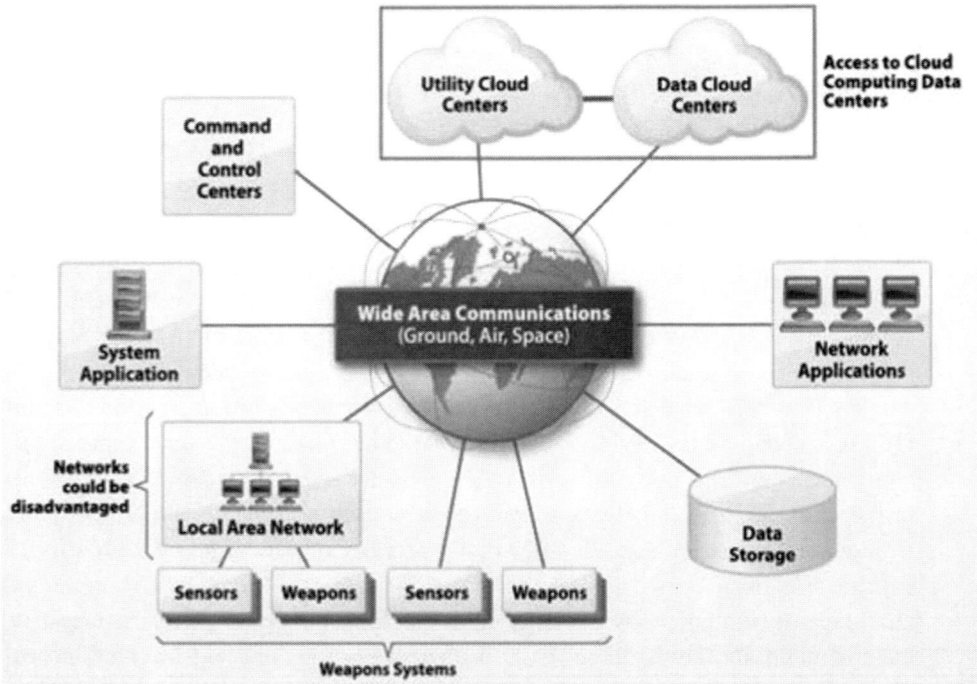

Figure 6. Cloud computing hardware and software as components of the GIG.

3. Cloud Computing Architecture and Implementation

Cloud computing architectures have developed to support the key benefits of cloud computing: elasticity, economy of operation, massive scaling of computing resources to solve critical problems, and real-time responsiveness.

3.1. The Building Blocks of Cloud Computing

Technology in several key areas has driven cloud computing architecture development and made cloud computing possible. A few critical developments are described here:

- **Commoditization of microelectronics**. Digital devices have become cheaper and more capable over time and, as a result, are now widely available and deployed in a broad set of contexts. Computing devices that cost millions of dollars in the 1960s have equally powerful descendants costing hundreds or even tens of dollars. The explosion of the personal computing market from 1975 through 2005 represents one outcome of this revolution in capacity and cost.

- **Networking**. Fast, cheap, ubiquitous networking between previously unrelated parties is critical for the success of cloud computing. The Internet fulfills this role by imposing interoperability requirements on its end-hosts. These interoperability requirements, in turn, have led to standards for protocols and services that have facilitated the emergence of a low-cost and widespread network infrastructure.
- **Virtualization**. A hypervisor provides an interface to implement VMs, giving each VM the appearance of exclusive access to a physical processor. The ability to run multiple, isolated virtual machines on a single hardware processor is fundamental to cloud because it enables multiple users to use the same physical node without interference, and it enables nodes to be rapidly assigned and reassigned as user computing demands ebb and flow. Virtualization facilitates the resource pooling and rapid elasticity that characterize cloud computing.
- **Commodity hardware**. Software is increasingly targeted at commodity computer hardware. A noteworthy outcome of this trend shaped high performance computing (HPC), where performance equal to or better than custom processor designs (*i.e.*, supercomputers such as Cray machines) has been achieved at much lower cost by using clusters built from commodity processors and high-speed interconnects. These clusters are the forerunner of today's cloud computing data centers.
- **Open source software**. Unix was among the first operating systems with widely available source code. This availability fostered broad community participation in the development of operating systems, applications, and tools that can be used as-is, or can be adapted by any developer. Open-source systems have, in many cases, outstripped expensive commercial software in function and quality, and many cloud computing systems, development tools, infrastructure, and applications are built from open-source components. Cloud providers routinely contribute labor and computing capacity to these open-source development efforts and the cloud community has several complete open-source frameworks.

3.2. The Scale of Cloud Computing

Combining the technology developments listed above would be a positive step but would yield only incremental improvements in cost and capacity. The signature characteristic of cloud computing is scale. Scale is the differentiator that brought a giant leap in computational and storage capacity in recent years. Search engines and other massive data applications were initial drivers for the evolution of cloud computing architectures, as exemplified by Google's mission "to organize the world's information and make it universally accessible and useful."[7] Today, cloud computing infrastructures support the large-scale storage and processing of many different types of data.

The scale of a modern cloud computing data center is sometimes difficult to comprehend. They are designed to support hundreds of thousands of central processing units, many petabytes of data on shared disk drives, and nearly a petabyte of dynamic storage of memory.

Thus, as is shown in Figure 7, cloud computing data centers are very large physical plants, sometimes with acres of computers. Even a small facility might consume several megawatts of electricity for cooling and powering the electronics, and some of the larger data centers today consume much more. A communications infrastructure is likely to support tens to hundreds of gigabytes per second of network ingress and egress; storage requirements dictate many thousands of disks.

3.2.1. Benefits and Challenges of Scale

One of the most attractive new capabilities of cloud computing is elasticity—the ability to rapidly and dramatically increase the computing resources assigned to solve a problem. Elasticity is achieved mainly by designing resilient infrastructure and applications and by deploying uniform hardware and standardized operations so that tasks can be redistributed and relocated within the computing substrate.

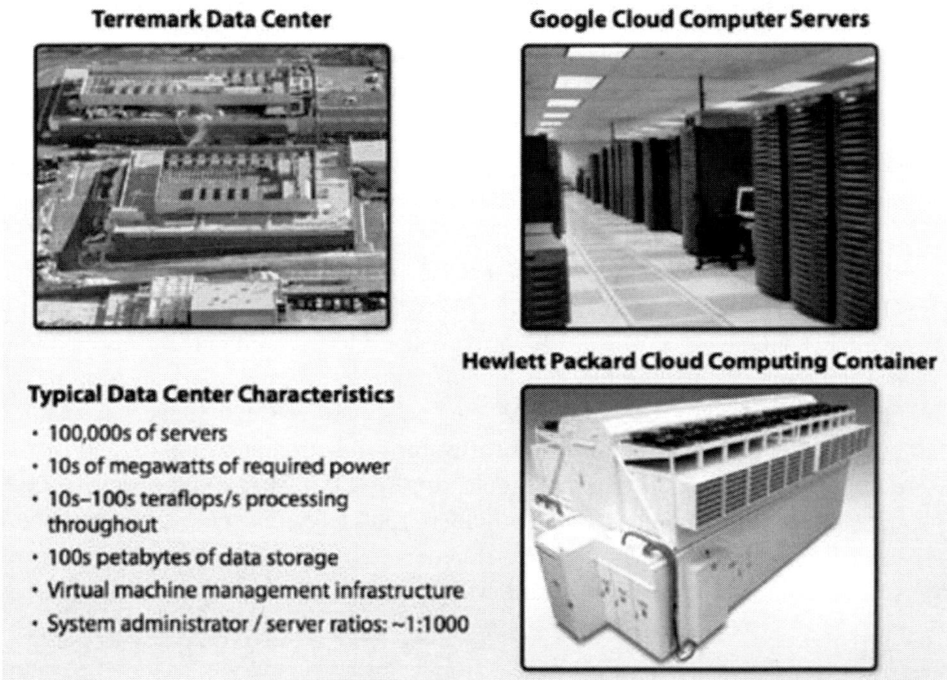

Figure 7. Cloud computing data center characteristics and examples.

The ability to scale seamlessly can also enable rapid processing and analysis of very large datasets through using highly parallel operations. This is an important capability for DoD.

Using scale to achieve reliability as well as performance leads to profound changes in application design and application management. Many cloud computing applications are long-running and have thousands of software components that cooperatively and continuously execute across multiple data centers. In a typical cloud computing data center, even with high quality parts, hundreds of disks and electronic components fail every day. Homogeneity of hardware, infrastructure, service, deployment, and operation of applications is crucial for achieving the efficiencies of a cloud.

Assembling a large facility at an enormous capital expense dictates that different parties with different goals and objectives must be able to use the facility efficiently and securely, despite none having physical access to the facility. This style of sharing could be accomplished through strict physical isolation between tenants, or through strong but flexible access controls to support collaborative access to shared data.

Another potential benefit of scale is cost savings. Applications that may experience the most cost benefit from cloud computing architectures are those used in the same way by large numbers of people, such as email. Many, if not most, DoD applications, however, are not standardized.

Designing more specialized applications to operate efficiently in a cloud computing environment can require large up-front development costs. Even slight customizations, such as the ability to find and erase any unintentionally transmitted classified material, could quickly and dramatically reduce potential savings of using an existing email application. However, even addressing all of the technical challenges, large cloud data centers have been shown to achieve a factor of ten cost savings over smaller installations. Cost savings are discussed in more detail in Chapter 6.

3.3. Specific Cloud Characteristics Affecting Architecture and Implementation

Each of the following characteristics informs cloud architecture design tradeoffs that materially affect performance and security. These tradeoffs will be explored further in the discussion on security in Chapter 5.

3.3.1. Automatic Provisioning and Infrastructure Management

Commercial cloud computing data centers have developed an operational model that requires few visits by human operators to individual computers or nodes. Many operations can be automated and the physical configuration for all the machines in a data center is generally homogeneous. No application can rely on special setup of a particular machine or continuity of execution on the same computer. Some installations simply disable nodes as individual components fail, but many providers have excellent diagnostic software that can help to forecast and avoid hardware failures proactively.

Applications must be packaged to support automated data center operations. Typically this involves expressly specifying provisioning requirements—what resources are required to run the application—and designing software to tolerate the full range of resource assignment within the scope of the specified requirements. Data center personnel generally do not know application behavioral patterns; hence the operations staff cannot detect or fix anomalous behaviors *except* when problems are expressly registered with data center operations software. When such a report is made, a pre-specified automatic procedure is performed without human intervention.

3.3.2. Application Development and Scale Out

Existing application software sometimes does not perform efficiently when it is simply deployed on a cloud computing system. Well-architected cloud computing applications must detect failures, incorporate failover alternatives, and provide sufficiently robust diagnostic support to allow remote analysis and debugging of problems as well as implementing automated contingency planning and reconfiguration. Conventional computing, conversely, generally deals with component failure using lower-level mechanisms, such as redundant hardware, mirrored storage, and automatic failover. These are more costly and more time-consuming.

Many cloud applications are accessed through Internet browsers, which can be challenging to secure. For these applications, there is a performance premium on reducing data exchanged between the browser front-end and the cloud deployed back-end. Network round-trips must also be reduced, and if disconnected operation is required, provisions may be designed to cache data at clients.

When applications deployed in cloud computing share data and infrastructure, they must use standard protocols, which can limit flexibility and can make application development, debugging, and testing expensive. As a result, the expense of customizing some legacy applications for cloud deployment can be substantial.

Redesigning a legacy application so that it benefits from scaling can sometimes require significant effort. An application developer must carefully consider shared volatile state management and full system effects such as latency, network and storage failures, and correlated hardware failures.

3.3.3. Application Centralization

Because cloud data centers involve replication of hardware, systems software, and application software elements, care must be exercised to avoid the risks that monocultures bring. Fortunately, the uniformity also means that changes and security updates can be installed very quickly. Moreover, one impediment to installing updates—backward compatibility—is less of a problem in cloud computing because data can be migrated at the same time as the software update is deployed.

Because cloud-based applications typically are partitioned between a client front-end and a cloud back-end server, security issues arise that do not occur when client and server are deployed within the same enclave. In particular, in cloud deployments, strong client and server authentication must be used.

3.3.4. Data Collection and Centralization

Cloud computing is a natural repository for large and complex datasets that cannot be easily managed or accessed using traditional database management tools. Indeed, cloud computing services, such as Facebook, Google, and Amazon, rely on such centralized data repositories. Central repositories are attractive attack targets—both by insiders and outsiders. For this reason, special attention must be paid to data provenance for damage control, forensics, accountability, and data-quality control.

3.3.5. Clients

Almost all cloud computing services are accessed through a client—an application or system that accesses a service made available remotely. Client design is thus an integral part of any cloud application. Many reported cloud security failures have been attributed to bad or compromised client machines.

3.4. Architecture of a Modern Cloud Data Center

When building a cloud data center, a prospective designer must specify the machine and cluster configurations, storage architecture, network connectivity and management, and physical infrastructure, such as power and cooling. Often data centers are built near hydroelectric facilities to exploit the cheap power and near major fiber links to facilitate high-bandwidth remote access to the cloud. Site characteristics conducive to cooling, as well as access to a trained support staff, are important. The expected frequency of natural disasters (*i.e.*, earthquakes, floods, or hurricanes) and proximity to transportation are also key factors in site selection. In addition, the buildings and campus themselves must be built to ensure physical security.

Designing data center software to manage and monitor machines and the network, as well as providing software for common tasks, is just as critical as physical construction details and hardware procurement choices. In fact, how DoD obtains, develops, maintains, and evaluates software will have a big impact on cloud security, economy, and performance. Key software elements include:

- storage systems software, including access control
- network management software
- software to help detect and correct malfunctions or malicious activity
- resource allocation software to assign tasks to hardware elements
- system software to isolate tenants, be they clients or clouds, so that a malicious tenant cannot affect any other tenant
- plant software to manage power and cooling in the data center
- software for load balancing within and between data centers

A notional design of such a data center is depicted in Figure 8. This data center uses virtualization technology, which is common in data centers, but is not required. Key elements in Figure 8 are:

- **Network head node**: These components provide external data center network access.
- **Network forensics analytics**: These components monitor network behavior to detect attacks and failures.
- **Data center network**: This is a high performance network connecting all machines within a data center.
- **Portal**: This component registers new data center users, obtaining billing and authentication information. Tenants access the portal to transfer software and data to the cloud, negotiate resource assignments (*e.g.*, how many machines are needed, when, how much storage capacity, networking characteristics, and special requirements).
- **Storage**: A high speed, fault-tolerant storage system for the data center.
- **Infrastructure Controller**: This component allows data center operators to assign physical resources, monitor hardware and software health and operations, and detect

and remedy attacks and failures as they arise. All data center software is deployed and managed through the infrastructure controller.

- **Node instances**: These machines run the applications for tenants. Tens or hundreds of thousands of nodes are in a typical cloud data center. Each node has a hypervisor to manage machine resources and to isolate and protect user software from other software sharing the node. A management partition obtains, configures, and starts user software on the machine, and monitoring software monitors node heath and operations.

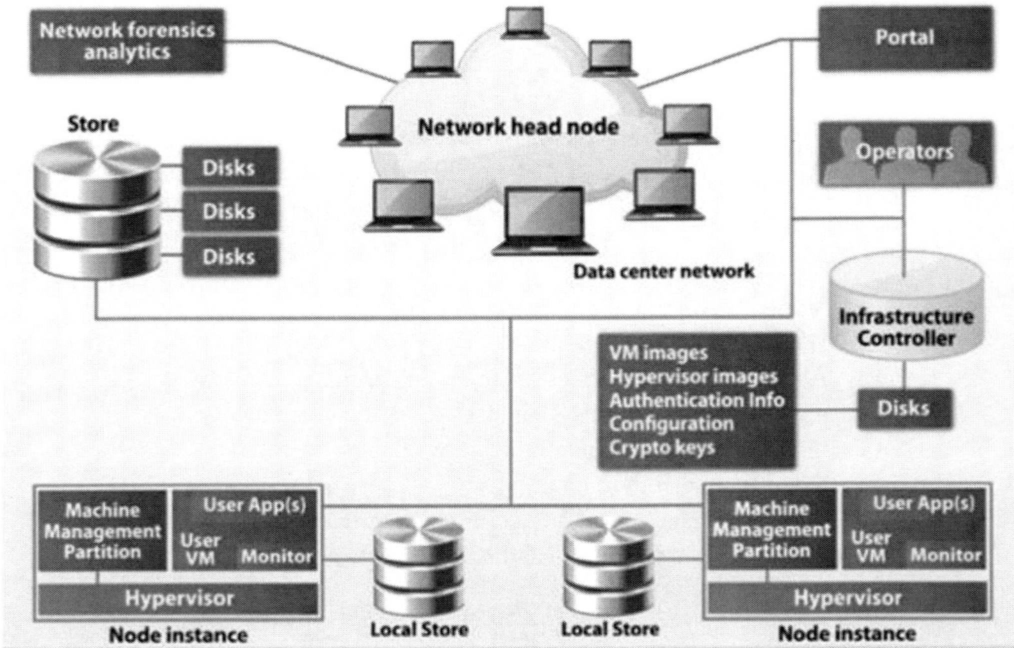

Figure 8. Example of a cloud computing data center architecture.

Each of these elements represents design choices that affect cost and performance. For example, the network might allow one cluster within a data center to become partitioned from another but will not allow a partition within a cluster. Management software, in conjunction with user-supplied information, would then be knowledgeable about this clustering and allocate to each application only those elements located within the same cluster. Similarly, a data center may provide some heterogeneous computing elements— powerful processors that can perform computations such as fast Fourier transforms— much more quickly than normal computing units. This heterogeneity will also be visible to the management software so that appropriate resource allocations will be made.

3.4.1. Modular Data Centers

One innovation in the design of data centers is to use pre-assembled modular units that together create a data center of varying size, depending upon the number of units used.

Early versions used standardized shipping containers and contained racks of computers and all the associated power distribution and cooling units required. These containers were simply hooked up to power, chilled water, and networking cables to make them ready to be used. A simple concept for such a modular data center is shown in Figure 9.

Today, new variants of modular data centers include those that use custom racks for greater densities, separate containers for the associated cooling, and custom containers that are easier to maintain. New designs may also assemble modular units of different configurations that, as an aggregate, provided all the required computing, power distribution and cooling required. As an example, a single modular data center might contain 44 racks with 7,000 servers and require 1.3 megawatts of power.

Although it would be less expensive to build a full-size data center rather than construct it entirely from modular units, in practice, modular data centers are much faster to install. They can also make it much easier to add incremental or refreshed computing capacity by building them a container at a time. Modular data centers can also be easily transported to where they are needed. For these reasons, modular data centers are often used in cloud computing.

Alternatives to modular data centers include data center designs in which entire rows of preconfigured racks can be quickly snapped into place by simply connecting the appropriate electrical cables and cooling hoses.

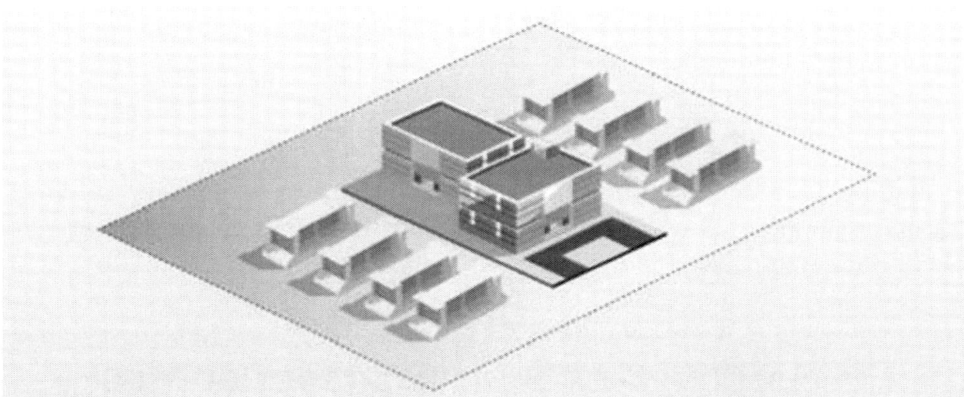

Figure 9. Concept for a modular DoD data center.

3.4.2. Critical Cloud Computing Design Choices

A well-designed cloud computing data center will reflect its projected uses. The degree of automation and flexibility in the management software of a cloud computing data center will depend on the applications that are run there.

For example, a single, large SaaS application (such as search) may be operated and used by a single organization, and as such will require only modest data security. The need for a hypervisor to provide isolation between tenants becomes less compelling, because only a single application is being run with no need to co-locate with different— and potentially adversarial—applications. By contrast, when an application involving highly sensitive data is deployed in a cloud computing data center running many other programs, the system design will include a hypervisor on each processor to assure isolation. If multiple tenants share a facility, it becomes important to manage resource usage quite strictly to assure responsiveness for all.

Social networking or search applications will interact almost exclusively with client machines through internet browsers. Data center and application design in this case would focus on protecting data leaks from one user to another, which may be achieved at the expense of availability.

In some special cases, a cloud data center may be used for software development. The design will need to allow access and control of running programs to facilitate debugging, with the understanding that speed may suffer. Other data centers may be designed to minimize latency, support high interactivity, or maximize physical security. These may benefit most from locating a small cloud computing data center near the user, either as the sole source of computing capabilities or as an intermediary.

Finding

Finding 1: Although cloud computing is an overloaded term, cloud computing providers are offering services that are fundamentally new and useful, typically encompassing the:

- ability for massive scale-up of storage and computing
- rapid, agile elasticity with the ability to increase and decrease storage and computing capacity on-demand, when the community of tenants don't all require that capacity at the same time
- metered services where the user pays only for what is used
- self-service start-up and control

Finding 2: Modular data centers offer an approach to quickly set up cloud computing capacity, add additional capability to existing cloud computing data centers, and easily refresh or update existing capability.

4. Cloud Computing Benefits to the DoD Mission

Cloud computing offers the DoD new ways to provide computational capabilities for missions. DoD missions most likely to benefit from cloud computing services will satisfy one or more of the following:

- **Scalable, on-demand computing.** The elasticity and resource-pooling provided by cloud computing is useful to applications that involve varying or unpredictable computing capacity. This model works well for applications that do not require highly correlated computing capacity, so it may not be useful for active missions or intensive exercises.
- **Integration of many, high-capacity data feeds**. The DoD collects high-capacity data from sensor networks and other sources, and data clouds have proven effective for the large-scale ingestion and integration of this kind of data. If cloud computing data centers are not used, custom-designed large-scale computers would be required to support these applications, and the construction of such machines is far more costly.

- **Analysis of very large datasets**. The DoD has the requirement to analyze large datasets. Over the past several years, a number of cloud computing applications have been developed, including Hadoop, Accumulo, Cassandra, and Hive, that scale to many thousands of processors and support easy-to-program parallel computing frameworks. These make big data analysis a practical enterprise.
- **Connections to common services.** Such applications as email, shared calendars, unclassified training, or document-preparation can benefit from SaaS, PaaS, or IaaS. Accessing these applications through cloud computing results in lower computation cost, lower software management costs, and enforced uniformity and interoperability. DoD has already begun to move some common services into private and public cloud computing architectures.

In this chapter, five examples of defense applications are discussed that have proven to be well-suited for cloud computing data centers.

4.1. Example: Communication and Networking

Email, calendars, and contact lists are applications found in many of today's commercial cloud-based computing services with millions of regular users. These applications rely on redundant storage to enable widespread availability, many identical processors for interactive performance, and a simple and uniform user interface across different internet browsers. The required bandwidth from client machines to the cloud computing data center is relative low, so the internet suffices. These services are also easily accessed from highly portable devices—cell phones and tablets—that are useful in many DoD scenarios.

Technologies for e-learning will also be increasingly important to the warfighter. As applications such as YouTube and Netflix have demonstrated, commercial cloud computing is a reliable, economical, and highly scalable way to provide video to users. The ability to access a YouTube-like system for virtual training sessions is an integral part of the Army Training Concept. New ways to deliver multi-media content will be needed in all locations that the DoD operates.

4.2. Example: Analysis of Large Datasets

A wide variety of cloud-based applications have been developed to support the analysis of extremely large datasets. Specialized clouds are being built to process, manage, and analyze signals, imagery, and other types of intelligence.

One example is Hadoop, which consists of a distributed file system and a simple to use parallel programming framework called MapReduce. Hadoop is widely used by the DoD and other U.S. government agencies, as well as in commercial applications. The Hadoop Distributed File System is designed to run on top of unreliable computer servers, and uses replication in order to safeguard the data it manages. One of the reasons for the popularity of Hadoop is that there is a rich ecosystem of applications based upon Hadoop, including Hive, a data warehouse infrastructure; HBase, a distributed database; and Pig, a high-level data flow language.

Accumulo, is a distributed database that is built over Hadoop, and includes cell-level security. Accumulo has proved effective for several DoD applications.

Another example of applications working with large datasets is sometimes called NoSQL databases. These applications relax some of the characteristics usually required for databases, such as transactions, in favor of scale. A widely used example of this type of application is Cassandra, which is a highly scalable key-value store.

Hadoop and NoSQL databases are currently used effectively to support intelligence analysis applications. These applications range from simple search to more sophisticated queries that look for patterns of interest in the data.

4.3. Example: Operational Support for the War Fighter

Cloud computing can offer great benefits to warfighters, especially when they have adequate connectivity back to a cloud computing data center. Useful services that can be provided by the cloud include translation, maps and navigation, searchable stored images, and specialized analyst applications. Smaller-scale, modular data centers can be used to support these types of applications in theater.

With the poor and uncertain communications that sometimes occur in the field, cloud architectures are needed that include thick clients and other components, such as local caches, that enable continued, though degraded, operations when network connectivity is not available.

4.4. Example: Situational Awareness for Cyber Security

The DoD continuously monitors the health of their computing systems to ensure that these information systems are capable of supporting DoD missions. A part of that monitoring process involves analysis of data reporting adversary activities against DoD networks, both on the boundaries and inside them. A notional architecture for supporting this situational awareness would array analytic, foundational, and enterprise services with associated sensor applications, as they are made available to users. Data flows into the system from multiple sensors, including client and server logs and network traffic capture. Various services analyze and process the data, providing risk and mission readiness assessments, malicious activity analyses, and anomaly detection.

Some of the challenges faced by engineers building such situational awareness systems include the high rate of data ingest from a multiplicity and variety of data sources. Data is produced by each host, server, network device, and process on the network being monitored. In addition, raw network traffic is also collected at many points within the network and at network boundaries.

Some types of data analytics are compute-intensive. Further, the computing capacity required will vary, depending on the data ingest rates, which themselves may vary depending on time of day, day of the week, time of year, world events, and so on. A good example of compute-intense algorithms are graph-based algorithms that look for anomalies in graphs built from the cyber data. In one study, an enterprise with 3,500 users and 9,500 hosts on its internal network accessed more than 200,000 web servers during the course of one month, producing 7.5 million unique connections and more than 500 million proxy log entries.[8]

4.5. Example: Wide-area Persistence Surveillance

Over the past ten years, DoD has built a large inventory of airborne battlefield sensors. Examples of the kinds of data being collected include signals intelligence and full-motion video of moving targets. These sensors are capable of collecting large amounts of data, which require subsequent processing before they can be exploited and disseminated. Figure 10 shows that data rates for a variety of advanced sensors are growing exponentially as a function of time. At times, the amount of data collected can exceed the DoD's ability to perform processing, exploitation, and dissemination.

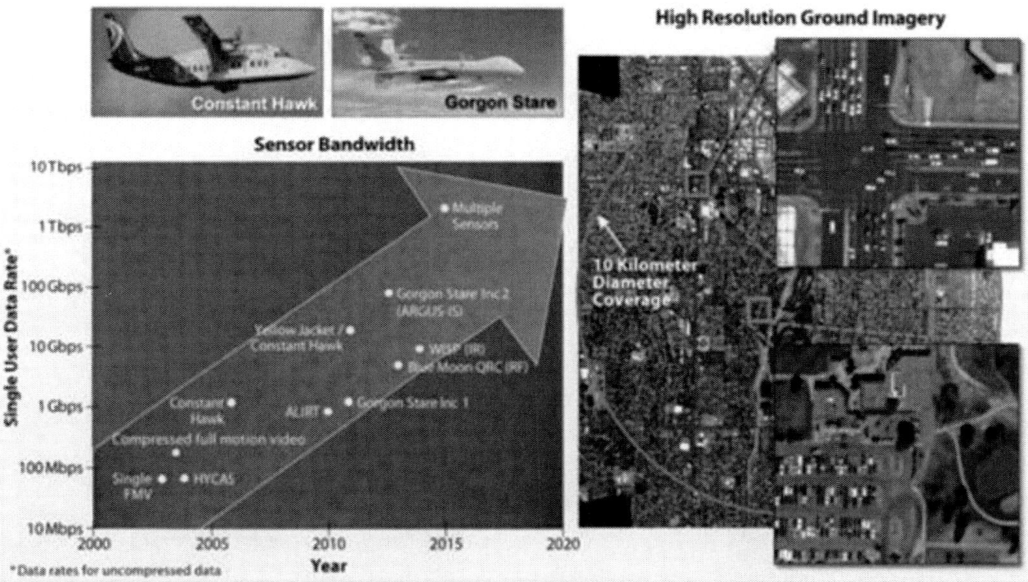

Figure 10. Exponential growth of data readouts from advanced DoD sensors.

One example of the new generation of airborne sensors is the Autonomous Real-Time Ground Ubiquitous Surveillance Imaging System (ARGUS-IS).[9] The ARGUS-IS video sensor produces 1.8 billion pixels per frame at 12 frames per second, providing continuous coverage of a large field of regard—up to a 100-square kilometer area. A single ARGUS-IS class sensor can produce more than a petabyte of data per day. Processing video data from sensors such as ARGUS-IS requires stitching the images from the individual cameras, rectifying the data according to known geographic references, removing the effects of motion by the airborne platform, modeling the unchanging background, detecting and tracking vehicle motion, selectively compressing the raw data, and archiving the results. This processing chain might require 100 operations per pixel.

Finding

Finding 3: Cloud computing services can scale to data centers or “warehouse-scale" computing. Elastic, warehouse-scale cloud computing is fundamentally new and can provide DoD with important new capabilities.

5. Cloud Computing Security

Enhancing today’s cloud computing security is emerging as an important priority for the DoD.[10] This chapter discusses needed enhancements and discusses assumptions about hardware, software, people, and physical plant that are part of the security operating picture for a cloud computing system.

Security experts evaluate real systems through careful analysis, accurate auditing, and vigorous red teaming. Most current software is poorly suited for forensics and auditing, even though these capabilities are extensively used in security analysis. As a result, most DoD software today is not amenable to accurate operational risk assessments. With current software, the defensive and offensive roles in systems are highly asymmetric, favoring the attacker who succeeds by finding a single vulnerability over the defender who must eliminate all vulnerabilities in a large system.

Despite uncertainties about security, new capabilities enabled by cloud computing could provide significant benefits to the DoD. In many cases, the DoD could achieve some cost savings when using cloud computing, even though secure cloud operations may involve additional work and expense.

With the requirements and risks in mind, three questions emerge:

- How should DoD build secure cloud environments?
- How can DoD take advantage of cloud benefits in the near future by careful risk management involving existing technology?
- What should DoD do to ensure access in the future to secure, efficient, and effective cloud technology?

5.1. Security Assessment

Security assessment provides the decision-maker with a basis for selecting a cost-effective computing system that provides sufficient assurance for completing assigned missions, despite the plausible actions of the anticipated adversaries. The assessment must be based on both the material and activity that must be protected, and the resources and access of the adversaries. A worthy long-term goal is to make all security-critical functions remotely verifiable by the user through simple technological means.

A security maxim is that the worst enemy of good security is the delay and expense caused by an insistence on perfect security. No activity is unconditionally secure against an adversary with unlimited resources. In this light, risks and tradeoffs must be carefully examined and security decisions must be realistic.

To be effective, security must be described in terms of specific, concrete goals. None of the goals listed here can, unfortunately, be purchased off-the-shelf or simply marked off on a checklist:

- **Preserving confidentiality and integrity of data.** Confidentiality means the data should not be disclosed to unauthorized parties. The integrity requirement is concerned with ensuring that unauthorized parties cannot corrupt data.
- **Protecting the computational confidentiality and integrity of the software.** This requirement means that program execution must not be visible to adversaries. The integrity requirement means the software should operate in accordance with what its designers intended. Adversaries should not be able to tamper with a program and cause subsequent execution to produce incorrect output or undesired side effects. In some cases, it may be important to keep code confidential, because it discloses techniques and methods.
- **Ensuring resiliency, availability, reliability, and predictability of operation.** Under actual operating conditions, the target computer services must recover quickly from potential failures, operate reliably, be available when needed, execute in a predictable way, and deliver results in a predictable time frame.
- **Avoiding single points of failure in applications.** Code for many of today's applications is vulnerable to intentional or accidental modification by insiders. In one case, an unintentional incident crashed major data centers for hours because an error condition accidentally triggered a flaw in a single protocol that many data centers were running. Application diversity and formal fault analysis are promising approaches for mitigating these types of risks.
- **Retaining agility.** Security measures should not limit the rapid development of new programs or create unreasonable delay in the deployment of existing programs in other suitable environments.
- **Detecting system failures and enabling ongoing evaluation of system performance and safety.** This is sometimes called situational awareness, and it requires audit and forensics. It means detecting failures and, when they do occur, collecting information that helps assess ongoing operational security posture. Systems, processes, and skilled staff must be in place so that an intrusion will be detected quickly and its effects rapidly and thoroughly remediated.

5.1.1. Comparing Cloud and Conventional Computing Approaches

Cloud computing is not intrinsically more secure than other distributed computing approaches, but its scale and uniformity facilitate and enable the wholesale and consistent application of security practices. Secure aspects include large scale monitoring and analysis of data to detect attacks, and automated and persistent provisioning and re-provisioning to foil intrusions. For these reasons, well-operated cloud computing facilities can exhibit better security hygiene than conventional data centers.

Cloud computing deployment can offer potential for improvements over the security found in some existing DoD systems. For many current DoD applications, moving to a well-implemented cloud computing data center would improve both the overall security and security of individual applications. On the other hand, for applications that were built with attention to security, a cloud deployment environment, in which security is not a priority, would likely decrease the security of the application.

Some threats are exacerbated by cloud computing deployments, absent further security provisioning. For example, cloud computing data centers are generally large in scale and, therefore, they present attractive targets. Insiders often have access to immense resources, and determined, well-funded adversaries could exploit even generally trustworthy insiders to compromise a cloud system. Cloud services often rely on connectivity; for many applications, a network outage—perhaps due to an attack—would render that application completely unusable. Poor development practices are also more damaging in a cloud environment, because tenants share resources, which means tenants execute in close proximity to other's programs and data. Note that these threats are not unique to cloud computing. They would be present in any large-scale DoD computing system that relies on network connectivity.

For a system to be built with today's technology—which is notoriously insecure whether in a cloud or conventional deployment—it may be more productive to compare the relative security of existing conventional and proposed cloud computing systems rather than the absolute security of either one.

5.1.2. Classifying Threats

Threats refer to specific opportunities by identified adversaries to defeat security goals. It is useful when thinking of threats to separate them into the categories shown in Table 1.

5.1.3. Classifying Adversaries

Adversaries are entities that may or may not be intentionally malicious, but either way an adversary is a person or group that undertakes actions that will cause one or more of the security goals to be violated. Under this definition, adversaries include well-intentioned operators who improperly configure systems, as well as outsiders who can access computer systems, and insiders who are entitled to access computer systems but in an unauthorized manner. Perhaps the most powerful adversaries are skilled and well-financed nation states that can exercise attacks ranging from exploiting software vulnerabilities to corrupting operational elements of a system either before or after deployment.

Table 1. Example Threat Classifications

Threats that apply to computing systems in general:

- Malicious insiders who take sensitive data or knowingly interfere with the proper operation of the system adversely.
- Benign insiders who accidentally leak sensitive data, improperly configure components, fail to carry out responsibilities, or commit unintentional errors in the handling or analysis of system infrastructure or information.
- Provisioned elements of the system, such as computers, storage disks, or software, that are modified to provide back-door access to an adversary.
- Provisioned components, either hardware or software, having vulnerabilities that may be exploited.
- Data that is stored unencrypted on disks and, therefore, available to anyone with physical access to the disk.

- Data may be encrypted, but underlying cryptographic keys may be managed in a way that allows them to be observed by insiders with varying degrees of difficulty.

Threats that apply to remote data centers:

- Networks may fail or experience unpredictable delays.
- Tenants must rely on the trustworthiness and competence of personnel to safeguard data—sometimes in unencrypted form—that is being stored or physically transported.

Threats that apply to computer systems with multiple tenants:

- Co-tenants and service users who pierce isolation boundaries to compromise confidentiality or integrity of the data, code, or communications of another tenant.
- Authorized service users who access the services from insecure clients.
- Co-tenants and service users who compromise availability in a cloud infrastructure, for example, by consuming too many resources.
- Access to shared infrastructure is denied.
- The failure of access control mechanisms to grant authorized access to shared resources.
- A service provider who underestimates the aggregate resource demands of all tenants and, as a consequence, under provisions resources.
- Malicious tenants and service users who damage the reputation of infrastructure components or other tenants, thus raising concerns about the integrity or reliability of data or operations.

Threats that apply to public clouds:

- Public clouds have many, many tenants, thereby increasing the threats experienced by systems with multiple tenants.
- Tenants in public clouds cannot generally control who their co-tenants are, even when cotenancy requirements are specified.
- Tenants in a public cloud computing data center generally have little visibility into operations that might create potential or actual vulnerabilities.
- Tenants in today's public cloud computing data centers have little or no ability to review and assess the hardware and software that must be trusted for their applications to execute safely.
- Tenants have only minimal situational awareness and limited awareness of data leakage.

Each computing application will have different security requirements and must be defended against different classes of adversaries. Differences among adversaries stem from the resources, access, and knowledge they can employ in an attack, as well as the expected value from a successful attack. The decision to deploy a specific system in a cloud computing environment becomes a question of balancing risk against opportunity and cost for that specific system and anticipated adversary attacks.

Figure 11 presents a notional taxonomy of cyber adversaries. The pyramid shape is meant to convey the number of adversaries for each class in the taxonomy, showing that adversaries today mostly operate at Tiers I and II—so-called "script kiddies"—using malicious code developed by others. The primary defense against these types of attacks is improved computer hygiene, meaning user best practices for passwords, firewalls, and links. Tier II actors have some ability to develop their own malicious code. Their actions may be directed at achieving specific business or political objectives, such as the theft of information or alteration of financial data. These lower-tier actors can be effective because sophisticated tools and techniques developed and exposed by others are widely available.

Tier III and IV actors are characterized by their abilities to employ a broad range of technical capabilities to penetrate cyber systems. The distinction between Tiers III and IV is scale—Tier IV is characterized by larger, well-organized teams, either state or criminal.

Tiers V and VI comprise actors who are able to go beyond introducing malicious software via internet access. They are able to create new vulnerabilities in otherwise well-protected systems. Tier V actors can insert corrupt software or hardware at various points during a system's lifecycle for later exploit, including supply chain attacks. Tier VI organizations can employ full spectrum techniques, such as persons engaged in bribery and blackmail, as well as proximate physical or electronic means to gain system penetration. Tier VI adversaries may conduct many operations concurrently and benefit from coordinated attacks.

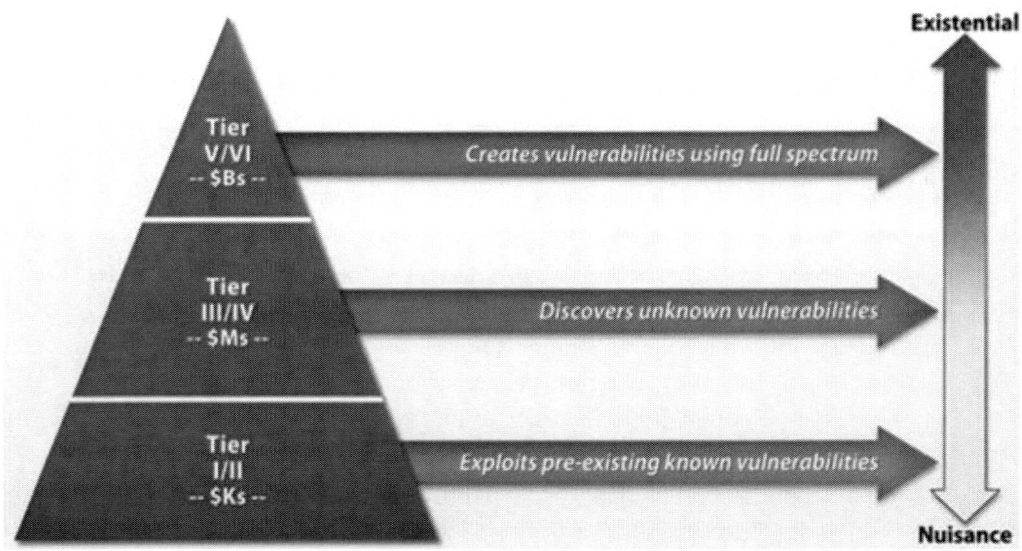

Figure 11. A notional cyber threat taxonomy.

5.1.4. Security Decision Parameters

The operational environment of a data center, including a cloud data center, can be described by the following considerations:

- **Physical siting.** Where is the cloud data center located, and what are its physical security characteristics? What provisions have been made for availability of reliable power; local supply and support; proximity to high capacity, reliable network fibers; and protective measures for the equipment and surrounding area against kinetic attacks and electromagnetic eavesdropping?
- **Operator affiliation.** Who runs the data center? DoD personnel? Coalition partners? Conventional DoD contractors? Commercial providers?
- **Tenant population.** Does the data center only serve activities associated with a single mission? Diverse missions within DoD and intelligence community? Only U.S. Government applications? Commercial applications (which might or might not involve affiliations with foreign powers)?
- **Hardware.** What is the physical plant and hardware architecture? Who manufactures hardware components? Who assembles and integrates hardware components? How are hardware components tested, qualified, and monitored for secure operation?
- **Software.** Who develops and tests data center infrastructure software (resource allocation, provisioning, hypervisor, operating system)? Who supplies application components? Who provides software components? How are software components tested, qualified, and monitored for secure operation?
- **Data.** What is the value of the data? What are the consequences if there is a loss of data integrity?
- **Architecture.** Is forensic information that that can provide insight into safety and performance of the systems collected regularly? Can redundant data centers provide resiliency and consistent performance? Can operational data that is critical to carry out mission critical activities be staged or cached for access under network-disadvantaged circumstances? Is there enough information to make a well-informed forward risk assessment?
- **Clients.** Who can access cloud resources? What are the client machine security requirements?

Making computing deployment decisions requires careful consideration of these factors. In each case, these decision parameters must not only be verified at design and installation, but must be meaningfully and effectively verified during ongoing operation.

5.2. Data Center Security

Security goals, as noted above, will depend on the application, and the means of enforcement will depend on the threat, so there can be no single answer for the characteristics of a data center used by DoD. The following lists some considerations for DoD cloud computing data center security.

5.2.1. Physical Security

Large commercial cloud computing data centers observe excellent physical security measures, and the amortized cost of good physical security in a large cloud computing data center is relatively modest. Data centers live and breathe on connectivity, so a cloud data center's management of network activity is usually quite good. They are often located far away from populated areas, and few, well-authenticated people are granted admittance. Good perimeter security is in place, including intrusion detection, electronic physical access control, and video surveillance.

To host very high security applications at a cloud computing data center, the DoD would undoubtedly take direct military control of a physical plant and add physical security measures. Fortunately, protection and risk assessment of kinetic attacks as well as physical security is comfortably within DoD competencies. Most commercial data center facilities do not protect as rigorously against snooping via electronic emanations as is customary in high-value DoD location, nor do they protect against sophisticated kinetic attacks.

The DoD could also employ multiple data centers to provide resilience against attacks. Balancing the economics of much stronger physical protection for a small number of sites versus the protection derived from having many data center sites requires careful, mission-specific analysis.

5.2.2. Personnel Security

The most important element in ensuring information security is having a highly skilled, adequately resourced team, backed by management that takes security seriously. Personnel security practice is usually good at commercial data centers, and they are staffed by well-trained professionals. The DoD will almost certainly employ even more stringent personnel security practices in their data centers. The DoD would likely also develop and deploy additional technology to reduce access to confidential data by data center personnel, as well as to remotely verify operations. As with physical security, requirements for personnel security will vary based on classification of what is being protected.

In addition to a core security team, red teams are needed, made up of experts who try to attack systems in an effort to determine risks. Modern computing systems are too complex for direct analysis alone to determine all real-world risks. Finally, incident teams are needed that are skilled in mitigating ongoing attacks quickly and identifying root causes.

For application software, DoD must employ individuals skilled in developing scaled and secure cloud software so that applications will be written to the same rigorous security standards as systems software. Many cloud applications will be developed using a small number of common frameworks and libraries, so investments in secure coding of these building blocks can be leveraged.

5.3. Secure Cloud Computing Software

Software is possibly the most critical security element for cloud computing deployments. The critical components include image management and resource allocation software, hypervisor and management partition software at node instances, and audit and forensic software.

Conventional DoD software, acquired over many years and written without specific concern for resisting cyberattacks, is often vulnerable to attack by relatively unsophisticated adversaries. Even if properly updated, such software is likely to have easily exploited vulnerabilities. Further, its complexity makes proper configuration of most software difficult and time consuming—even for experts—providing yet another avenue of attack for an adversary. Software that is employed in a DoD cloud computing data center is likely to come from the same sources as software used by commercial data centers, and the high costs of software development suggest this is unlikely to change.

Today, these may be a combination of commercial-off-the-shelf (COTS), open source, and custom software.

- **Commercial software** such as VMware and Windows are commonly used in cloud computing data centers. It is important to realize that all such commercial programs have proprietary source code and are opaque to security specialists, both in terms of source code and in their manufacturing provenance.
- **Open source software** is also likely to be used. These programs are maintained by an international community and under the condition that all source code is published. Open source software offers the advantage of transparency to facilitate security assessments, but currently available offerings might not have all of the features required by DoD.
- **Custom operating software** may also be developed specifically for DoD cloud computing data centers. However, custom software has proven to be more expensive than either commercial or open-source and can lead to very long deployment delays.

Whether commercial software or open source software is being run, DoD must carefully examine these software components to ensure that they can provide sufficient operational security assurance. It is critical that DoD develop a well-conceived process for analyzing and gaining assurance when using open source and commercial proprietary software. The DoD must have some basis to believe that a chosen operating system is trustworthy.

The task force found that it is unlikely to be economically feasible or even advisable for the DoD to write or buy all of the software it runs in cloud computing data centers. The task force found that the best strategy will likely leverage existing commercial and open source development. If such a hybrid case were pursued, DoD would only need to develop software when commercial and open source communities are unlikely to offer the needed functionality in a timely manner.

If DoD-authored improvements are contributed to the open source community, the normal community processes will mean that the improvements remain usable as the software evolves, and the DoD-authored improvements could be adopted by commercial cloud providers, improving their security. The DoD, in fact, already has taken important steps by making contributions, albeit somewhat inconsistent and uncoordinated, to review and assess the security of open source systems. Of course, certain sensitive DoD software might have to be developed by the DoD itself, without disclosure. This route should not be taken casually, because the DoD then incurs all subsequent costs of maintaining this software.

Reasons that the DoD might consider partnering with public cloud service partners to develop cloud computing software include:

- The DoD can leverage software capability and security capabilities developed by the open source community, including existing schemes for isolation of tenants, key management, and strong authentication and authorization.
- Even in a DoD cloud computing data center, the best commercial security practices developed by large scale commercial cloud service providers with deep experience will contribute to running a more secure system. That is, as compared to less

experienced contractors with experience limited to building small-scale, private clouds. In fact, large commercial cloud providers face a threat profile that has many of the same elements as the threat the DoD faces. For example, insider threats are critical in public cloud data center operations just as they are for the DoD.

5.4. Secure Cloud Computing Hardware

5.4.1. Hardware Supply Chain Security

Commercial cloud providers and the DoD generally buy COTS hardware from commercial vendors, although some large commercial cloud providers increasingly build custom hardware made from COTS components. Thus, commercial providers and the DoD are today at risk to supply chain attacks by well-funded organizations (*i.e.*, tier V and VI adversaries). A supply chain attack can be perpetrated at any point in a production—design, manufacturing, testing, distribution, or installation—and this life-cycle exists concurrently for components, boards, subsystems, and entire systems.

Some hardware components, like central processing units, can be economically designed and manufactured by only a very few vendors, who must manufacture at scale to recover development costs. While DoD has relied on trusted foundries for the production of certain sensitive parts with minimal exposure to supply chain risks, this strategy is not feasible for all of the parts that comprise a cloud data center.[11] Today, many critical components in computers are manufactured only outside the United States and some are especially vulnerable to supply chain attacks.

Testing and procurement strategies will be needed to mitigate supply-chain risks.[12,13] Among other strategies, a DoD cloud data center design could limit the number of components in each design required for secure operation, could vary the sources of components it procures, or could attempt to be secretive about procurement sources. By far, the best solutions—in analogy with software—are designs that focus on reducing the trusted computing base for hardware.

5.4.2. Client Hardware Security

Client hardware security is just as essential for cloud computing as is the security of cloud servers. In fact, many famous cloud computing security failures were caused by compromised client machines. Client machines operated by authorized persons can initiate critical operations in cloud computing data centers and transmit sensitive data to other clients. For these reasons, client hardware and client software must incorporate the same level of protection as other cloud components.

For example, a client must be able to quickly verify the identity and security posture of a server running in a cloud computing data center, just as that server must be able to authenticate the client system. Even thin client components must still be capable of authenticating to the cloud and being authenticated by the cloud.

5.4.3. Building Secure Cloud Computing Environments

In addition to physical security, a secure cloud computing data center must run reliable components to ensure isolation and facilitate remote authentication of software components. It must also support authentication of clients and servers, authorization for access to software and data, verified audit of data access and resource usage, secure and flexible key management, safe and effective resource management, and provisioning—of images, network configuration and partitioning and storage management—that can be verified under circumstances that support economical and agile data center operations.

Two interconnected capabilities can be deployed to provide confidentiality and integrity of both data and software. The first is an ability to authenticate that a critical software component is one that appears on a list of well-understood, trusted implementations that have been isolated from other software. The second is a basis to have assurance that an application was loaded and executed without tampering. Because cloud computing resources will be used freely by developers, all software executed by the cloud cannot be expected to come from a short "white list" denoting approved components. Rather, system software must automatically ensure that the developer's code, even though it might exhibit bugs, does not have the power to access or corrupt production software or data in the system.

Assurance that an application was loaded and executed without tampering can be achieved if the system can store cryptographic keys in such a way that these keys can be used only by some pre-specified uncorrupted software element executing in an environment that ensures it is isolated from other tenants. The isolation environment and key management scheme must be resilient to insider attack and must be remotely verifiable.

Modern processors often have hardware that can be used to enable these two interconnected capabilities. These processors are typically not deployed in cloud data centers despite the low incremental hardware cost of technologies. These hardware attestation technologies are known as hardware security modules, or Trusted Platform Modules. The DoD has mandated the use of this technology in most client computers.

Where hardware attestation is available on cloud computing processors, the basic approach for secure isolation and key management is to employ encryption and cryptographic integrity verification for all data in transmission and storage, coupled with secure access control that enables decryption only within those isolated software components that are run by authorized users under policy control enforced by cryptographically protected credentials issued by data owners. These same isolation and key management facilities then also provide an environment for implementing secure forensics and audit.

5.5. Secure Data Center Operations

Many security considerations apply whether the DoD is using dedicated data centers for specific mission, shared defense clouds, vendor or coalition operated clouds or, indeed, public clouds. Commercial cloud data centers must have efficient means for deploying applications, which lead to timely installation of updates—something that is particularly valuable for patches that mitigate against newly discovered vulnerabilities. Centralization in cloud data centers enables better and more comprehensive forensics, especially for detecting subtle attacks that are less visible in a small environment. Moreover, the naturally dynamic nature of resource assignment in a cloud data center makes persistent attacks on critical functions much more expensive.

Security requirements and gaps in current technology, however, will likely force the DoD in some cases to operate their own private clouds under operational conditions similar to those of existing, non-cloud systems. Regardless, the following operating guidance is offered to any cloud computing data center implementation.

5.5.1. Data Sharing, Confidentiality, and Integrity

Data centers employ cryptographic mechanisms and operational procedures to ensure confidentiality and integrity of data and program code. DoD, in conjunction with NIST, has done an admirable job in contributing to interoperable algorithms, protocols, and format standards to support cryptography. Yet data is still often stored in unencrypted form on data center disks, or it is transmitted within or between data centers with no encryption.

Current data centers also often employ poor key management. For example, cryptographic keys that form the basis for protection may be stored in a way that makes them visible to insiders. Even when it has been encrypted, data at rest and data in transit can remains vulnerable to attacks by operators, technicians, and even other tenants. Inadequate key management is not unique to cloud computing, and these vulnerabilities are not always easy to remedy without impacting performance. Ultimately, the use of encryption creates trade-offs between confidentiality and legitimate monitoring for abuse or other kinds of situational awareness.

Robust, flexible, and verifiable authentication and authorization frameworks to enable secure data sharing among authorized applications have been developed, but are not widely employed in today's cloud computing systems. A good example is provided by the Accumulo system and the associated authentication, authorization, and access control framework. Strong authentication of software components in a data center and end-clients is crucial for ensuring that the principals requesting access to data are legitimate.

To improve verifiability and gain protection from insider attacks, operators should require appropriate processes for making hardware changes and to deploy system initialization routines that do not depend on the competency or altruism of insiders. The goal is to allow safe key management and remote verification of operation. Keys used by programs should be available only to user programs that have been authenticated and whose execution is isolated from potentially malicious programs. In most traditional and cloud computing systems, this isolation is implemented by the operating system software and database-level file and process access lists, which are difficult or impossible to protect from insider tampering. However, such complete trust in software is not necessary—hardware such as TPMs exists to strengthen access controls. Without it, confidentiality and integrity of programs and data is difficult to assure. The DoD could lead the way in fostering the widespread availability of cloud data centers that incorporate these features.

5.5.2. Forensics, Monitoring, and Intrusion Detection

Many cloud architectures provide data collection and analysis functionality to support detection, analysis, and rapid remediation of attacks, although such capabilities vary widely among providers. Indeed, one possible security benefit of cloud architecture is the ability to gather such comprehensive situational data.

Cloud computing data center providers generally are not, however, economically motivated to provide the data to their tenants, nor to release the information, because it could adversely affect their reputation or reveal information to attackers attempting to avoid detection. Discretion is sometimes required during assessment and investigation to avoid alerting adversaries; other times, complex equities must be balanced. Some providers and vendors have very good incident response teams; others share information under *ad hoc*, personal arrangements and publish vulnerabilities only after they are fixed. Sharing this information more rapidly allows others to learn about threat signatures and potential vulnerabilities and make repairs. Silence about attacks can mean that risk is poorly understood by those responsible for overall mission results.

5.5.3. Red Teaming and Incident Response

Vulnerabilities often are the result of subtle design and implementation problems, and historically the most effective mechanism to assess the security of a system is red teaming. Unless a system is regularly subjected to red teaming, there is no way to understand the security risks. Because systems tend to evolve over time (as software components are updated, for example), a system's vulnerabilities will also change over time. A list of problems identified in prior red team attacks might say little about a current system. The need for recurring security assessment is a major issue in cloud data centers where operations are opaque and vulnerabilities and successful intrusions are sometimes either undetected or unreported.

Figure 12 depicts a block diagram for one red and blue teaming model. Effective red teaming includes reviewing the current threats, assessing the current system performance, and extrapolating to estimate future threats and system vulnerabilities. Blue teaming investigates techniques for reducing the impact of current and future threats and vulnerabilities. The results of blue teaming can then set the direction for future cyber system developments, new tactics, techniques and procedures, and improved technology investments. The benefits of red and blue teaming are improved significantly when soldiers, sailors, airmen, and marines with recent operational experience participate.

Commercial, government, and DoD cloud providers currently have widely varying expertise in red teaming, incident response, and analysis. There are pockets of deep knowledge in industry, the intelligence community, and in the DoD. Improved and coordinated efforts to systematically build a basic understanding, principles, tools, and procedures for evaluating security of cloud systems would benefit both DoD and commercial providers.

5.5.4. Operating under Degraded Conditions

Cyber attacks, system failures, and human error all can cause operational cyber systems to exhibit degraded performance. Cloud computing systems are not immune to most of these disruptions and, in fact, in some cases may be more affected. While commercial cloud computing providers have developed effective detection and mitigation techniques for degradations in communications, network outages can still result in complete service disruption for many commercial cloud computing services. Such disruption could be catastrophic for some DoD applications.

Before any cyber system becomes central to DoD military operations, it is essential that the operational community understand the implications of degradation of that system. The goal is to use realistic training and exercising to develop tactics, techniques, and procedures (TTPs) to ensure adequate mission assurance under the degraded conditions. These TTPs may include such changes as more distributed cloud computing resources or more redundant cyber and communication systems.

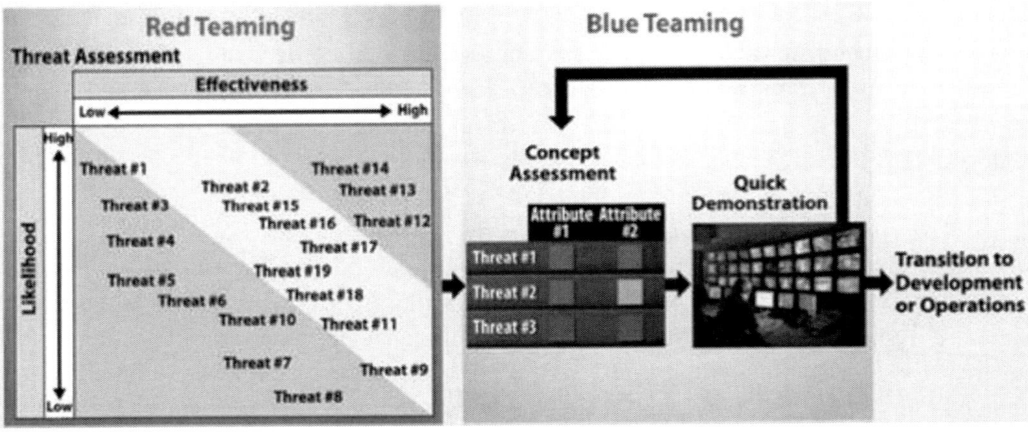

Figure 12. A red-blue teaming model for enhanced assessment of advanced threats and possible mitigations.

The 2010 Defense Science Board Summer Study on Enhancing Adaptability of our Military Forces investigated the prevalence of military training and operational exercises with degraded cyber and communication system conditions.[14] The study found that most military operational exercises did not include scenarios with realistic examples of degraded cyber system conditions. At the time of the study, the U.S. Pacific Command's *Terminal Fury* series of exercises was a notable exception because of its incorporation of an increasingly complex set of cyber threats.

The DoD conducted a number of support exercises during fiscal year 2012 that included degraded operations. Several commands participated, including the U.S. Strategic Command in *Global Thunder and Global Lightning*, the U.S. Cyber Command in *Cyber Flag*, the U.S. Pacific Command in a follow-on to *Terminal Fury*, the U.S. European Command in *Austere Challenge*, and the U.S. Transportation Command in *Turbo Challenge*. Although incorporating degraded cyber operational conditions improved these exercises, stronger red and blue teaming will be needed to improve the realism of degraded cyber systems in training and operational exercises.

To effectively design and deploy cloud computing services, DoD will need to train and exercise under degraded conditions and to incorporate mitigating actions in those activities. Effective mitigations for communications outages might include the use of local data centers that have cached mission-critical information, the use of alternative network provisioning, and the fielding of thick clients that can provide local, albeit degraded, support for mission critical capabilities, or restricting some applications from deployment on cloud computing systems.

5.5.5. Operating in Partnership with Public Cloud Computing Providers

Many of the risks discussed in this chapter can be reduced or eliminated by using in-sourced or out-sourced private cloud computing facilities, or non-cloud local computing resources.

The vast information resources available in public clouds, however, is also important to the DoD. In addition, some DoD missions will appropriately operate in the public cloud. Working in partnership with public cloud computing providers also offers some operational advantages. As the U.S. government encourages more secure public cloud computing infrastructures, these facilities may become an important option for the DoD in emergencies. As well, large public clouds may have more secure software stacks, and larger and better-trained security teams than newly constructed private clouds. Further, careful development of critical software that takes economic advantage of shared benefit in development may make critical cloud components more naturally resilient to hardware and software vulnerabilities.

If a public cloud data center implemented the best practices recommended here for DoD private facilities, then public cloud computing would not generally be any less safe than in-house operations. These practices may include externally verifiable key management, verifiable reliable access control over tenant-owned-but-shared resources, adequate isolation of execution, verification of critical data center operations, and reliable authentication of client systems to ensure their safety and identity. In addition, the naturally dynamic nature of resource assignment in a large public cloud computing data center might make persistent attacks on critical functions much more expensive.

Today, commercial data centers do not generally disclose hardware infrastructure in sufficient detail for a potential tenant to reasonably assess risk. To work in partnership, therefore, the DoD must be prepared to negotiate contractual provisions with commercial data centers to ensure the integrity of the hardware infrastructure.

Findings

Finding 4: Cloud computing is not intrinsically more secure than other distributed computing approaches, but its scale and uniformity facilitate and enable the wholesale and consistent application of security practices. Secure aspects include large scale monitoring and analysis of data to detect attacks, and automated and persistent provisioning and re-provisioning to foil intrusions. For these reasons, well-operated cloud computing facilities can exhibit better security hygiene than conventional data centers. However, the centralization of resources in a huge data center also encourages more determined attacks, especially on critical components broadly affecting security, just as in conventional systems, attacks are observed to focus on central directories.

Finding 5: The scale of cloud computing enables the analysis of packet and log data that provides new capabilities for event forensics and real-time detection of malicious behavior. The ability to manage very large, diverse datasets facilitates a data-centric security model, in which users are authorized to work with data based upon their security credentials and the security markings on the data, rather than the conventional enclave-centric security model in which users are provided access to an enclave and can access all the data in the enclave.

Finding 6: No cloud computing deployment model is uniformly suitable for hosting all DoD applications. In general, sensitive, classified, and time-critical DoD applications should be deployed only in private clouds or conventional non-cloud approaches.

Finding 7: The case for transitioning a DoD application to a cloud computing data center must include a security assessment detailing the impact of the transition.

Whether security will be improved by transitioning an application to a cloud computing data center will depend on factors specific to the application, to the cloud computing data center, and to the transition process.

Finding 8: The DoD has not established effective plans for cloud computing facility backup, or for dealing with any anticipated degradation of communications between the cloud computing facilities and the end user.

6. The Economics of Cloud Computing

The movement to cloud computing is an oft-cited contemporary strategy for achieving efficiencies within information system enterprises. In the past three years, dramatic price reductions have been offered by commercial cloud computing service providers. As depicted in Figure 13, Amazon Web Services (AWS) lowered prices consistently over three years. Moreover, the commoditization of infrastructure resources by commercial cloud service providers has created a new marketplace with ever decreasing price floors and a trend for increasing service fungibility.[15,16]

Significant differences in management models (*i.e.*, private, in-sourced private, out-sourced private, and public); service models (*i.e.*, software as a service (SaaS), platform as a service (PaaS), and infrastructure as a service (IaaS)); and support for security and compliance introduce architecture and implementation differences that impact investment and operating costs of cloud data centers. Hence, when examining the economics of cloud computing, decision-makers must be wary of unsubstantiated estimates for return on investment. Consequently, a careful analysis that incorporates expected cost and expected security is essential in order to ensure savings and function for DoD mission.

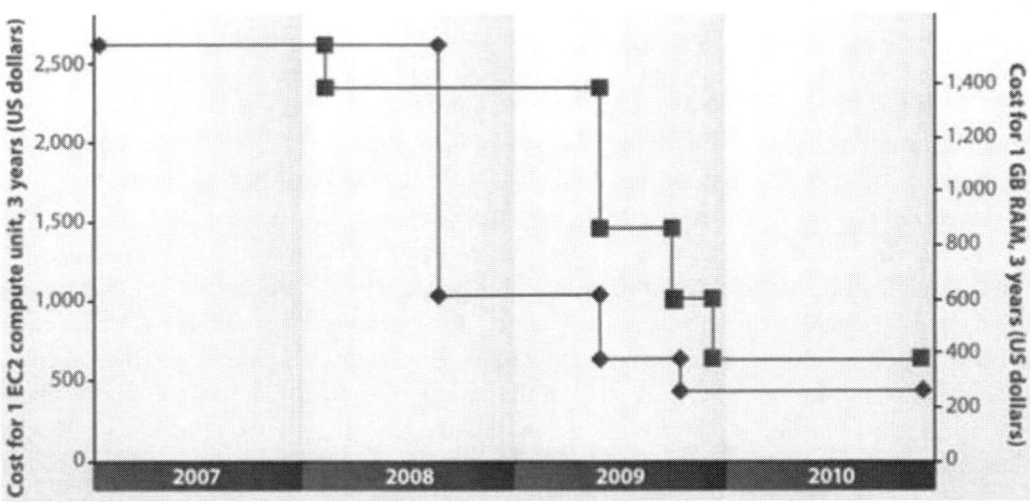

Figure 13. Price in U.S. dollars for a 3-year rental of Amazon Web Services resources, 2007–2010.

6.1. Cloud Service Economic Drivers

Online pricing of commodity cloud providers suggests lower prices for consumers. How service providers are achieving these cost reductions is discussed here, as well as the changes to traditional data center practices, technology, and information technology culture that have resulted in these savings.

6.1.1. Improving the Administrator to Server Ratio

Changing the number of servers that a system-administrator can effectively support has significantly affected costs. In traditional data centers, this ratio has averaged around 20 to 30 machines per administrator, depending on the types and complexity of machines, the commonality of underlying system software, and the similarity of machine configurations.

This machine-to-operator ratio improves for cloud computing architectures. The use of a small number of approved baseline machine images simplifies configuration management and the operation of the machines.

The ratio in the average enterprise of administrators to VM is about one to 77.[17] For most organizations this effectively halves the number of operations staff required. Trade press reports routinely suggest even higher numbers for public commodity cloud computing providers.

6.1.2. Increased Automation

Many commodity cloud service providers are taking advantage of substantially increased automation to lower labor costs for operations staff. Automation in a cloud data center can supplant many labor-based data center processes. For example, provisioning activities for cloud computing resources is typically fully automated and made directly available to the consumer. This saves on center operations staff time.

Some cloud data centers include automatic support for scaling the numbers of processors in response to system demand, recovery of failed application components, automated metering and billing, and automated backup of server states and images.[18] All of this frees the operations staff to focus on other concerns.

6.1.3. Leveraging Virtualization

With server virtualization, multiple VMs, each running their own, perhaps different, operating system, can share the same underlying hardware within separate, isolated partitions. The cost savings when applications use virtualized resources may include:

- **Reduction in data center rack space**. If the applications are lightly or occasionally used but need to be available to users continuously, then sharing the resources of the underlying hardware can reduce the number of servers needed to host a given set of applications. A recent survey of 346 CEOs found cloud computing adoption is widespread. The primary reason given for adoption was reducing total cost of ownership.[19] In one example cited, the equivalent of thirty traditional servers could be placed in one rack-mounted computer because they have low processor utilization.
- **Reduction in total cooling and power requirements**. A reduction in the underlying number of servers also reduces the air conditioning (HVAC) required for cooling, the backup batteries required, and the kilowatts (kWs) required for powering the infrastructure. This savings includes one-time costs for building the HVAC and power support structures, and the continuing operational costs.
- **Supports straightforward continuity of operations**. VMs can be saved off-site and quickly re-started if needed for continuity of operations purposes. Because the entire

VM, containing a specific instance of an operating system at any patch level with any combination of applications, can be saved as an image, the installation can be quick and low-risk. This can be a cost-effective approach to ensuring availability versus active-active failover or multi-site clustering for some applications.

6.1.4. More Effective Power

Electric power impacts cloud computing basic economics in at least two significant ways. First, the more efficient use of processing resources and associated HVAC reductions, due to virtualization and better utilization of hardware, changes the total amount of power required for the same computing. Second, many service providers move their data centers to take advantage of lower power costs prices at certain locations.[20] Figure 14 shows how the cost of power varies across the United States— with numerous locations where the cost of power is relatively low.

Moving data centers to locations where electrical power is less expensive is a very effective way to keep the costs of cloud computing low. Further, moving to locations where colder air is abundant and can be used to augment cooling and reduce HVAC costs can also have a considerable impact on the bottom line.

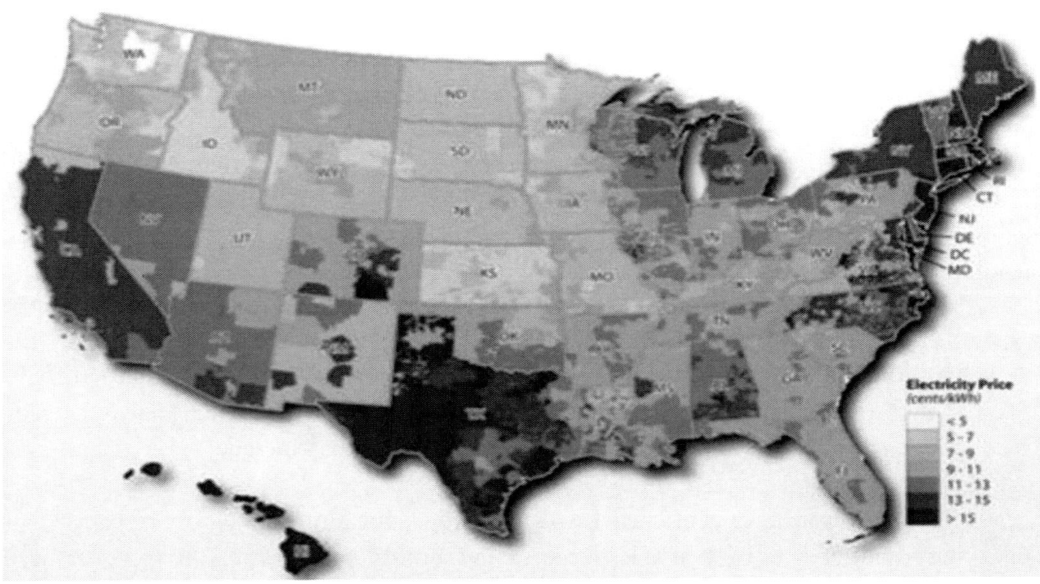

Note: The average electricity price data is based on 2008 EIA data.

Source: The map was produced by the National Renewable Energy Laboratory for the U.S. Department of Energy. Author: Billy Roberts, March 30, 2010.

Figure 14. Map of average U.S. residential electricity price by utility service territory.

6.2. Business Case Considerations for Cloud Service Use

In deciding to deploy applications into cloud computing data centers, the size of the investment, performance, risks, and investment characteristics (*i.e.*, capital investment versus operating expense, fixed versus variable costs) must all be factored into the business decision model.

Transition to cloud-based services must consider initial investment costs as well as recurring costs. Moving applications to clouds may require licensing and maintaining virtualization software. The use of virtualization may require new security software, identity management software, and management software for provisioning and backups. Data migration, integration, and testing costs associated with moving applications to a virtualized environment must also be incorporated in the cost model. Depending on the architecture of legacy applications currently deployed, there may also be porting costs.

Figure 15 shows a notional graph of the investment over time required to move an application to cloud computing. Some initial investment may be required initially, but over time the overall costs should be expected to decline.

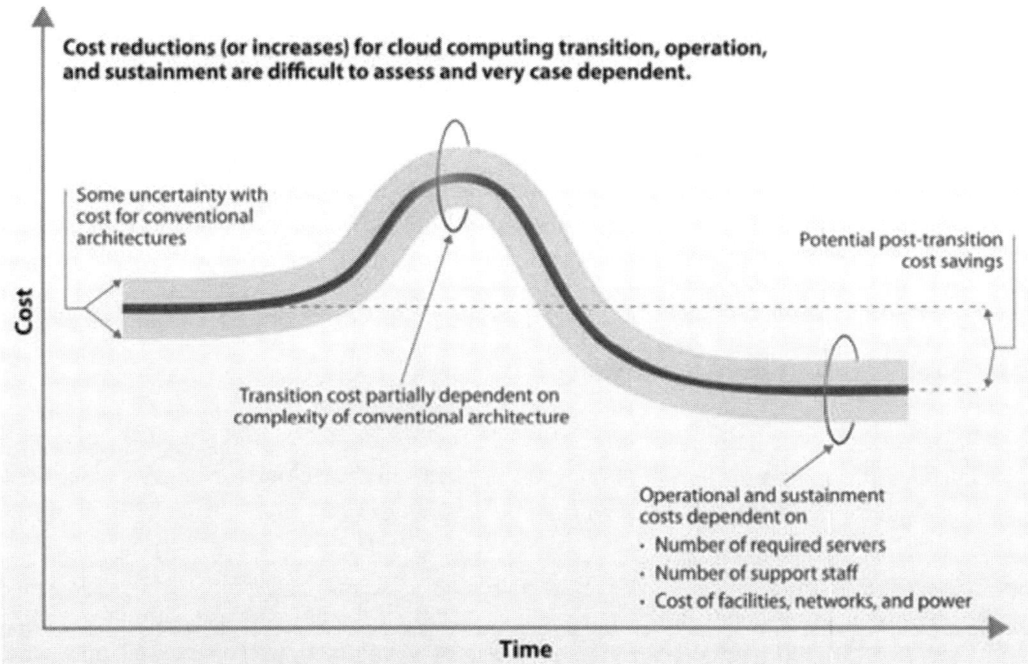

Figure 15. Notional cost over time to implement cloud computing.

As mentioned, users generally access cloud computing applications over browsers. This may impact network loads and, in turn, increase costs if upgrades to networks are needed to meet agreed-upon service level agreements (SLAs).

6.3. Service Level Agreements

SLAs affect in-sourced private, out-sourced private, and public cloud computing. Well-understood SLAs are essential for mission success, and they can directly drive costs for the service provider. When SLAs are negotiable, contractual terms for SLAs can include characteristics such as:

- response time
- hours of operation
- service availability
- expected throughput and utilization ranges
- maximum permitted down-time
- performance measurement and reporting requirements
- performance-based pricing
- problem resolution thresholds
- problem escalation and priorities

When possible, an SLA should specify steps the consumer can take when service is not meeting terms specified in the SLA. These remediation steps should include points-ofcontact, contact information, and escalation procedures. The time-to-resolve performance should be specified in the contract based upon the severity of the problem.

It is useful to be precise in the definition of metrics, and specify when and where they will be collected. For example, network performance metrics could have different values when measured from the consumer or provider, due to the propagation delay of the network. Performance metrics should measure characteristics under the control of the vendor or they will be unenforceable. Finally, the SLA should describe a mutual management process for the service levels, including periodic reporting requirements and meetings for management assessments.

6.4. Cloud Computing Case Studies

Case studies can be helpful for understanding the business case and potential cost savings associated with deploying or re-deploying an application to a cloud computing data center. The case studies cited here indicate significant cost savings.[21]

6.4.1. Cloud Providers

- The U.S. Air Force's 45th Space Wing at Patrick Air Force Base estimates that they save $180,000 annually through their use of virtualization. They found that even at peak load times, very few of their servers were running at more than 5 to 6 percent of load according to Glenn Exline, manager of enterprise networks at Computer Sciences Raytheon, which supports the 45th Space Wing.[22] To improve utilization, and lower hardware and energy costs, the Wing reduced 60 physical servers to four running a VMware virtualization solution. Here, the elements of cost savings were: $104,000 in hardware costs, $30,000 in power to cool what used to be 60 file servers, $28,000 in maintenance costs, and $18,000 in other expenses.[23]
- Over a four-year period, the Department of Energy Los Alamos National Laboratory has removed 100 physical servers and replaced them with 13 servers running hundreds of virtual machines, resulting in a cost savings of $1.4 million.[24] Recently they launched private cloud capabilities that allow employees to request and provision Windows, Linux, or Sun virtual server environments through a self-service portal. They've implemented management and chargeback capabilities as well. Chargeback is also important because users have an idea that virtual servers are free,

comments Anil Karmel, solutions architect at Los Alamos' Engineering Division in an interview with *Federal Computer Week*.

6.4.2. Cloud Consumers

- The Recovery, Accountability, and Transparency Board moved Recovery.gov to Amazon's Elastic Compute Cloud (EC2) for a projected savings of $334,000 in 2010 and $420,000 in 2011.[25] Recovery.gov is the official website for Recovery Act data and EC2 is a commercial, publicly available IaaS cloud offering. Additionally, there is additional value to the Board in the capabilities EC2 provides, including uptime and backup capabilities.
- The General Services Administration (GSA) moved 17,000 users to cloud-based Google Apps for Government in 2011 to provide email and collaboration capabilities.[26] Martha Johnson, GSA Administrator, said, "We expect that using a cloud-based system will reduce email operation costs by 50 percent over the next five years and save more than $15.2 million for the agency in that time. A large part of these savings will come from a decrease in the number of costly data centers requiring hardware, software licenses, maintenance, and contractor support."[27] Google Apps for Government has received an authority to operate at the FISMA-Moderate level and includes more secure versions of cloud tools like Google Docs, Google Sites and Google Reader.[28]

Finding

Finding 9: Potential cost reductions, or increases incurred during the transition to and sustainment of cloud computing infrastructure, depend on the specifics of the implementation. Potential cost-reduction factors include a higher utilization of servers, lower professional support staff needs, economies of scale for the physical facility, and the flexibility to locate data centers in areas with lower-cost power.

7. TECHNOLOGY INVESTMENT AND RESEARCH OPPORTUNITIES

Cloud computing technologies developed in the private sector provide significant capability. In particular, these capabilities include utility computing for business services on public clouds, and large scale analytics to process increasing amounts of web traffic, and search and user data on private clouds. In this context, security is not the main concern, while business agility is. Additionally, many applications supported by today's clouds are embarrassingly parallel (employing simple parallelism). While it is certainly possible to encode parallel sparse linear algebra in MapReduce or over a collection of EC2 instances, it is inefficient.

In this chapter, research investments are discussed in key areas, such scalability, security, and usability, that could take cloud computing from predominantly embarrassingly parallel utility computing to computing that is secure, reliable, and more tightly coupled with adequate support at the tactical edge. Many technology challenges highlighted in this chapter are active research areas with often decades of relevant results (such as scheduling, performance optimization, fault tolerance, databases, and statistical learning techniques). However, the scales of current and emerging computing systems and the DoD and intelligence community application requirements dictate the need for new technical approaches to these, at times, classical problems.

It is important to note that DoD's computing requirements are quite broad, ranging from applications that are well-served by today's utility, data, and storage clouds, to applications that use specialized high performance computers, computing clusters with high performance specialized interconnects, and computing clusters with graphic processing units. In addition, today's clouds were never designed to support war fighters at the tactical edge, in which communications may be interrupted or seriously degraded.

An interesting development is the emergence of commercial high-performance computing cloud offerings, in which midrange symmetric multiprocessor clusters are being offered as infrastructure as a service, as well as computers with large memory and high performance storage. In addition, clouds at universities and research laboratories are being prototyped that incorporate graphic processors, solid state memory, and other specialized hardware. This is changing the type of applications that can be supported by infrastructure as a service.

Also in this chapter, a survey of research is discussed that may lead to a broader range of applications that can be supported by today's cloud, as well as clouds built from some of the more specialized types of hardware just mentioned.

As an example, today there is a significant amount of work being done so that clouds can support mobile clients, which may experience degraded communications or, at times, be disconnected. Some of this work may prove useful in the future to supporting clients at the tactical edge. From this point of view, supporting devices on the tactical edge using clouds for DoD has some similarities to supporting mobile clients using commercial clouds in the private sector. With the appropriate research and development, thick clients with intelligent caching policies may be used in order to mitigate bandwidth constraints so that remote clouds can more effectively support devices at the tactical edge.

For many potential users of public cloud computing data centers, security is still one of their most important concerns. There are significant differences between how security is implemented and managed between different commercial clouds. Some of the large commercial clouds have security groups that are larger than the security groups at many DoD facilities, while other commercial clouds pay much less attention to security. As mentioned in Chapter 5, users of commercial cloud computing services are usually not given sufficient information about the computing infrastructure, monitoring of the infrastructure, forensic investigations, and so on, to satisfy the security requirements required for DoD applications.

Within the DoD, DARPA is currently making investments in several relevant technical areas. For example, its Mission-Oriented Resilient Cloud program is developing technologies to detect, diagnose, and respond to attacks in the cloud, effectively building a "community health system" for cloud computing. The DARPA Programming Computation on Encrypted Data (PROCEED) program is developing methods that allow computation on encrypted data without first decrypting it. One approach, homomorphic encryption, would have a client encrypt the data before sending it to the cloud. The client would also provide the cloud with executable code to allow it to work on that data without decrypting it. Current homomorphic encryption approaches are computationally infeasible, and researchers at DARPA are seeking to make them practical. DARPA is also funding other related approaches that may incur less overhead.

Table 2 lists recommended technology investments, categorized into three areas For each column, the list is presented approximately in order of increasing difficulty. In the section that follows a few particularly high-impact technology areas are described in more detail (with emphasis on security). While the technology areas are broken down into the three categories, technologies often require advancements across categories. Furthermore, progress within a category has impact in other categories. For example, while scalable runtime code optimization will benefit from improvements in program analysis, such improvement will also benefit research and development of malicious code detection.

7.1. Scalability

7.1.1. Quality of Service and Fault Tolerance

While existing technologies provide fault tolerance through elasticity (replication) of computing resources, this is not sufficient to run competitive DoD applications that use high performance computers. To address the needs of these applications, fault tolerance must be achieved in the context of complex parallelism or distribution, as opposed to simple parallelism models and parallel computations. To continue scaling with both data sizes and computation complexity, one must address computational efficiency—achieved operations per second as compared to peak operations per second—and scalable application-to-computing-architecture mapping.

Table 2. Recommended DoD Research and Development for Cloud Computing Technology

Scalability	Security	Usability
• Quality of service metrics and guarantees	• Security instrumentation and metrics	• Fused data representation
• Dynamic scheduling and resource allocation	• Authentication and access control	• Data and resource visualization
• Program analysis	• Efficient, secure hypervisors	• High-performance, massively parallel databases
• Dynamic program analysis	• Traffic and data flow analysis	• Optimized indexing, search, and retrieval
• Automated diversity	• Hardware provenance and remote program authentication	• Heterogeneous client—thin, thick—programming models
• Software, middleware for heterogeneous hardware	• Key management	• High-level composable application programmer interfaces (APIs)
• Automated performance optimization	• Data/information flow labeling, isolation, and tracking	• Cloud-client application partitioning
• Compute optimization	• Cyber offense	• Scalable parallelization-distribution framework
• Memory, communication optimization	• Streaming analytics	• Specialized, general code generation
• Power optimization	• Statistical analytics	
• Automated diversity, fault tolerant runtime environments	• Formal methods for correctness	
• Resilient, scalable storage systems	• Secure multiparty protocols	
	• Tractable, practical homomorphic encryption	
	• Specialized hardware architectures, co-processors for homomorphic encryption	

*The ordering in each column is in approximate order of increasing difficulty.

Technology initiatives to address this include development of instrumentation tools that could measure performance in context of the SaaS cloud computing paradigm, distributed and heterogeneous programming models, parallelization techniques that are agnostic and separate from the nature of the computation, and check-pointing tools (similar to traditional high performance computing).

7.1.2. Program Analysis

Advances in program analysis tools and techniques would benefit both scalability and security. Efficient program analysis would allow performance prediction and optimization of data-intensive codes, analysis of security flaws in the code, and detection of injected malicious software (given signatures or family of signatures). As many large software systems within the DoD leverage open source components, program analysis tools could significantly increase safety and reliability of those components.

Program analysis challenges that are specific to DoD cloud computing include highly heterogeneous software and hardware environments, virtualization (analyzing code within a virtual machine), and efficiency at scale (developing program analysis techniques with minimal overheads).

7.1.3. Automated Diversity

Even with the most diligent attention to preventing software flaws, some exist. Often exploiting these flaws depends critically on specific implementation-artifacts that must be present in every copy of the program. Cloud computing applications, with high development costs and wide distribution, are especially vulnerable. Artificial diversity techniques, such as address space layout randomization, have been developed to provide economical resistance to some attacks.

Additional techniques, like control flow integrity, offer further protection with limited human investment in individual program copies. Attackers respond to defenses, so the defense remains useful only if development continues. And, given the vulnerabilities, this research is critical for cloud computing.

7.1.4. Automated Performance Optimization

Cloud data-intensive computing can be highly inefficient by classic performance measures. Reasons for inefficiency include the common use of languages that trade off computational efficiency for programmability (Java); coarse parallelism programming models (MapReduce); data characteristics (sparse, massive data); and hardware inefficiencies (hardware platforms that are designed for high locality of data accesses).

One way to address some of these challenges is runtime performance optimization of existing codes. Research efforts in this area could include a runtime optimization environment for MapReduce, leverage of flexible communication models for parallel codes such as publish-subscribe, and leverage of flexible programming models such as message passing interface and array-based programming. Additionally, for utility computing, tools can be developed to optimize power efficiency and provide guarantees for quality of service.

7.2. Security

7.2.1. Instrumentation and Metrics

Often, there simply is a lack of available data regarding a wide range of security incidents. Instrumentation that minimally interferes with performance could significantly improve the development of meaningful metrics, provide data for development of analytics, and enable effective remediation of security incidents. Research efforts could focus on instrumentation at different levels in the software stack—from virtual machine to specific services or computation modules.

7.2.2. Authentication and Access Control

Cloud users and providers are rarely co-located and, yet, establishing their identity is foundational to all access control. While there are good cryptographic techniques for doing this authentication, wide-scale use of these techniques incurs all sorts of problems, from the manipulation of physical tokens, to corruption of central databases like Active Directory (whose compromise can defeat an entire enterprise's security in one fell swoop), to sensor-based confirmation or audit of identity (biometrics, gaze tracking), and so on. Further, access control in cloud systems and mobile devices depends not only on authenticating the human user, but also on authenticating some program performing the task. In fact, most mobile applications and cloud applications depend solely on program identity to determine access rights. Passwords are problematic, and usability of authentication mechanisms represents a major issue. Much work remains to be done.

The ability to read or write data, run programs, enter physical facilities, and receive keys to decrypt information must be controlled so that only authorized parties (people, programs, organizations), under authorized conditions (location, time) have the access. As with authentication, access control with clouds is an inherently distributed systems problem, requiring high assurance and flexibility (to describe who has what rights to what objects under what conditions). Cryptographic techniques using supporting infrastructure (physical tokens, isolated, measured software components, and perhaps a public key infrastructure) have been employed but, as with authentication, current deployments are fragile in the face of use by real people trying to get their jobs done. This is a large research area.

7.2.3. Labeling, Isolation, and Tracking

As stakeholders become physically remote from the computers that run programs on their behalf, technology must play a larger part in ensuring the isolation, confidentiality, and integrity of those computations from other cloud users, as well as the data center operators. Hardware has already been developed to enable programs to "prove" isolation and integrity properties to their providers and remote users.

This technology also allows cryptographic key provisioning in a manner that ensures even data center operators cannot access keys. Programs can now encrypt all stored and transmitted data as a means to ensure confidentiality and integrity. This technology also can be employed by data center framework components—that can be remotely verified by users—to ensure fair resource allocation, inter-job sanitization, and reliable auditing.

However, there is much work to do to make this existing technology useful to DoD, as well as to ensure usability by clients and by datacenter managers. Further research and software development is required to enable cloud-client systems to leverage these mechanisms for enforcing isolation boundaries that are crucial for ensuring confidentiality and integrity of data, results, and provenance of information. Further investigation related to the resilience of these systems is also needed, to address implementation flaws and environmental factors; for example, those that enable side channel attacks. A further area of interest is compositional vulnerabilities introduced when two otherwise safe components interact in an unexpected way.

7.2.4. Cyber Adversaries

Cyber security is often described as computing in the presence of an adversary. Economics often involves the study of parties competing for resources. In both cases, understanding adversarial capabilities is critical to defense. Security experts often place confidence in assessments of system vulnerabilities as a result of diligent attacks by well-informed and well-trained red team members. This sort of analysis is much more representative of the actual threat environment than contrived, piecemeal analyses. Red team attacks have proven to be the best source of information about improvements in the design and operations of a security system.

For security reasons, this knowledge is often not widely held or employed by system researchers. Further, other parties, such as antivirus vendors, are occasionally better positioned to discover attacks and attack techniques. While some techniques should properly be closely held, developing capable attack techniques is surely critical to developing safer systems and this research must proceed.

7.2.5. Streaming Statistical Analytics

Existing streaming analytics, whether for detection of cyber security events or analysis of large-scale datasets and databases, usually either perform relatively simple computations on large datasets or complex computations on small portions. However, the application of complex analytics to large datasets is needed to address the challenges presented by big data, namely detection of weak signature events in multi-intelligence or multisource datasets in an efficient and timely manner, in absence of a cue. Technology efforts could focus on developing novel algorithmic techniques along with data representations. These algorithms would detect statistical anomalies at global scale and alert either human analysts or another algorithm layer. This approach would fundamentally change the current analytic paradigm where the initial processing step is either omitted, based on reliance on an external cue, or performed manually. New algorithmic techniques would also benefit from new programming models and performance optimization tools.

7.2.6. Hardware Provenance

A disturbing trend is the increased susceptibility of hardware components to attack by unknowingly using attacker-supplied circuits in fabrication. Most DoD components— and almost all national infrastructure components—are manufactured by commercial suppliers, operating on thin economic margins, with the associated motivation to economize with respect to security and assurance. These commercial suppliers operate largely in foreign countries that may themselves have good reasons to interfere with equipment used by DoD. Limiting the number of critical components required to "fight through" a corrupt hardware chain is a new design imperative, and the area is one that requires new research. Discovering hardware modifications or assuring their absence is also an important area for further research.

7.2.7. Methods for Assurance

The customary DoD processes for testing, verifying, and certifying software systems are inadequate. Certified systems often delay deployment until long after vulnerabilities are discovered and much safer (but not-yet-certified) versions are available. Certification cost is prohibitive, driving innovation out and, worse yet, delaying availability of key new capabilities (like big data analysis tools) that are rapidly developing. Every single element of this process must change. Better and more automated testing; automated verification and risk assessment; and an economical, streamlined certification process are absolutely critical research areas.

7.2.8. Homomorphic Encryption

Homomorphic encryption enables operations on the data in encrypted form (performing multiple functions without decrypting the data). A key challenge in homomorphic encryption is computational tractability. Existing techniques have demonstrated the capability for simple operations such as addition and multiplication; however, the computational complexity is currently prohibitive. Advances in tractable homomorphic encryption could enable both highly secure utility computing and data intensive computing across multiple classification levels. These techniques could also provide situational awareness and aggregate statistics without sacrificing privacy or sensitivity of the original data sources. The research challenges need to be tackled algorithmically through design of novel hardware. Near-term research targets could include advances in searchable encryption, where recent results already allow practical database-like operations on encrypted data in a cloud, preserving the confidentiality of the data.

7.3. Usability

7.3.1. Data and Resource Visualization

A key challenge in processing massive datasets is visualizing both the raw data and the results of computations on the data. Similarly, when distributing applications and computations across multiple resources, it is often desirable to visualize those resources and data distributions. Research efforts into visualization (especially combined with statistical analytics of data) could significantly improve analysts' ability to understand massive datasets and detect events of interest (for example, malicious activity or exfiltration).

7.3.2. High Performance Massively Parallel Databases

While existing distributed database technology enables ingest of large datasets, complex queries still present a significant challenge. As algorithms for processing large data continue to advance, support for increasingly complex queries will become necessary. Research efforts could focus on database architecture, query language, and performance optimization.

7.3.3. Composable, High-Level Application Programmer Interfaces

Ability to interact with large datasets in context of data-intensive cloud computing requires efficient, scalable, and intuitive APIs. While existing APIs (such as MapReduce) provide reasonable capabilities, they do not naturally allow for implementation of complex parallelism and support for array-based algebra operations. Array-based algebra allows for both implementation of complex analytics (principal component analysis, feature extraction, large graph analysis, complex queries) while providing an intuitive parallelization interface (mapping the array). Research efforts could focus on developing novel languages, creating libraries using existing languages, developing parallelization frameworks, and performance optimization techniques.

7.3.4. Cloud–Client Application Partitioning

Cloud computing does not exist in a vacuum—it must be provisioned, and often it provides value by supplying information to remote clients. Service is often delivered to users by browser-based clients or moderated through productivity applications, such as Adobe Reader or Microsoft Office, that can hide attacks, promulgate them, and deliver exfiltrated information to attackers or corrupt information to users. Browsers are particularly worrisome, given the large and unending stream of catalogued exploitable vulnerabilities. A cloud application is really the combination of a cloud component and a client component, and the security goals should be to protect this combined system— not to protect just the cloud. Increasing the proportion of processing done on a safe cloud can improve updates and maintenance; however, the remaining components on a client must also be made safe. Research into safer browsers and browser-extension safety is required. Access policies, configuration safety, and verification of client components are needed, as well as the ability of both client- and cloud-computing components to mutually verify partner code. This is clearly a critical research area prior to deploying a broad set of applications between client devices and a cloud computing center.

7.4. Combining Technologies

As described here, these technology areas can provide significant improvement in scalability, security, and usability in their own right. However, combining these technologies could lead to revolutionary changes in computing. For example, combining homomorphic encryption with a high-level composable, parallel API (such as an associative array) could enable processing of massive, multi-intelligence datasets, thereby providing actionable intelligence to the user at the tactical edge without concern for mixing classification levels. Being able to provide big data analytics at the tactical edge (without a cue, which is consistent with the changing nature of the conflict) is an example of significant capability that could be enabled by investment in cloud computing technologies.

Finding

Finding 10: The DoD has active research and development efforts in technology areas applicable to cloud computing performance and security.

Sustained DoD investment in cloud computing security technology is critically important to allow DoD data centers to continue improving their defenses against evolving threats. Research and development in software stack protection, monitoring, and forensics of very large datasets, secure hypervisors, and advanced encryption offer significant possible security benefits.

8. FINDINGS SUMMARY AND RECOMMENDATIONS

8.1. Findings Summary

The Significance and Impact of Cloud Computing

Finding 1: Although cloud computing is an overloaded term, cloud computing providers are offering services that are fundamentally new and useful, typically delivering the:

- ability for massive scale-up of storage and computing
- rapid, agile, elasticity with the ability to increase and decrease storage and
- computing capacity on-demand, when the community of tenants don't all require that capacity at the same time
- metered services where the user pays only for what is used self-service start-up and control

Finding 2: Modular data centers offer an approach to quickly set up cloud computing capacity, to add additional capability to existing cloud computing data centers, and to easily refresh or update existing capability. This concept is illustrated in Figure F-1.

Finding 3: Cloud computing services can scale to data centers or "warehouse-scale" computing. Elastic, warehouse-scale cloud computing is fundamentally new and can provide DoD with important new capabilities.

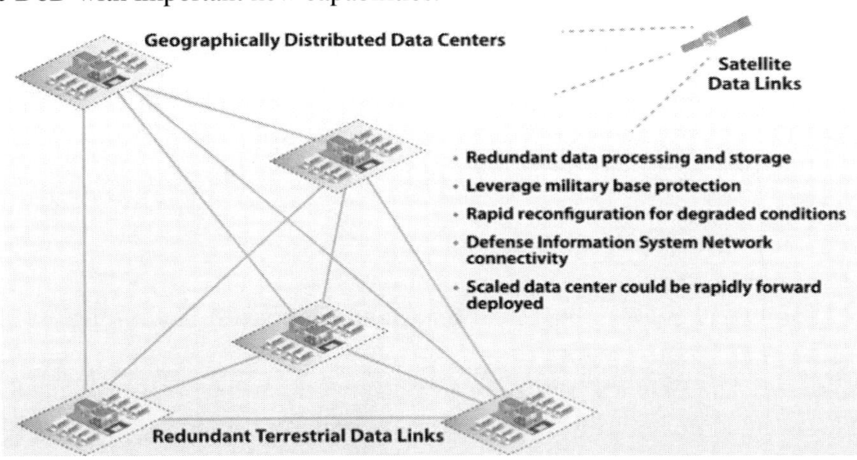

Figure F-1. Concept for a geographic distribution of DoD data centers.

The Security of Cloud Computing

Finding 4: Cloud computing is not intrinsically more secure than other distributed computing approaches, but its scale and uniformity facilitate and enable the wholesale and consistent application of security practices. Secure aspects include large scale monitoring and analysis of data to detect attacks, and automated and persistent provisioning and re-provisioning to foil intrusions. For these reasons, well-operated cloud computing facilities can exhibit better security hygiene than conventional data centers. However, the centralization of resources in a huge data center also encourages more determined attacks, especially on critical components broadly affecting security. This is similar to conventional systems where attacks are observed to focus on central directories.

Finding 5: The scale of cloud computing enables the analysis of packet and log data that provides new capabilities for event forensics and real-time detection of malicious behavior. The ability to manage very large, diverse datasets facilitates a data-centric security model in which users are authorized to work with data based upon their security credentials and the security markings on the data rather than the conventional enclave-centric security model in which users are provided access to an enclave and can access all the data in the enclave.

Finding 6: No cloud computing deployment model is uniformly suitable for hosting all DoD applications. In general, sensitive, classified, and time-critical DoD applications should be deployed only in private clouds or conventional non-cloud approaches.

Finding 7: The case for transitioning a DoD application to a cloud computing data center must include a security assessment detailing the impact of the transition. Whether security will be improved by transitioning an application to a cloud computing data center will depend on factors specific to the application, to the cloud computing data center, and to the transition process.

Finding 8: The DoD has not established effective plans for cloud computing facility backup or for dealing with any anticipated degradation of communications between the cloud computing facilities and the end user.

The Costs Associated with Cloud Computing

Finding 9: Potential cost reductions or increases incurred during the transition to and sustainment of cloud computing infrastructure depend on the specifics of the implementation. Potential cost-reduction factors include a higher utilization of servers, lower professional support staff needs, economies of scale for the physical facility, and the flexibility to locate data centers in areas with lower-cost power.

Research and Development for Cloud Computing Technologies

Finding 10: The DoD has active research and development efforts in technology areas applicable to cloud computing performance and security. Sustained DoD investment in cloud computing security technology is critically important to allow DoD data centers to continue improving their defenses against evolving threats. Research and development in software stack protection, monitoring, and forensics of very large datasets, secure hypervisors, and advanced encryption offer significant possible security benefits.

8.2. Recommendations

Overarching Recommendations

Recommendation 1: For some sensitive, classified, and time-critical applications, the DoD should pursue private cloud computing, provided that strong security measures are in place.

In particular, cloud computing-based solutions should be considered for applications that require the agility, scale-out, and ability to integrate and analyze massive data that cloud computing can provide. Examples of such applications include: big data analysis and all-source intelligence integration; processing, exploitation, and dissemination of data gathered through intelligence, surveillance, and reconnaissance (ISR); large-scale modeling and simulation; open source data collection, storage, and assessment; and advanced decision support systems.

Recommendation 2: The DoD CIO in partnership with the military Services should deploy interconnected, modular cloud computing data centers located at secure locations, such as military bases.

The development of large, private community clouds in DoD will enable greater computing and storage elasticity and the improved ability to operate under degraded conditions. The DoD CIO should guide this development with an eye on both current and future DoD computing needs.

A DoD private community cloud may include in-house, in-sourced, or out-sourced private clouds. Implemented through interconnected, modular cloud computer data centers, this can be operated as an integrated unit to improve the potential reducing costs. Because large data centers can also be attractive targets, geographically distributed modular data centers are recommended that are operated as a single, large-scale, distributed cloud. The design should include a distributed data center architecture that allows access by multiple Services and Agencies. Cost savings would be achieved through shared development, operations, and maintenance support.

These modular data centers could be located on military bases in order to provide good physical security. The location should also be influenced by the cost and availability of reliable electric power. It is anticipated this will be similar to the National Security Agency private cloud models. Shared cyber security event response and rapid forensics would be an enhanced capability. By designing and acquiring these data centers as a system, the DoD can achieve the economies of scale typically associated with large data centers.

Recommendation 3: The DoD CIO and DISA should establish clear security mandates for DoD cloud computing.

Security mandates should be aimed at reducing the number of cloud compromises and to mitigate those that occur. Some examples of potential mandates include:

- Hypervisors hosting DoD operating systems should have effective cryptographic sealing, attestation, and strong virtual machine isolation.
- Data at rest should be stored in encrypted form with keys protected using hardware attestation, such as a trusted platform module (TPM).

- Data in transit on communication lines should be encrypted with keys protected using hardware attestation, such as a TPM.
- Access to cloud computing systems should require multifactor authentication.

Recommendation 4: The DoD CIO should establish a central repository to fully document cloud computing transition and sustainment costs and best practices for programs underway or completed.

Because the cost savings to be gained through cloud computing are case-dependent, a central repository documenting DoD cloud computing programs is needed. The goal of this repository is to improve the understanding of the following:

- system costs before the switch to cloud computing, costs during transition, and sustainment costs
- enhanced functionality attributable to cloud computing architectures
- best practices for cloud computing security
- issues surrounding service license agreements
- metrics for availability and reliability

This repository will enable leveraging the lessons learned from several DoD cloud computing initiatives underway, including:

- NSA development and use of private clouds
- DISA Rapid Access Computing Environment (RACE)
- Army Enterprise Email

Recommendations to Improve DoD's Implementation of Cloud Computing

Recommendation 5: The DoD USD AT&L and the DoD CIO should establish a lean, rapid acquisition approach for information technology infrastructure, including cloud computing hardware and software.

Acquisition guidelines for all information technology—not only cloud computing hardware and software—should strive to create a lean, capabilities-based approach with strong, clear security mandates. Rapid certification and accreditation (C&A) and other characteristics to streamline acquisition of cloud computing hardware and software should be developed and implemented quickly.

Recommendation 6: The DoD CIO and DISA should establish standard service level agreements for private and public cloud computing.

Key attributes that should be included in service level agreements include availability, authentication and authorization approaches, data processing and storage locations, software and data back-up approaches, cyber attack event notification, required staff clearances and background checks, software and data disposition, risk disclosure requirements, and contingency plan. Transparency in all of these aspects for DoD service providers will help set standards for secure cloud computing across the economy.

Recommendation 7: The DoD CIO and DISA should participate in the public development of national and global standards and best practices for cloud computing.

A key outcome of this activity will be to inform the private sector and open source developers about the agility and auditability requirements for DoD cloud computing.

Recommendations to Improve Cloud Computing for Degraded Operations

Recommendation 8: The DoD and the intelligence community leadership should develop a unified approach for training and exercising with degraded information infrastructure, including cloud computing hardware and software.

Degraded operations in a realistic operational exercise must be implemented organically, *i.e.*, beyond simply holding up a white card to introduce a cyber event to an exercise. Advanced cyber security threats should be exercised, including a gradual ramp-up of threat and loss of disadvantaged communication and data links as well as primary capabilities. Enhanced red and blue teaming should be established along with operational exercises incorporating degraded cloud computing infrastructure. Participants should demonstrate a rapid forensics response and effective backup plans.

Recommendation 9: The Joint Chiefs of Staff and Combatant Commands should establish effective back-up plans for operations with degraded information infrastructure, including cloud computing hardware and software.

Candidate plan attributes include implementing thicker clients and forward caching of data as well as backup data networks, processors, and storage. Each organization should also develop operational contingencies for degraded networks. Potential strategies also include using local network connectivity for forward clients and narrowband, analog communication links for situational awareness and warning.

Recommendations for Investment

Recommendation 10: The DoD should continue investing significantly in information security research and development, including research and development for secure cloud computing technology.

To best leverage state-of-the-art cloud computing technologies for DoD, significant investment should continue for technology research and development activities in areas such as: efficient operations of cloud computing data centers; cloud security; secure, lean hypervisors; micro-virtualization; advanced TPMs; homomorphic computing; and cloud situational awareness software.

CONCLUSION

The DoD should pursue cloud computing to enhance mission capabilities, provided that strong cyber security measures are in place. Stronger red teaming and realistic exercises are needed to provide critically important improvements to DoD cyber security. Missions that may enjoy new capabilities as a result of cloud computing include: big data analysis and all-source intelligence integration; ISR processing, exploitation, and dissemination; and large-scale modeling and simulation. New modular cloud data center hardware offers the DoD an opportunity for rapid enhancement of the overall computing enterprise in a secure and resilient manner. The potential to reduce costs or to increase them through implementation of cloud computing is very case-dependent. Some factors that can lead to cost reductions include higher usage of data center, lower support staff-to-server ratios, better management of peak loads, and economies of scale.

TERMS OF REFERENCE

DEPUTY SECRETARY OF DEFENSE
1010 DEFENSE PENTAGON
WASHINGTON, DC 20301-1010

MAY 1 9 2011

MEMORANDUM FOR CHAIRMAN, DEFENSE SCIENCE BOARD

SUBJECT: Terms of Reference – Defense Science Board (DSB) Task Force on Cybersecurity and Reliability in a Digital Cloud

You are hereby directed to establish a Task Force to evaluate all aspects of providing reliable, secure, and responsive services for military and intelligence applications using these technologies. Specific purposes of this Task Force include:

- Characterize the operational properties of clouds and virtualized infrastructure, and the quality of service that can be delivered to connected users, paying particular attention to attacks on communication that would destroy or delay delivery of services and information for time-critical uses;
- Consider alternative designs and implementations of these technologies and evaluate their use for varied military and intelligence applications;
    - Discuss options for inter-cloud services and other communications between clouds, especially between clouds that operate at different classification levels, have different authorities, or are operated on behalf of different agencies and organizations;
- Evaluate the vulnerability and risk mitigations of a cloud infrastructure to various attacks, compared to alternative infrastructures;
- Evaluate the vulnerability and risk mitigations of virtualized infrastructure to various attacks, compared to alternative infrastructures;
- Determine how to avoid the danger of concentrating data and computation; for example, suggest how diverse (non-homogeneous) software and hardware can be deployed in the cloud to enhance reliability and security;
- Review and project the consequence of current trends in digital technology on cloud deployments, including social computing;
- Comment on customer practices and modes of interaction with the cloud that might aid in increasing security;
- Make recommendations on what dimensions (pros and cons) of these technologies should be considered to increase reliability and to ensure security as the military and intelligence communities evolve their digital infrastructure;
- Comment on workforce implications (skills, qualifications required, etc.) the Department might expect in transitioning from current environments to cloud implementations;
- Identify research opportunities and estimate the level of investment to achieve results consistent with DoD needs;

OSD 04475-11

- Assess cost/benefit and effectiveness/suitability issues associated with Software as a Service, Platform as a Service, and Infrastructure as a Service, as those technologies apply to both garrison and deployed computing requirements; and
- Identify methods to leverage the rapid innovation and operational maturity being delivered by public cloud providers while maintaining the Department's ability to service its own IT needs effectively and operate at multiple classification levels.

The military and intelligence communities are increasingly articulating a need for information systems that rely upon cloud computing, virtualization, and related technologies. A digital cloud has a richly networked, distributed core of data storage and computational resources that provides shared information and services on demand to individual users located outside the cloud, but connected via a network. Cloud advocates assert that infrastructure incorporating cloud-based technologies and virtualization can deliver both higher reliability and more assured cybersecurity.

Administration support and funding will be provided by the Under Secretary of Defense for Acquisition, Technology, and Logistics. Additional support will be provided by the Assistant Secretary of Defense for Networks and Information Integration/DoD Chief Information Officer (ASD(NII)/DoD CIO), the Director, Operational Test and Evaluation (DOT&E), the Vice Chairman of the Joint Chiefs of Staff, and the Commander, U.S. Cyber Command. All Task Force members, consultants, and supporting personnel will be appointed or designated in accordance with DoD Instruction (DoDI) 5105.04, "Department of Defense Federal Advisory Committee Management Program."

The Task Force will be established and operated in accordance with the provisions of the "Federal Advisory Committee Act" (5 U.S. Code Appendix, as amended), DoDI 5105.04, the DSB Charter, and all applicable laws, policies, and regulations. It is not anticipated that this Task Force will need to go into any "particular matters" within the meaning of section 208 of title 18, U.S. Code, nor will it cause any member to be placed in the position of acting as a procurement official.

TASK FORCE MEMBERSHIP

Co-Chairs

Dr. Eric Evans, MIT Lincoln Laboratory

Dr. Robert Grossman, University of Chicago and Open Data Group

Executive Secretary

Mr. John Mills, Department of Defense CIO

Members

Mr. Gregory Neal Akers, Cisco

Dr. Wanda M. Austin, Aerospace Corporation

Dr. Ron Brachman, Yahoo!

ADM William J. Fallon, USN (RET), Private Consultant

Mr. Al Grasso, MITRE Corporation
Dr. Eric Grosse, Google
Hon. (Dr.) Anita K. Jones, University of Virginia
Mr. Larry Lynn, Private Consultant
Dr. John L. Manferdelli, Intel
Mr. Larry Meador, MGI Strategic Solutions
Mr. Alden V. Munson, Jr, Potomac Institute for Policy Studies
Dr. Fred B. Schneider, Cornell University
Mr. James D. Shields, Draper Laboratory
Mr. Steve Schmidt, Amazon
Dr. Marc Zissman, MIT Lincoln Laboratory

Senior Advisors
Dr. Craig Fields, Private Consultant
Dr. Theodore S. Gold, Private Consultant
Hon. R. Noel Longuemare, Private Consultant
Hon. (Dr.) William Schneider, Jr., International Planning Services

Government Advisors
Mr. Lee Badger, National Institute of Standards and Technology
Dr. Patrick W. Dowd, Department of Defense
Ms. Cecilia Phan, Department of Defense CIO

Defense Science Board
CDR Doug Reinbold, U.S. Navy

Staff
Dr. Toni Marechaux, Strategic Analysis, Inc.
Ms. Kelly Frere, Strategic Analysis, Inc.

PRESENTATIONS TO THE TASK FORCE

	Organization	Title of Brief
May 17–18, 2011		
Ms. Jennifer Bayuk	Stevens Institute of Technology	Systems Security Engineering
Mr. Brad Bleier	National Cyber Investigative Joint Task Force	National Cyber Investigative Joint Task Force
Ms. Jamie Dos Santos	Terremark, Inc.	National Capital Region NAP
Dr. Timothy Fraser	Defense Advanced Research Projects Agency	Dynamic Quarantine of Worms; Cyber Gnome

	Organization	Title of Brief
Ms. Margie Gilbert	Office of the National Counterintelligence Executive	National Counterintelligence
Dr. Keith Gremban	Defense Advanced Research Projects Agency	Cloud to the Edge
Mr. Barry Horowitz	University of Virginia	Research Roadmap
Mr. Dan Kaufman	Defense Advanced Research Projects Agency	Cyber Analytical Framework
Dr. Carl McCants	Defense Advanced Research Projects Agency	TRUST, ISIS Programs
Dr. Jenendra Ranka	Defense Advanced Research Projects Agency	National Cyber Range
Mr. Tony Sager	National Security Agency	Vulnerability Assessment: Virtual Machine
Mr. Steve Stone and CAPT Mike Murray	U.S. Transportation Command	TRANSCOM Security issues
June 15–16, 2011		
Mr. Lee Badger	National Institute of Standards and Technology	U.S. Government Cloud Computing Technology Roadmap
Mr. Patrick W. Dowd	National Security Agency	Cloud Computing Architectures
Mr. Steve Schleien	Office of the Secretary of Defense	DoD Strategy for Cyberspace
Mr. Rob Vietmeyer and Mr. John Shea	Department of Defense CIO	DoD Cloud Computing for the Defense Science Board
Mr. Greg Wilshusen	Government Accountability Office	Information Security Issues for Cloud Computing
Mr. Jim Young and	Google	Overview
Ms. Michelle		
WeslanderQuaid		
July 12-13, 2011		
Mr. Asher Aziz	FireEye, Inc.	Advanced Persistent Threat Landscape and the Subversion of Existing Defenses
Mr. Rod Beckstrom and Mr. Whitfield Diffie	Internet Corporation for Assigned Names and Numbers (ICANN)	Internet Corporation for Assigned Names and Numbers (ICANN)
Mr. Bill Burns	Netflix	Netflix Cloud Security
Mr. Edmundo Costa	Catbird	Security and Compliance for Virtual and Cloud Infrastructure

(Continued)

	Organization	Title of Brief
Mr. Michael Donovan	HP Enterprise Services	Cloud Security Issues; HP Fortify
and Ms. Kelly Collins		Federal: Protecting the Software that Runs the Mission
Mr. Bret Hartman	RSA	The Intelligent Security Operations Center and Advanced Persistent Threats
Mr. Chris C. Kemp	OpenStack Cloud Software	OpenStack Cloud Software
Mr. Pravin Kothari	CipherCloud	Cloud Data Protection
Dr. John C. Mitchell	Stanford University	Innovation in the Big Cloud
Mr. Eric Olden	Symplified	Small Business Innovation in the Big Cloud
Mr. Don Proctor	Cisco Systems	Cisco Systems
Mr. Justin Somaini	Yahoo!	Yahoo!
Mr. Rich Tener	Zynga	Public Cloud Security Topics
Dr. Pete Worden	NASA Ames Research Center	Welcome to NASA Ames Research Center
Mr. Ken Xie	Fortinet	Small Business Innovation in the Big Cloud
August 10–11, 2011		
Mr. Lonny Anderson	National Security Agency	View from the CIO
Mr. Phillip Bodkin	National Security Agency	NSA Threat Operations Center
Mr. Justin Christian	National Security Agency	OZONE Cloud Interface
Mr. Simon Crosby	Bromium	Three Tales of the Cloud
Dr. Patrick W. Dowd	National Security Agency	Cloud Strategy
Mr. Oren J. Falkowitz	National Security Agency	ABR
Mr. Sterling S. Foster	National Security Agency	Data Cloud; Metadata Repository Increment 2
Mr. Glenn Gaffney	Office of the Director of National Intelligence	Cloud Computing: Key Questions
Ms. Melissa Hathaway	Hathaway Global Strategies	Observations on Cyber Strategy
Dr. John D. Howard	Defense Information Systems Agency	DISA Common User Services: The "Cloud" and the Future of DoD IT
Mr. Brian Hughes	National Security Agency	IT Efficiencies at NSA
Mr. John Ingliss	National Security Agency	Overview of NSA

	Organization	Title of Brief
Mr. Jaime Jenandez-	National Security Agency	Human Language Technology
Cordero		Demonstration
Ms. Catherine Lotrionte	Georgetown University	Georgetown Cyber Law and Policy
Ms. Stacey Olexy	National Security Agency	Content (PRESSUREWAVE)
Ms. Teri Takai	Department of Defense CIO	DoD CIO Challenges and Priorities for the DoD Enterprise
Mr. Neal Ziring and Mr. Adam P. Fuchs	National Security Agency	Cloud Security
September 14–15, 2011		
Mr. Kevin Cooley	U.S. Navy	U.S. Navy, Fleet Cyber Command Information Officer
Mr. John Hale	Defense Information Systems Agency	DoD Enterprise E-Mail
Mr. Frank Konieczny	U.S. Air Force-Chief Technology Officer	Air Force Perspectives on Cloud Computing
Mr. John McLaughin	IBM Corporation	Mission Oriented Cloud Architecture Overview
Mr. Mike McCarthy	U.S. Army-Brigade Modernization Command	Connecting Soldiers to Digital Applications
Brig. Gen. Linda R. Medler	The Joint Staff	Cloud Services for the Warfighter
RDML Jan Tighe	U.S. Navy	Cyber security in Military Exercises
November 30–December 1, 2011		
LTC Arthur Sellers and Mr. Tony Gillespie	U.S. Special Operations Command	U.S. Joint Special Operations Command
Ms. Jamie Dos Santos	Terremark	Overview of Terremark's National Capital Region Network Access
Dr. Howard Shrobe	Defense Advanced Research Projects Agency (DARPA)	Cloud Investigations at DARPA
MG Mark Bowman and Col Gary Langston	U.S. Army, G6	Enterprise Email

(Continued)

	Organization	Title of Brief
January 18–19, 2012		
Mr. Kevin Dulany	DoD Office of the Chief Information Officer	Federal Risk and Authorization Management Program
Mr. Kevin Gates	House Armed Services Committee	Data Servers and Centers
Mr. John Howard	Defense Information Systems Agency	Technical Strategy, Target Architecture, and RACE
Mr. Gus Hunt	Central Intelligence Agency	Cloud Strategy
Gen. Stanley McChrystal, USMC (RET)		Observations on Operations
Mr. Mark Morrison	Defense Intelligence Agency	DNI IT Efficiencies
Mr. Albert Reuther	MIT Lincoln Laboratories	Some Cloud Computing Economics
March 14–15, 2012		
Mr. George Slessman	IO Data Centers	IO -Intelligent Control
Mr. Bill Newhouse	National Institute of Standards and Technology	An Overview of the Cloud Assumption Buster Workshop
Mr. Orv Stockland	National Reconnaissance Office	Cloud Computing
Mr. Rob Vietmeyer	Office of the Secretary of Defense	Cloud Update
Mr. Neal Ziring	National Security Agency	Cloud Security

ABBREVIATIONS AND ACRONYMS

ALIRT	airborne ladar imaging research testbed
API	application programming interface
ARGUS-IS	Autonomous Real-Time Ground Ubiquitous Surveillance Imaging System
AWS	Amazon Web Services
C&A	certification and accreditation
CIO	Chief Information Officer
COTS	commercial off the shelf
DARPA	Defense Advanced Research Projects Agency
DISA	Defense Information Sysytems Agency
DISN	Defense Information Systems Network
DoD	Department of Defense
EC2	elastic compute cloud
EIA	Energy Information Administration

GIG	Global Information Grid
GSA	General Services Administration
HPC	high performance computing
HVAC	heating, ventilation and air conditioning
HYCAS	hyperspectral collection and analysis system
IaaS	infrastructure as a service
IEEE	Institute of Electrical and Electronics Engineers
ISR	intelligence, surveillance, and reconnaissance
kWs	kilowatts
NIST	National Institute of Standards and Technology
NoSQL	not only structured query language
NSA	National Security Agency
PaaS	platform as a service
PROCEED	Programming Computation on Encrypted Data
RACE	Rapid Access Computing Environment
RAM	random access memory
S3	Amazon Simple Storage Service
SaaS	software as a service
SLA	service level agreement
TPM	trusted platform module
TTP	tactics, techniques, and procedures
USD AT&L	Under Secretary of Defense for Acquisition, Technology, and Logistics
VM	virtual machine
WISP	wideband infrared scene projector

End Notes

[1] L. Leong and N. MacDonald, "Mitigating Risks in Cloud Infrastructure as a Service" (Gartner Research G00235858, July 11, 2012). Available at time of press at http://goo.gl/oIeq5

[2] United States Department of Defense, "Cloud Computing Strategy" (DoD Chief Information Officer, July 2012). Available at time of press at http://goo.gl/MfFQg

[3] IBM. "X-Force 2011 Trend and Risk Report," IBM Security Collaboration (March 2012). Available at time of press at http://goo.gl/MW0qH

[4] V. Winkler, "Securing the Cloud: Cloud Computer Security Techniques and Tactics" (April 2011). Available at time of press at http://goo.gl/AVEIO

[5] P. Mell and T. Grance, "The NIST Definition of Cloud Computing" (September 2011). Available at time of press at http://goo.gl/eBGBk

[6] D. Gottfrid, "The New York Times Archives + Amazon Web Services = TimesMachine," *New York Times* (May 21, 2008). Available at time of press at http://goo.gl/G7uvG

[7] "About" Google. Available at time of press at http://www.google

[8] B.A. Miller, N.T. Bliss, and P.J. Wolfe, "Toward signal processing theory for graphs and non-Euclidean data, in Proc.," IEEE Int. Conf. Acoust., Speech and Signal Process (pp. 5414–5417, 2010).

[9] A. Heller, "Autonomous Real-Time Ground Ubiquitous Surveillance Imaging System," *Science & Technology Review* (Lawrence Livermore National Laboratory, April/May 2011). Available at time of press at http://goo.gl/w4H2D

[10] A. Sternstein, "NSA Chief Endorses the Cloud for Classified Military Cyber Program," *Nextgov* (June 13, 2012). Available at time of press at http://goo.gl/bUrS5

[11] Trusted Foundry Program. Available at press time at http://www.trustedfoundryprogram.org/

[12] Defense Science Board, "High Performance Microchip Supply" (2005). Available at press time at http://www.acq.osd.mil/dsb/reports/ADA435563.pdf

[13] W.J. Lynn, III, "Defending a new domain," *Foreign Affairs* (September/October, 2010). See also, "The Pentagon's Cyberstrategy, one year later," *Foreign Affairs* (September, 2011).

[14] Defense Science Board, "Enhancing Adaptability of our Military Forces" (2011). Available at time of press at http://www.dtic.mil/docs/citations/ADA536755

[15] Amazon Web Services blog, "Dropping Prices Again—EC2, RDS, EMR and ElastiCache" (March 5, 2012). Available at time of press at http://goo.gl/lGZHs

[16] B. Howe, "Cloud Economics: Visualizing AWS Prices over Time" (eScience Institute, November 28, 2010). Available at time of press at http://goo.gl/ASGbS

[17] Enterprise Management Associates, "Best Practices in Virtual Systems Management: Virtualization Metrics and Recommendations for Enterprises," (2009, page 2). Available at time of press at http://goo.gl/N8xEV

[18] As an example, see a commercial offering for cloud automation solutions from enstratus. Available at time of press at http://goo.gl/biAx0

[19] J. McKendrick, "Cloud Providers Pitch Cost Savings, But Enterprises Want More: Survey," *Forbes* (August 16, 2012). Available at time of press at http://goo.gl/QVkxV

[20] Energy Information Agency, "Electricity: Wholesale Market Data." Available at time of press at http://www.eia.gov/electricity

[21] Federal Chief Information Officer, "The State of Public Sector Cloud Computing" (May 20, 2010). Available at time of press at http://goo.gl/alOzh

[22] R. Yasin, "Virtualization Takes Wing at Patrick Air Force Base," *GCN* (April 1, 2010). Available at time of press at http://goo.gl/NAm94

[23] D.M. West, "Saving Money Through Cloud Computing" (Brookings Institute, April 7, 2010, page 9). Available at time of press at http://goo.gl/ZJH3y

[24] R. Yasin, "Los Alamos Lab Launches Private Cloud," *Federal Computer Week* (September 8, 2010). Available at time of press at http://goo.gl/4zkMc

[25] J.N. Hoover, "Recovery.gov Moved To Amazon Cloud," *InformationWeek Government* (May 13, 2010). Available at time of press at http://goo.gl/cE7LL

[26] R. Yasin, "GSA wins race to the e-mail cloud," *GCN* (October 18, 2011). Available at time of press at http://goo.gl/XehEj

[27] M. Johnson, "GSA Is In the Cloud," U.S. General Services Administration blog (July 26, 2011). Available at time of press at http://goo.gl/N217t 28 Google, "Google Apps For Government." Available at time of press at http://goo.gl/iRM3P

INDEX

D

G

H

I

J

L

Q

R

S

T

U

V

W

Y